Harley Sherlock, RIBA, AA Dipl., FRSA, has been involved in urban housing in London for most of his working life, and for the last twenty years he has also been actively involved in the related issues of transport and land-use planning.

His architectural practice, Andrews Sherlock & Partners, grew from an experiment in living and working on co-operative lines in the 1950s. Attempts to interest the London Co-operative Society in social housing on the Swedish model failed, but the partners then became, in effect, architect developers. They gained awards and commendations from the Ministry of Housing and from the Civic Trust, which won them work in the public sector on low-rise, high-density housing and on the rehabilitation of nineteenth-century streets.

Mr Sherlock's interest in transport grew from a realization that, even when people were benefiting from improved conditions within their homes, the urban environment outside was becoming more hostile than ever, due mainly to the excessive use of the motorcar. From 1972–80 he was chairman of the London Amenity and Transport Association and from 1980–85 he was chairman of Transport 2000, the national campaign for a transport policy that is compatible with a decent environment. Mr Sherlock was chairman of the Royal Institute of British Architects' London Region from 1984–86.

HARLEY SHERLOCK

Cities Are
Good For Us

Paladin
An Imprint of HarperCollins*Publishers*

Paladin
An Imprint of HarperCollins*Publishers*
77–85 Fulham Palace Road,
Hammersmith, London W6 8JB

Published simultaneously in hardcover
and paperback by Paladin 1991
9 8 7 6 5 4 3 2 1

A catalogue record for this book
is available from the British Library

ISBN 0 586 09092 4
ISBN 0 586 09054 1 (paper covers)

Set in Caslon 540

Printed in Great Britain by
HarperCollinsManufacturing Glasgow

ACKNOWLEDGEMENTS

In collecting material for this book and in getting my prejudices checked or corrected, I have made life a misery for my friends and colleagues. Some of them had helped me with a report for Transport 2000 on the same subject, but if they felt they had already given me enough of their time they hid their feelings well. I am particularly grateful to Malcolm Andrews, Terence Bendixson, Peter Bibby, Keith Buchan, Mick Hamer, Judith Hanna, Alastair Hanton, Tom Hart, Mayer Hillman, Stephen Joseph, Tim Pharoah, Stephen Plowden and Stephen Potter.

Apart from Figure 30 the illustrations are my own, but when it came to illustrating points about buildings my task was made easier with material supplied by some of the architects concerned. I am most grateful to them. The buildings illustrated, and those responsible for their design or conversion, are listed below.

Fig. 25 The Lanes shopping centre, Carlisle – Building Design Partnership

Fig. 33a & b High-density housing in Islington – Andrews Sherlock & Partners

Fig. 33c High-density housing in Richmond – Darbourne and Darke

Fig. 34 Conversion of Georgian houses in Islington – Andrews Sherlock & Partners

Fig. 35 Conversion of Liverpool's Flower Streets – Edmund Kirby and Sons

Fig. 36 Upgrading of Islington's inter-War estates – Islington Architects' Department

Fig. 37 Wood Lane housing, Hammersmith – Darbourne and Darke

Fig. 38 Odhams Walk, Covent Garden – GLC Architects' Department

Fig. 39 Princes Reach housing, Preston – Brock, Carmichael Associates with BCA Landscape

Fig. 40 Infill housing, Clerkenwell – Islington Architects' Department

Fig. 41 Infill housing, North Kensington – Jeremy Dixon

Fig. 42 Byker housing, Newcastle – Ralph Erskine

Fig. 43 Housing at Bohnenviertel, Stuttgart – Darbourne and Darke

I am also grateful to London Regional Transport for material for Figure 16; to the Greater Manchester Passenger Transport Executive for material for Figure 28; to the authors mentioned in the Bibliography without whose ideas I would have been unable to develop my own; and, particularly, to Transport and Environment Studies, whose library and publications provided me with material for Figures 2, 18–21, 23 and 29–30.

My greatest thanks, however, must go to those who have read, commented on and almost rewritten passages of the book: to Dr David Allan, former librarian at the Royal Society of Arts, for attempting to correct my rose-coloured view of history; to David Hall, director of the Town and County Planning Association, for (almost) converting me to his way of thinking on garden cities; and to Nick Lester, the planning and transport officer of the Association of London Authorities, not only for commenting on the whole book but also for patiently reminding me of information he had given me before.

My final thanks are due to my wife Fionnuala for keeping me going, to Stanley Alderson, without whom the project would never have started, and to Wendy Andrews, without whom it would never have been finished.

CONTENTS

Illustrations and Tables 11
Introduction 13

PART I   The Growth of Cities

1   CITIES BEFORE THE INDUSTRIAL AGE   25

1 (i) ANCIENT BEGINNINGS
Urbanism Defined – Dependence on Agriculture

1 (ii) TOWNS IN MEDIEVAL ENGLAND
Saxon Villages, Danish Burghs and London – Towns and
Guilds – The Independence of Medieval Towns

1 (iii) RENAISSANCE GRACE AND SQUALOR
City-states and Capital Cities – The City as a Work of Art –
The City as Somewhere to Live – Privacy and Public Open Space

1 (iv) TRADING, MANUFACTURING AND FARMING
Systems of Manufacturing – Markets and Fairs – The Wool
Trade – The Growth of European Trade – Agriculture

2   THE INDUSTRIAL REVOLUTION   57

2 (i) INDUSTRY AND TRANSPORT
Rural Changes – Iron and Coal – Textiles – Rural Poverty –
The Steam-engine – Roads, Canals and Railways – *Laissez-faire*

2 (ii) URBAN REFORM
Reform before 1700 – Georgian Estates and Spa Towns –
Growth of the Urban Population – Salubrious Suburbs – Urban
Transport and Geographical Expansion

2 (iii) NINETEENTH-CENTURY REFORM
Parliamentary and Municipal Representation – Public Health
Acts – Housing by Paternalist Employers – Housing Trusts
and Bye-laws

PART II   The Present Impasse

3   FAILURES IN PLANNING AND HOUSING   83

3 (i) SUBURBS, GARDEN CITIES AND TOWER BLOCKS
Ebenezer Howard, Patrick Geddes and Raymond Unwin –
'Private' Suburban Sprawl and 'Public' Cottage Estates – New
Towns after World War II – Abercrombie's Greater London
Plan – The *Ville Radieuse* and the Demise of the Street

3 (ii) THE DESTRUCTION OF COMMUNITIES
Comprehensive Redevelopment – Planning Blight –
Demolition, Gentrification and Suburbanization

3 (iii) THE RISE AND FALL OF STRATEGIC PLANNING
The Town and Country Planning Act 1947 – The Local
Government Act 1972 – The Abolition of Metropolitan
Counties

3 (iv) THE CONSEQUENCES OF DISPERSAL
Central Decay and Peripheral Expansion – The Location-of-
Offices Bureau – Shops: Bigger, Fewer and Further Away

4   THE MOTOR AGE   112

4 (i) 'UNIVERSAL' CAR OWNERSHIP
Tarmacadam, Motor Vehicles and Ribbon Development –
The Buchanan Report and The Greater London Development Plan

4 (ii) FREIGHT
The Switch from Railways to Roads – The Cost of Lorries to
the Community

4 (iii) ANARCHY AS A POLICY FOR URBAN TRANSPORT
Political Timidity and the Freedom of the Motorist –
Company Cars – Trend Planning, Cost-Benefit Analyses,
Public Inquiries and Assessment Studies – Fragmented
Responsibility – Roads without Reason

4 (iv) SIDE EFFECTS
Communities Dispersed and Industries Concentrated – The
Decline of Public Transport – Treatment of Pedestrians and
Cyclists

PART III   Urban Revival

---

5   STRATEGIC PLANNING   147

5 (i) CONCENTRATION – v – DISPERSAL
Old Cities and New Towns – Urban Communities –
Interdependence of Businesses – Derelict Land – Public
Open Space – Cities, Fuel Efficiency and Pollution

5 (ii) DIVERSITY AND MARKET FORCES
A Balance of Land Uses – Old Buildings for 'Downtown'
Activities – The Need for Housing in City Centres

5 (iii) CITY CENTRES FOR PEOPLE
The Urban Environment and Pedestrianization –
Urban Planning in Europe

5 (iv) THE FUTURE OF RETAILING
Retailing in the Right Place – Shops Where People Live

5 (v) METROPOLITAN GOVERNMENT
Strategic Planning, Land-Use Planning and Transport

6   URBAN TRANSPORT   181

6 (i) MOBILITY AND ACCESSIBILITY
Unnecessary Travel – The Perceived Cost of Motoring –
The Need for Traffic Restraint – Area Bans or Road Pricing? –
Do We Need Cars in Cities?

6 (ii) WALKING AND CYCLING AS TRANSPORT
The High Proportion of Urban Journeys Made on Foot – The
Healthy Journey to Work – Cycling as a Mode of Transport

6 (iii) PUBLIC TRANSPORT
Land-Use Planning Comes First – Subsidies and Comparisons
with Europe – Buses and Re-Regulation

6 (iv) THE MOVEMENT OF GOODS
Avoidance of Unnecessary Freight Traffic – City-Friendly
Lorries

6 (v) ACCOMMODATING TRAFFIC AND TAMING IT
Streets as Places, and the Dutch 'Woonerf' – Car-Free Areas
and Traffic Priorities

7   URBAN HOUSING   214

7 (i) DENSITY AND COMMUNITY
What is Meant by Density? – Densities in London and Paris

7 (ii) THE ENGLISH HOUSE AND STREET
Renaissance of the Street – Street Densities Illustrated

7 (iii) NEW HOMES FROM OLD HOUSES
Nineteenth-Century Houses – Inter-War Council Estates

7 (iv) NEW URBAN HOUSING
Low-Rise, High-Density Housing – New 'Street Housing' –
New Housing in Central Areas

Summary and Conclusions   243
Bibliography   248
Index   251

ILLUSTRATIONS AND TABLES

1	A typical medieval town		35
2	The Renaissance piazza – Bologna		41
3	Renaissance vernacular – Amsterdam		45
4	Renaissance vernacular – Bedford Square, London		46
5	The Thames as seventeenth-century transport corridor		65
6	Radial cities: London 1914 and Washington Plan 1950		66
7	'Model Homes for the Working Classes'		79
8	Ebenezer Howard's Slumless, Smokeless Cities		86
9	LCC cottage estate at Acton		89
10	Roehampton's *Ville Radieuse*		96
11	Incongruous low-density housing, Wilton Square, Islington		101
12	The Buchanan Report – Three-level local shopping street		117
13	A large lorry stuck in a small street		123
14	Road freight in the United Kingdom	(Table)	134
15	Heritage damaged for a pointless road – St Benets, London		135
16	Rush-hour journeys to central London	(Table)	139
17	The City of London as townscape		153
18	A small urban open space, Copenhagen		157
19	Old buildings for 'downtown' activities – Covent Garden		163
20	Freiburg residents' mode of travel to shops	(Table)	168
21	Central Copenhagen		169
22	The West End of London		169
23	Vienna – journeys to work and school	(Table)	170
24	Princes Street, Edinburgh		171
25	The Lanes shopping centre, Carlisle		173
26	Car ownership related to population density	(Table)	190
27	Financing public transport in Paris and London	(Table)	198
28	Manchester's Metrolink		200
29	Heavy lorries compared (typical lengths shown)		206
30	The people-friendly street in Germany		211

31	Traditional high-density street	220
32	New high-density street housing	222
33	Examples of low-rise, high-density housing	224
34	Conversion of Georgian houses in Islington	227
35	Liverpool's Flower Streets	228
36	Upgrading of Islington's inter-War estates	230
37	High-density housing in Hammersmith	233
38	Odhams Walk, Covent Garden	234
39	Princes Reach housing, Preston	235
40	Infill housing, Clerkenwell	237
41	Infill housing, North Kensington	238
42	Newcastle's Byker housing	239
43	Central-area housing, Stuttgart	241

INTRODUCTION

Men came together in cities in order to live.
They remain together in order to live the good life.

Aristotle
Politics

No city has ever meant 'the good life' for all its inhabitants. In some
ages Aristotle's maxim has been true for some people; in most ages
reformers have seen it as an achievable aim; and immediately after
World War II it seemed on the verge of attainment. Yet, half a
century on, it seems further from attainment than ever. Cities are
now seen at best as a great social problem, and at worst as obsolete,
in the approaching age of advanced information technology.

I have been a Londoner all my life, having been born and bred in
the London Borough of Croydon and having lived in the (inner)
London Borough of Islington since 1952. I was a student of
architecture at the height of the period of post-War idealism which
saw the introduction of the National Health Service and the 1947
Town and Country Planning Act. Like students everywhere we
talked about and campaigned for a fairer society and, in the other
sense of the word, for a fairer environment. Although we argued
about the means (and the style) we were enthusiastic about the ends
proclaimed by the 1951 Festival of Britain which we saw as
symbolizing the New Age; culture for all exemplified by the
Festival Hall, and housing for all exemplified by the Lansbury
Estate in Poplar, which was as much a part of the Festival as was the
South Bank site itself.

During the 1950s and 1960s the fairer society began to manifest
itself, but the fairer city did not. In getting rid of bug-infested

slums we unwittingly threw out the baby with the bath water. Many buildings were demolished that needed to be demolished, but so too were many that could have been repaired to provide more homely housing than the tower blocks that replaced them. Worse still, the street community and its local shops and pubs were destroyed along with the slums.

To start with it was misplaced idealism that led to the dashing of our hopes for an improved environment. The London County Council did not wish their tenants ill when they housed them in tower blocks, any more than the City Fathers of Birmingham and Worcester deliberately set out to destroy the centres of their cities as they did, or the Ministry of Transport deliberately built roads to destroy the environment. But as time went on (or perhaps just as my generation grew older) idealism seemed to give way to political opportunism, which in turn bred doctrinaire planning and a vain search by planners and architects for universal panaceas and new gimmicks.

We were given fair warning of what was happening by the Danish author Steen Eiler Rasmussen, when the third edition of his book *London: the Unique City* (Jonathan Cape) was published in 1948. Sensing that the French architect Le Corbusier was seducing us with his ideas, Rasmussen wrote, 'Le Corbusier is a modernist in his artistic form but a conservative in his planning of a city. When he plans to rebuild Paris with rows of skyscrapers he is merely keeping up the old tradition of the Bourbons and the Bonapartes.' But we took no notice of Rasmussen's warnings and even invented an anti-people style of building to go with the new dogma. The term 'New Brutalism' may have been coined in jest but the method of building which it described was carried on in earnest, and its effects are still all too visible in the unrelieved concrete of some of our tower-block estates.

The one aspect of the post-War rebuilding programme that worked well was the machinery for making sites available. The Medical Officer for Health had only to notice that the timber floors of a house were a bit 'springy' for it to be condemned as unfit for human habitation and therefore worth only its site value. The occupants were happy because they would be rehoused; the land-lords were only too pleased to get rid of their unprofitable fixed-rent tenants and to sell their homes to the Council as building land; and the Council bureaucrats, for their part, were remarkably unencumbered by red tape when it came to boosting the housing figures for their political masters.

Here lay the stuff of real tragedy. The vast majority of people who were moved from dirty, war-shattered streets to new, clean tower blocks were initially very pleased with the change. By the time second thoughts had arisen the machinery of change was virtually unstoppable. In normal circumstances reaction from householders would have prevented the process from going so fast or so far.

If architects had had the benefit of feedback from such second thoughts we might have seen what an asset the street community had been and how difficult it was to replace; we might have appreciated before it was too late that the space between buildings divided up into the yards and gardens of terraced houses was more useful than the no-man's-land between tall blocks of flats; we might have seen that you cannot exchange greetings with someone passing your flat in a lift, in the same way that you can with someone passing your window facing the street; and we might also have seen that mothers cannot have any contact with children playing in the street if they are twenty floors up. Because of our understandable but unthought-through obsession with light and air, we went too far and gave up our street communities for the sake of open views that were sometimes spectacular but were more often than not simply views of other blocks. And it was not as if tall buildings were cheaper than streetscale housing. They were in fact very much more expensive, and the Government gave out large subsidies to ensure that they were built.

If housing is one of the twin urban disasters of the last forty years, transport is the other. At the age of ten I was asked, with other members of my class in the 1930s, to write an essay on transport fifty years hence. Only one of the class (and it was not me) had the imagination to see us all in the 1980s travelling at a brisk walking pace in motorized beds (inclined at thirty degrees for visibility's sake)! The rest of us settled boringly for versions of the 'people's helicopter'. I maintain that, as children, we could not be blamed for failing to see the possible social consequences of our prophecies; but I never cease to wonder at our failure as adults a generation later to foresee the consequences of mass car ownership and, even more, at

our failure to do anything about it when the consequences were
already upon us.

In spite of its undoubted usefulness and its liberating effect on
many people, the motorcar has been a very mixed blessing. Not
only has it caused atmospheric pollution and serious damage to our
physical environment, it has also caused a great deal of damage
indirectly. It has encouraged people to live further from their work.
It has also encouraged retailers to concentrate on fewer and larger
outlets further from where people live, and it has allowed planners
to site hospitals, county offices, etc., remote from the members of
the public who need to visit them. The result is that instead of
saving time through use of the car we now waste more time than
ever on travelling. Furthermore, although the car has the rather
dubious distinction of making mobility for its own sake available to
car owners, it has also had the effect of removing all mobility from
people living in the country who were dependent on once-profitable
bus services which have now been driven out of business. It is often
forgotten that those affected are not just the members of carless
families but also the members of single-car families left at home
when one of the family has taken the car to work.

If the motorcar has been a mixed blessing in the countryside it has
been an unmitigated disaster in our cities. It is now much more
difficult to get around London (or to get goods collected and
delivered) than it was thirty years ago, and yet the total number of
people travelling and the weight of goods being moved has
remained more or less constant. Our transport policies, or lack of
them, have resulted in an appalling degradation of the environment
outside our homes. Many residential streets, and, even more
noticeably, shopping streets, have lost their sense of place and are
now almost totally given over to their role as traffic arteries. Not
surprisingly in such circumstances the number and quality of our
local shops have deteriorated to the extent that many people, at
great inconvenience to themselves, make long and difficult journeys
on congested roads to find alternatives – thus adding to congestion,
damaging the environment further and making it even more difficult
for local shops to survive.

The greatest sufferers from this upheaval have been our children.
They have lost their freedom to play in the street where they live, or
to cycle to their friends' houses or to school. As a ten-year-old in

outer London I enjoyed all those freedoms, in addition to the ability to make trips into the country by bike or by bus, always knowing when we went by bus that there would be no difficulty in getting a bus back even if we finished up on a different route. No children could do such things today whether they lived in town or country. My own children, brought up in Islington in the 1960s and 1970s, were not allowed to cycle to school because of danger from the traffic, although they were lucky enough to live in a street where they could play football. But that is no longer possible because all inner-city streets are now clogged with parked cars or moving traffic, or both. City children have not only lost their street community, they have also lost the freedom to move around at will. Now, wherever they go, for safety's sake they have to be under adult supervision.

If I had been told in 1950 that urban society was going to become more fair, it would have been nothing more than I expected. But if I had been told that our air would become even more poisonous than it was then; that our physical environment was going to be drastically degraded; that our mobility was going to be reduced; that vital service industries were going to be driven out of central areas by doctrinaire planning laws; that our children were going to lose their freedom to play in the street and travel independently; and that changes in the retail trade were going to force many of us to make tediously long journeys to do our shopping, I would simply not have believed it.

Jonathon Porritt, former director of Friends of the Earth, has made the point that by using up the planet's resources at an unsustainable rate we are stealing from our grandchildren. Clearly one essential way of making amends is to reduce our need to travel; and one way of doing this is to live in cities where the necessities and pleasures of life are close at hand, so we use our cars less. But while the threat to the planet must be our greatest long-term concern it is not the theme of this book. The case for revitalizing our cities was a sound one even before we were so forcibly made aware of global warming.

This book is an attempt to explore why we came to live in cities in the first place; why our cities grew as they did and the influence that this had on the way they are now; why everything went so desperately wrong in the latter half of the twentieth century, just when we thought we were on the verge of getting it right; why we still need our cities; and what we must now do to make amends for past mistakes.

In examining the development of cities I look not only at Britain but at Europe and beyond. However, when considering the legacy of the Industrial Revolution, and the more recent developments of the twentieth century, I concentrate on Britain and particularly on England and London: on England because our urban traditions, and especially our housing traditions, are different from those of almost every other country (except perhaps Holland), and on London partly because I know it best and partly because so many national policies have followed from policies originally applied to the capital. I have discussed this with friends living outside London who are sick of London-dominated arguments, and even they agree that they have a working knowledge of London that they lack for other cities outside their own. I have therefore decided, as a rule, to use as illustrations of my argument examples that are known to me, in spite of the fact that many are from London. They are not necessarily the best examples even from London, but I use them unashamedly to illustrate the environmental problems of all our towns and cities and to suggest solutions that could be applied generally.

The book falls naturally into three parts. The first two chapters briefly outline the development of cities up to the beginning of the twentieth century; the third and fourth chapters describe the developments in planning, housing and transport that have led to the present situation; and the last three chapters show how more rational policies on these three major issues could transform our urban environment. I reject the notion that cities are an anachronism in the motor age. On the contrary, I argue that they could be a sanctuary where people are given priority over cars, and that the close-knit city of the future could be not only the most stimulating place to live but also the means of preventing the surrounding countryside being swallowed up by an endless suburbia.

With the exception of fringe developments like the Docklands enterprise zones in London and Merseyside, the 1980s marked a period of remarkable inactivity in inner-city housing. My recurring nightmare is that when we resume attempts to improve urban housing we will again throw out the baby with the bathwater and, in our justifiable anxiety to avoid the mistakes of the 1960s, we will reject all forms of high-density housing: not just the tower block but also the traditional urban street (which it would be impossible to re-create at the 'suburban' densities proposed in some of the new Unitary Development Plans being drawn up by inner-city planning authorities). If this were allowed to happen and the urban population declined, we would lose more local pubs, shops and other services as their loss of customers would make them no longer commercially viable. We would then finish up with an urban wasteland that could become as great a social disaster as the tower-block estates of the 1960s.

On the other hand, if we were to retain our urban population, and perhaps add to it by bringing housing back to some central commercial areas, we would find it easier to revitalize both our cities and the services that support them. We do not have to build tall in order to do this. The towers of the 1960s were not built to increase densities (the taller the buildings the farther apart they have to be spaced because of the shadows they cast). They were built to get away from the concept of the street because the street had become associated with poverty and bug-infested slums. However, as Rasmussen points out, many English slums were once fashionable houses, and many now fashionable streets were once slums. Apart from the association of ideas, there is nothing essentially wrong with the urban street that cannot be put right, or emulated in a modern form. As I demonstrate in Chapter 7, even at the comparatively high densities of 300 to 375 people per hectare (120 to 150 per acre) it is still possible to provide everyone with a front door on to a public street and to provide gardens for all family dwellings. The challenge is not so much a search for new urban forms as one of developing our social, planning and architectural ingenuity to ensure that the advantages of inner-city living can be enjoyed by everyone.

My family lived in inner London for generations and moved to Croydon at the turn of the century to escape the 'smog'. I moved back to the inner city in the 1950s because I was prepared to put up with the smog for the sake of having work, friends, shops, pubs, etc., close at hand. The potential advantage of the inner city has increased since then as the decline of local shops and other services has become even more marked in the low-density suburbs and travelling, which is the essence of suburban living, has become more difficult. The reason that this potential has not been realized and that many people still want to move out is due almost entirely to our failure either to improve our public-sector housing or to find a successful alternative to it. For those fortunate enough to be well-housed, inner London still retains most of its advantages – as is clearly demonstrated by the high cost of residential property there. Although my local shops are neither as good nor as inexpensive as they used to be, I still have plenty of good ones within five minutes' walk. I therefore escape the time-consuming chore of the massive weekly stock-up at a distant superstore. I can still get back from a party at night without having to drive. I can still get to work in fifteen minutes by bus (ten minutes by Underground but at great discomfort). And I have about twenty pubs, ten restaurants, three theatres and one cinema within ten minutes' walk. I am also fortunate, as many are not, to live in one of those intimate urban streets that is not yet overrun by moving traffic, although it is clogged with the stationary variety.

It is no great task to demonstrate that some parts of inner London and most of inner Edinburgh, for example, are good places to live. The object of this book is to demonstrate that *all* cities could be made attractive to *all* their citizens, and more people could be drawn to them – if strategic planning were restored, population densities maintained, public transport preferred to private cars, and urban street housing re-established and improved upon.

This cannot be achieved by market forces alone. Land for open space, low-cost housing and downtown industries has to be allocated out of public funds by a strategic planning authority. However, such costs would be nothing compared with the cost of urban failure and its consequences in terms of civil unrest and mass migration to the countryside just outside the cities.

Homo sapiens is a sociable species that likes to live in a community but also likes access to privacy. England's traditional urban housing, with its street-cum-meeting place at the front and private yard or garden at the back, provides such an environment: sometimes well, more often badly, but always with the potential for improvement. I maintain that to forsake our cities, or to turn them into something else by suburbanizing them, would be a national disaster. Air pollution from car exhausts would make the smog of the Steam Age look like clean air; shops, pubs and schools (and even the countryside) would be more inaccessible than ever; and our social life, including that of our children, would have to hinge on the use of the car.

If on the other hand we could realize the potential of our cities by ensuring through sensible land-use planning that everyone and everything was reachable by public transport, walking, or cycling (which it once was), and if we could also make available the sort of low-cost housing that people want to live in (for which since the 1950s we have had the resources, but not the wit to use them wisely), we could have a virtually car-free, people-friendly urban environment with all the pleasures and necessities of life within easy reach.

PART I The Growth of Cities

1 CITIES BEFORE THE INDUSTRIAL AGE

> One was either in or out of the city; one belonged or one did not belong. When the town gates were locked at sundown, and the portcullis was drawn, the city was insulated from the outside world. As in a ship, the wall helped create a feeling of unity between the inhabitants.
>
> Lewis Mumford
> *The Culture of Cities*

1 (i) ANCIENT BEGINNINGS

Urbanism Defined

We all have strong views about cities. We tend to love cities in other countries and hate our own. We visit the former and take photographs of them to show to our friends. The latter we visit occasionally for pleasure but more usually for work, and we get out of them as quickly as we can. But why do we have cities? How did they come about, and what exactly are they?

Paul Bairoch in his book *Cities and Economic Development* (Mansell Publishing, 1988), claims that most writers agree that urbanism at its origins could be said to exist only if one or more of the following conditions is met:

1. The existence of full-time craftsmen furnishing evidence of a division of labour.
2. The existence of fortifications or walled enclosures, thus distinguishing the city or town from the village, which remains open.

3. A population of sufficient size and, above all, density.
4. A specifically urban habitat: houses built of durable materials, habitations arranged so as to form streets, and so forth.
5. Permanent settlements as opposed to transient encampments.

Bairoch argues that all these conditions can be modified to some extent except the first one – the division of labour and inter-dependence of people doing different work being the very essence of urbanism.

But even supposing that we can define urbanism, can we say how, when or why it first came about? According to Bairoch, Jane Jacobs once put forward the interesting thesis that townships of a sort may have existed before settled agricultural communities. The theory was that Neolithic hunters, grouped with their families in semi-permanent encampments, came across the idea of sowing crops as a means of supplementing their food supplies as their numbers expanded. Certainly settled agriculture would have supported many more people in a given area than could have been supported by hunting.

It is more generally assumed that agriculture developed as the Ice Age receded, land became more fertile, and hunting was displaced as the means of supporting the larger population. Urbanism then grew from the needs of agriculture as the farmers acquired the ability to 'pay' for those needs from their surplus produce. The craftsmen who served the agricultural villages would have originally lived in them, but as crafts became more sophisticated and crafts-men became more dependent on one another, townships would have grown up which served the agricultural community but were independent of it administratively. We know that the town even-tually became the focus of the community's defence and of its trading contacts with the world outside.

Dependence on Agriculture

Whether the needs of the 'town' led to the development of agriculture or whether the needs of agriculture led to the growth of towns, each has always been dependent on the other – and each has been a prerequisite for the development of the human race. 'Without cities there could have been no real civilization,' says Bairoch, but he adds that where there is no agriculture there cannot be the high concentration of people necessary for cities to develop.

It has been noted that human beings isolated from each other but with a similar problem to overcome will often solve it in a similar manner. (In the contemporary world it is often wrongly assumed in such circumstances that they have colluded.) It is reasonable to assume, therefore, that similar developments in agriculture and urbanism occurred in many parts of the world independently. The earliest towns known to us at present through archaeological research are the Sumerian cities of the 'urban revolution' in Mesopotamia around 3000 BC. They were sophisticated city-states, controlling the administration and religion of the agricultural region around them, and they probably represent the culmination of a process of population expansion going back several millennia.

It is hardly surprising that thriving communities should have sprung up around the fertile estuaries of the Tigris and Euphrates where they flow into the head of the Persian Gulf. The more fertile the land, the greater the number of people it could support and the easier it was to produce a surplus that could be exchanged for the goods and services provided by a city. It should also be borne in mind that if surplus produce was necessary to 'pay' for the services of a craftsman who was non-productive in agricultural terms, it was similarly necessary to employ someone to carry freight or drive a beast of burden. Thus to a primitive community which needed every available agricultural labourer, transport was a very large 'cost', and areas of dense population, where distances between communities were short, were likely to do a great deal more trading than scattered communities.

What does surprise most people is the comparatively large size of some of the early cities. The population of the whole world in the time of the ancients is estimated at less than a hundred million, compared with the population of the present world which is 10,000 times that figure. But Ur, the largest of the Sumerian towns, had a population of 24,000 by 2800 BC, while Babylon, which was further up the Tigris valley and succeeded the Sumerian cities as the leading light of civilization in the Middle East, had a population of 300,000 by 1700 BC. Ancient Rome (which in time is about halfway between Babylon and the present day, and much closer to us than it is to Ur) boasted about one million people by 200 AD.

The Egyptian civilization (at its height between 2500 and 500 BC) seems to be the exception that proves the rule, by existing without cities. It was ruled by despotic sovereigns and priests and kept its culture very much to itself. On the other hand the tiny Phoenician city-states spread their own and other peoples' knowledge far and wide through their seafaring trade, while, as Bairoch comments, 'The stunning achievements of Greek civilization had a great deal to do with the high level of urbanization exhibited by the population of the Hellenic World.'

Successful cities, however they developed in the ancient world, were always supported not only by the means to transport food and water but more particularly by sound agriculture. Sometimes this was based on a very local biannual crop, as in the case of Ur, sometimes on mountains of cheap grain imported from overseas, as in the case of Rome. It is not clear whether improvements in agriculture led to the growth of cities, or whether the growth of cities forced improvements on agriculture, but the development of the two has always been closely connected. Efficient farming in Tuscany made it possible for Rome to expand, but eventually the metropolis became so large that it had to import grain from North Africa. This became cheap through bulk purchase and was eventually distributed free to the citizens of Rome as a means of buying imperial popularity. Italian farming was thus destroyed, partly by market forces and partly by the loss of local labour attracted by the free bread and the elusive prosperity of the metropolis. However, the original need to feed Rome led to agricultural advances not equalled in Europe until the eighteenth century.

1 (ii) TOWNS IN MEDIEVAL ENGLAND

Saxon Villages, Danish Burghs and London

Although agriculture and urban development are now often seen as being in conflict, it was the practice of agriculture in Anglo-Saxon times that gave birth to the settled communities that now make up the majority of the villages, towns and cities in the fertile valleys of England.

Roman Britain was remarkable not only for its enormous influence on the primitive indigenous inhabitants but also for the suddenness with which that influence disappeared with the legions that had supported it. The function of a Romano-British town as a military and administrative outpost of a sophisticated empire was completely different from the function of the Anglo-Saxon settlements that followed them and that grew out of the needs of the people who, once they had forsaken seafaring, rape and pillage for farming, knew little of what went on outside their clearing in the forest.

It is true that in the three hundred years of the Roman occupation, the Celtic Britons of the southeast assimilated much that was Roman; but they were dependent on the Empire for their security. So long as the legions were at hand, the fortified towns and military roads provided a quick-response system of defence which rendered unnecessary the fortification of smaller towns and isolated villas. However, after the departure of the legions in 407 AD there was no co-ordinated defence of Britain from the ravages of the Anglo-Saxons. Although Romano-British civilization seems to have survived for up to fifty years in some towns remote from the east and southeast coasts, most of the fortified towns were quickly overcome. If the existence of the Roman roads had any influence on events it was to assist the attackers rather than the defenders. But in the long run neither roads nor sophisticated towns were of any use to the unsophisticated Saxons, until perhaps the ninth century when they started building in stone. Then both roads and towns made useful quarries!

No one really knows what happened to Roman Britain in the 150 years that followed the departure of the legions. Even before their departure there had been incursions from the Celtic tribes of Ireland and Scotland, and there is evidence that during the Dark Age the pre-Roman hilltop camps were reoccupied either by fleeing Celts (including Britons) or by invading Anglo-Saxons. In spite of extensive research by historians and archaeologists we still do not know for certain whether King Arthur was an invading Saxon, a fleeing Briton, the last of the Romans or pure mythology. What we do know is that by 600 AD the only remains of Roman civilization were ruined towns and roads. We also know that by then the Saxons were already transformed from invading warriors to settled farmers, bent on defending themselves from the next wave of Nordic invaders.

G.M. Trevelyan in his book *History of England* (Longmans, Green and Co., 1945), says of the period, 'The destruction of the Roman cities and villas was wholesale and almost universal. The early Anglo-Saxons were not city dwellers. They had no commercial instincts except for selling slaves overseas, and they lost their old sea habits when they had won themselves good farm lands in the interior. The most civilized of their ambitions was to settle in large rural "townships" and to till the soil on the open field system of village agriculture.' The newcomers preferred their log huts to the well-built Roman towns and villas that they could have occupied, and they virtually ignored the Roman roads. The life of the early settlers became centred on the forest clearing that contained their village and its surrounding farmland, and which was often connected to the outside world only by the river that had brought them there in the first place.

The one legacy from the Roman era that did survive the Dark Age was the site (though not much of the fabric) of London. The Romans chose this small Celtic village as their main trading centre in Britain because it provided an ideal inland harbour for trade with Europe, at the point nearest to the sea where the Thames could be bridged. It became the fulcrum of the road system, with Watling Street (to give it its Saxon name) running from Dover to Chester via London Bridge (and, for that matter, via the Old Kent Road and Edgware Road). Ermine Street ran from London to Lincoln and York, and there were other important roads radiating from London to Colchester, Portsmouth, Dorchester, Bath and Gloucester, while the Fosse Way from Exeter to York provided a link between the southwest and the northeast. As a result of its pre-eminent position, London survived the early Saxon era as the only town that existed because of its contact with other communities.

If the Saxons are best described as farmers once they had settled in Britain, the later Danish invaders are best described as traders. When they established the Danelaw in northeast England in the ninth century, their first thought seems to have been to build a town, fortify it, and open a market. Their life revolved around the town, or burgh, in the way that Anglo-Saxon life revolved around the village and its farmland. They rebuilt Roman York as their capital and established large fortified trading centres at Lincoln, Stamford, Leicester, Derby and Nottingham. The fortifications were built to ward off counter-attacks from the Anglo-Saxons under King Alfred of Wessex, who was quick to see the advantage of building military strongpoints of his own. A consequence of this policy was that Alfred repaired the Roman walls of independent London and charged the burghers with defending them. In effect he left London alone on condition that it was denied to the Danes, and thus he increased its independence.

Towns and Guilds

William the Conqueror made sure there was no resurgence of the squabbles between Saxons and Danes by transferring manorial power from the motley thanes to the Norman barons and knights, who owed William a more direct allegiance than was owed by the thanes to their Saxon kings. Nevertheless, in spite of the centralized power of the Norman monarchy (epitomized by the organization brought to bear for the Domesday survey), much that was Saxon and Danish survived: in particular the Saxon village and shire and the Danish burgh, together with the ecclesiastical parish which generally followed the boundary of village or burgh.

Apart from the fact that there would probably be a different lord of the manor, and that both manor house and church might be built of stone rather than timber, the English village was little changed by the Conquest. The serfs had secure tenure of their timber, thatch-roofed hovels and of their ten to twenty acres in strips of farming land. But their land and their homes were allocated to them rather than owned. They could not leave the manor, and if the manor were sold they were sold with it. The men were free to work their own land and graze their cattle on the village common but they were also obliged to do work on their lord's land. The women and children worked at home as spinners and weavers.

Among the serfs of the village there were thatchers, wrights (carpenters) and blacksmiths, who between them could make and repair the village buildings, furniture and farm machinery. The community was thus self-supporting and no one (apart from the lord of the manor, his family and perhaps the parish priest) was likely to leave the village except for a visit to the neighbouring market town which, itself, was nothing more than a similar rural village with a royal licence to hold a market, situated perhaps at a ford, river head or crossroads.

Life in the towns of the period was very different. Edward the Confessor had already reinforced London's pre-eminence before the Conquest by opening up trade with his native Denmark and moving his capital from Winchester to a completely new site at Westminster. The fact that the palace of Westminster was actually outside London was to have an important bearing on the latter's continuing independence from the monarchy. Although the other pre-Conquest towns, outside the Danelaw, were just rural villages with markets, the larger ones do seem to have enjoyed more freedom than the typical village, and as they grew in importance after the Conquest their merchants were able to turn some of their obligations to their lord into a form of rent. Responsibility for the payment of this rent rested with the merchant guilds, which in time became virtually indistinguishable from the town corporations. The granting of charters by the king, releasing the town's citizens from feudal obligations in return for rent, became a frequent way of raising revenue, especially at the time of the crusades. Because the rents were at a fixed level, as the town expanded so the burden per capita was reduced. The more the king needed money and the more charters he granted, the more the towns became independent and free to prosper.

By the twelfth century the craftsmen who made the goods for the merchants to sell were themselves organized in guilds on a craft-by-craft basis. Each guild regulated its particular craft through the system of apprenticeship, which obliged young people entering the trade to be apprenticed to a master craftsman for about five years, after which time they became independent journeymen with the hope, in due course, of themselves becoming masters. The guilds were originally established entirely for the benefit of their particular crafts. They protected their members' interests by controlling entry into the trade, limiting the hours that could be worked (to avoid unfair competition), and providing funds for those incapacitated as a result of accidents in the course of their work. But during the thirteenth and fourteenth centuries the guilds extended their powers well beyond the regulation of their own craft, and they shared with the merchant guilds the administration of the corporate boroughs. The master craftsmen who ran the towns came from humble beginnings. They seem to have made no attempt to become part of the nation's aristocracy, but they did establish an urban aristocracy of their own which became more or less hereditary. They built fine stone houses for themselves (at a time when timber-framed buildings were the norm) and they built guildhalls and almshouses, which served their overt purpose but also served as symbols of their patrons' power.

In England the guilds maintained the towns' independence from the monarchy until 1549, when all guild and church property outside London was confiscated by Edward VI. In London alone they retained their power after that date, and in 1642 the parliamentarians Pym and Hampden were able to thwart King Charles's attempts to arrest them so long as they remained within the city walls. Although the guilds no longer perform their original function of regulating their trades, their historical traditions survive to this day and they still control local government within the City of London's 'square mile'.

The Independence of Medieval Towns

By the twelfth century, towns throughout Europe had begun to make their corporate power felt. From the great historic cities of the old Roman Empire, which were recovering from the effects of Saracen piracy, to the more recent walled towns of northern Europe, merchants and craftsmen were beginning to demand conditions under which money could be safely made. H.A.L. Fisher in *A History of Europe* (Eyre and Spottiswoode, 1935) commented that they demanded the right to pay their taxes collectively (as a corporation) and 'to make their own bye-laws, to be relieved of onerous feudal servitudes, to have their civil suits tried in their own courts and within their own walls, to be able to select their own officers, and that serfs resident for a year and a day within a town or borough should be regarded as free'.

At this time London was a puny town compared with the city-states of Venice and Genoa. But in 1191 Richard the Lionheart mortgaged himself almost literally 'to the hilt' in order to take a leading role in the Third Crusade. His mortgagees were the citizens of London. While Richard was away crusading he entrusted the

Government of England to Hubert Walter, the Archbishop of Canterbury. Walter was no republican – far from it – but he perceived, in a way that the sovereign did not, that the monarchy (and therefore the state) would be stronger if the municipalities were strengthened, at the expense of the feudal barons. He consequently granted to several towns, including London, charters that recognized formally their right of self-government through elected officials. It is ironic that when Richard's brother John succeeded to the throne and embarked on a policy of extortion combined with mismanagement, Londoners were powerful enough to deny their city to the king, and open its gates to the barons. They thus helped to bring about the signing of Magna Carta in 1215.

Magna Carta appears at first sight to have done nothing for the towns or for ordinary people in general. According to Sellar and Yeatman in *1066 and All That* (Methuen) it said little more than that, 'Barons could be tried only by other Barons, who would understand.' Nevertheless, it is generally recognized that 1215 marked the end of absolute power for both king and barons, and the beginning of an ordered society in England. This gave the towns a freedom to act in their own right which was henceforth less dependent on strong fortifications.

Since the collapse of Charlemagne's Empire in the West (in the tenth century) and the steady decline of the Byzantine rump of the Roman Empire in the East, large parts of Europe from the Low Countries to Italy were nominally ruled by the Germanic Holy Roman Empire which, as our school history books told us, was neither holy, Roman, nor an empire. Its limited centralizing effect seems to have prevented the development of independent nation states, but for much of the time the only sort of power that the Empire represented was a power vacuum. In this vacuum thrived the independent cities of northern Italy and the small towns of northern Europe, which by necessity had to be well fortified and well organized to survive in the hostile world around them. The independence of English towns was more circumscribed because they were part of a sovereign state, but because from Magna Carta onwards the state was comparatively orderly, English towns avoided both the cost and the geographical restriction of the more elaborate fortifications that became necessary in the rest of Europe. They gradually became perhaps less powerful politically but more powerful commercially, and their growth during the late Renaissance and early industrial period was markedly different from that of their European counterparts.

During the Middle Ages the towns and cities of Europe grew from supplying their local communities to becoming the focus of international trade. They also rivalled the monasteries as centres of religion and learning, at least so far as the laity was concerned. In the more important towns the cathedrals became the objects of pilgrimage (usually because they held some grisly but holy relic), and the universities became the centres of an international system of education which thrived on the use of Latin throughout Europe by those fortunate enough to be educated. However, even the largest cities seldom held more than 40,000 people. Venice, with 100,000, was an exception and, like Genoa, it was really a city-state. It also had canals to provide a common means of transport other than walking.

Medieval cities were not overcrowded. True, the buildings were huddled close together, which achieved warmth as well as economy of construction. The people in the buildings were also huddled together, and that too achieved warmth. There was certainly no privacy in the houses – not even for sexual activity. Furthermore,

Fig. 1 A typical medieval town

there was little differentiation between home and place of work. Many of the townspeople were craftsmen working at home (or as apprentices or journeymen in their masters' homes) to serve the market in the town and the agricultural community round about. There was, however, open space between groups of buildings in the form of gardens, market gardens and thoroughfares (see Figure 1).

Sanitary regulations of a sort limited the indiscriminate dumping of human excreta. Organic waste was eaten by the town pigs, washed away by storms or, when all else failed (which was more often than not), dumped outside the city walls by gangs of 'rakers'. The paving of footways, although a Roman idea, seems not to have been reintroduced to Europe generally until the Renaissance city was well established in the sixteenth century. There is logic in the theory that the banning of pigs and the reintroduction of paved thoroughfares came about at much the same time.

For all their comparative freedom in a world of feudalism the medieval towns of Europe were primitive indeed compared with the great cities of the Roman Empire. The latter had generally been founded and administered under the centralized power of Rome, with proper supplies of fresh water (often brought great distances by aqueduct), with paved streets, and with properly maintained drainage (often provided in the form of brick sewers). H.A.L. Fisher deplored the collapse of the centralized order of the Roman Empire and of its pale imitation, the Holy Roman Empire but, writing of the twelfth century, he said, 'Who, when he considers the variety and brilliance of the Italian city life or the vigorous contribution of the Hanseatic League to the commerce and architecture of northern Germany, will be prepared to say that the breakdown of central government was in these regions an unmixed misfortune for the human race?'

1 (iii) RENAISSANCE GRACE AND SQUALOR

City-states and Capital Cities

There were clearly injustices in the medieval town but, at its best and in spite of its squalor, it represented a coming-together of merchants and craftsmen in the common cause of trade. It also became a small island of comparative independence and organization in a sea of oppression and anarchy. The Renaissance city, on the other hand, coincided not only (by definition) with the rebirth of learning but also with a trend towards political and commercial centralism, as weaker states and cities were absorbed by those that were more powerful.

In the Middle Ages building cities had been a means of achieving freedom and security; during the Renaissance it became a means of consolidating power. The medieval city was self-contained, self-supported and self-defended. It provided services for its surrounding agricultural villages but it had little dealing with the outside world. On the other hand the Renaissance city became the symbol of centralized power and looked outwards as it dealt politically and commercially with other centralized powers.

In historical terms the Renaissance period is generally reckoned to have begun in fifteenth-century Italy, but by the twelfth century there was a revival of the ancient trading cities of the Roman Empire and a sufficient restoration of law and order to allow Latin-speaking students of all nations to attend universities throughout Europe. The University of Salerno was famous for its medical school and, although its dubious medicine seems to have been based largely on astrology, it was here that Dante acquired his knowledge of Aristotelian philosophy. At the same time the University at Bologna was re-examining Roman law and the University at Paris, in defiance of the Church, was re-examining Christianity. It was with the help of academics from Paris that Oxford University was established at the end of the twelfth century.

It can therefore be argued that the Renaissance started in the twelfth century, and that it was simply the glorious but less fundamental 'flowering' that spread outwards from fifteenth-century Italy. According to Lewis Mumford in *The Culture of Cities* (Secker and Warburg, 1938), 'the so-called Renaissance of the fifteenth century is an illusion of its contemporaries who mistook the brilliant spray of the falling rocket for the energy that had lifted it into the sky'. The fact is that the Renaissance started much earlier than is generally recognized and, perhaps more importantly from the point of view of a study of cities, the customs of the Middle Ages carried on much longer.

Between the birth of Renaissance ideas in the twelfth century and their flowering in the fifteenth, Europe seems to have gone through a mini-Dark Age highlighted by wars and pestilence, and particularly by the Black Death. There was even a reversion to some of the superstitions of the Dark Ages, and with it an erosion of academic freedom. Belief in the power of witchcraft, which had been treated as a crime in the laws of Charlemagne in the ninth century, was positively encouraged by the Church in the fifteenth century and, as Mumford points out, it is ironical that the persecution of witches reached its height as Galileo and Newton were laying the foundations of modern science in the seventeenth century.

By the fifteenth century the 'capital city' had grown in influence at the expense of the small municipalities. In feudal times the court had moved round the country with the monarch, to whom mobility as well as vigilance had been the price of power. But as populations and territories increased, monarchs were forced to delegate their power and set up permanent courts with bureaucracies to serve them. They were also obliged to erect permanent buildings to house the bureaucrats and their archives. In time the capital city became the military, judicial, administrative and social centre of the realm, and as international trade expanded the capital grew in importance as a trading centre, at the expense of other towns. Economic privileges for individuals were henceforth to be obtained from the sovereign rather than from the burghers of the local town.

The death knell for the independence of small towns was the rapidly expanding use of gunpowder in the fifteenth century. The early cannons, which fired stone cannon-balls, were far too inaccurate to be effective against people but they had a devastating effect on buildings. Before gunpowder, the combination of a moat and simple walls built by the town's masons was sufficient to protect the town and could be extended without too much difficulty to embrace a suburb or to facilitate expansion.

From the fifteenth century onwards only the larger and more prosperous towns could afford the military engineering necessary to guarantee their independence. The fortifications of the new gunpowder age involved a complicated system of bastions projecting from the main walls so that the defending artillery could fire on the attacker from more than one direction. The earlier fortifications were built to suit the town and its growth. The new fortifications became a straitjacket within which the town had to be fitted.

Worse still, in order to provide a clear field of fire for defensive artillery the area outside the fortifications had to be cleared of buildings – a state of affairs that persisted in Paris until after the Franco-Prussian War of 1870. The clearing of suburbs outside the walls, and the consequential overcrowding within the walls, led first to the loss of the orchards and market gardens that had been hallmarks of the medieval town. It then led to the replacement of high-ceilinged, single-storey hovels with more substantial but more squalid structures of three or four storeys. No wonder that scavenging by the town's pigs was no longer a viable form of urban refuse disposal.

If the cost of defence contributed to the decline in importance of the small towns of Europe, its corollary was an increase in the power of the despots. Generally this meant a gradual dominance of Europe by national monarchies, but in Italy things were different. After the fall of Rome in 410 AD, the Italian peninsula had been under the tutelage of Gothic kings, Byzantine emperors, Charlemagne, the Pope and, for a short period, the Holy Roman Empire, which was centred on Germany. When the latter declined during the twelfth and thirteenth centuries it left Italy with no central authority but with half a dozen powerful, independent city-states, including Venice and Florence. While Venice had dominated seaborne trade for some centuries, Florence, famous for its banking, commerce and cloth manufacturing, emerged in the fifteenth century to give the first flowering of the Renaissance seeds that had been sown in the twelfth century.

Florence became the intellectual and artistic capital of Europe. Its rise marked the end of the medieval period of comparatively anonymous architecture and the beginning of the period of rich patrons seeking personal glory. Fisher points out that the Italian Renaissance thrived in an age that was still rife with cruelty and arbitrary power, but that its achievements were realized by a comparatively small minority of gifted and creative men working within an élite that was sensitive and intelligent.

The great men of Lorenzo de' Medici's Florence all possessed many talents. Lorenzo himself, a banker by trade and patron by his position, was also a talented statesman, poet and musician. Michelangelo, better known as a sculptor, painter and poet, actually made his name as a military engineer and builder of Florence's fortifications; while Leonardo da Vinci, better known for his painting and his science, was also a military engineer and town planner (and known to have recommended the separation of pedestrian and vehicular traffic in cities).

The City as a Work of Art

The link between Renaissance towns and military engineering was not fortuitous. Law and order, military order and architectural order were clearly linked and were in stark contrast to the anarchy (and greater individual freedom) that existed in the medieval town. Instead of seeing the town as a jumble of different buildings and different activities taking place wherever there was room (and the town expanding if necessary to accommodate them), the Renaissance rulers saw the town ideally as a work of art. It would be limited in size by its fortifications, and its important buildings around palace or parliament would be designed as a whole, with individuality sacrificed for the greater good of the concept and the greater glory of the state, prince or municipality. The great squares, or 'places', would be part of this concept – especially if they could be used for ceremonial purposes (see Figure 2).

There can surely be no better example of the ultimate Renaissance city than Paris, with its vistas of triumphal arches, processional avenues and terraces of individual buildings designed as part of a total concept. However, by the time Haussmann's tree-lined boulevards had been laid out in the mid-nineteenth century the Industrial Revolution was already in full swing.

Because of its boulevards we tend to think of Paris as a spacious and uncrowded city, but in fact its population density is much higher than London's due to the effect of its defensive walls described above. Thus when houses were demolished to make way for boulevards, the rehousing of the displaced inhabitants increased the population of the surviving residential streets. Paris epitomizes, if in exaggerated form, the limited geographical growth of Europe's cities before the nineteenth century. According to Bairoch they grew by an average of only twenty per cent between 1300 and 1800 but by 100 per cent between 1800 and 1900.

However enlightened the Renaissance prince might have been, if his city could not expand beyond its walls he could make the centre

more spacious only by making the rest of the city more crowded (see
the jumble in the foreground of Figure 2). As a result, apart from
new buildings in the classical style around their administrative
centres, most cities retained their essentially medieval (but more
crowded) character until the Industrial Revolution. Small areas of
medieval street pattern and many of the market places (and their
practices) survive to this day.

London's Great Fire of 1666 provided a golden opportunity for
breaking the mould of the old city, but it was taken only half-
heartedly. The replacements for St Paul's Cathedral and the other
city churches provided England with much of its best Renaissance

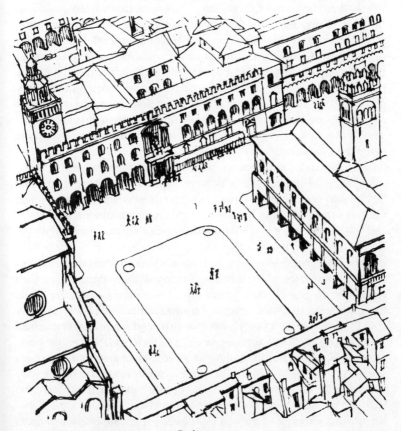

Fig. 2 The Renaissance piazza – Bologna

architecture. Wren's road plan for London was also implemented in part, and is notable for the fact that it gave precedence not to God in the form of St Paul's but to Mammon in the form of the Royal Exchange. London, however, like most other cities in northern Europe, was not transformed into a Renaissance city: it just had Renaissance bits added to it. It was a pleasant enough sight from the river (if not from within) but its essential character until the nineteenth century was that of a compact medieval town with its skyline punctuated by tall Renaissance spires and the one enormous dome of St Paul's.

English towns became less overcrowded during the Renaissance period than did most of their European counterparts, largely due to the lack of any need for fortifications, but even London, with its seventeenth-century population of 500,000 people, did not greatly expand geographically. Instead of being restricted by its walls it was restricted by the distance that people and goods could travel with no proper transport system other than that provided by boats and barges on the Thames. As a result London's overcrowded dwellings and congested streets, though less of a problem than in some cities, were still problem enough. Street congestion was greatly exacerbated by the increase in cart traffic that followed the replacement during the sixteenth century of the solid timber wheel by the rim-spoke-and-hub wheel, which required less timber in its manufacture and was easier to repair. It was claimed that roads intended for pedestrians and the occasional horse were unsuitable for heavy cart traffic, and there was a rigorous campaign against brewers' drays in London on the grounds that they caused extensive damage to the road surface. In 1563 the King of France was petitioned to the effect that all vehicular traffic should be banned from Paris. Like the campaigns to ban chariots from ancient Rome and motorcars from twentieth-century cities, neither was successful.

A further consequence of the fact that walking was the general mode of transport was that the centre of a city was clearly the best place to live. As a result, the medieval practice of letting the poor live on the periphery continued – no longer because the well-to-do wanted to be the best defended but because they wanted to have to walk the least. It seems strange to late-twentieth-century eyes, used to *inner*-city decay, that even in London the worst slums were *outside* the old walls until the nineteenth century. The nearest modern equivalent is perhaps the 'Third World' city, which for demographic or racial reasons sets a limit on the numbers allowed in and finishes up with a squatter camp outside.

The centralization of power and patronage that brought about the flowering of Renaissance art and town planning also had undesirable effects. Not only did it lead to the aggrandizement of the capital city at the expense of the provincial town, it also led to – or perhaps simply coincided with – the consolidation of industry and trade. We shall see in Chapter 1 (iv) that cottage industry actually continued until the nineteenth century, but political and industrial centralization eventually undermined and impoverished the local craftsmen who had been the backbone of the medieval town. The craftsman was still needed in the Renaissance capital city but he represented a smaller and less influential part of the community, which increasingly included large numbers of servants and people seeking the employment that they could not obtain in the provinces. The result was that the average town dweller not only lived in more crowded accommodation than his medieval counterpart but was also worse off financially.

The City as Somewhere to Live

If England provides the exception to the rule that Renaissance towns were constrained by their defensive walls, Holland provides the exception to the rule that the burden of such constraint was an unmitigated disaster for the lower orders. Until the end of Spanish colonialism in the Netherlands in the late sixteenth century, Dutch towns had more need for fortifications than most, and there had been no opportunity to expand beyond their walls. Fortunately, however, they had been generously laid out in the first place, and there were no Dutch despots bent on urban aggrandizement at the expense of their citizens. Gerald Burke in *The Making of Dutch Towns* (Cleaver-Hume, 1956) put it thus: 'The gap between ruler and ruled, between aristocrat and common citizen, was not nearly so pronounced in the Netherlands as, for instance, in France and Germany; the rich of Holland were never so arrogant, the poor never so abject. One look at an old Dutch city or town will suffice to show that the dominating component in its structure was the house: the solid, undemonstrative homely house built to last, like the family, for many generations. The ruler's palace, if it merited such a name, did not stand in majestic aloofness, but side by side with the houses of the burghers . . . Houses of the common man were never swept away to make space for a processional highway or monumental piazza.'

The medieval Dutch towns had been founded later than most in Europe. They altered little during the Renaissance and stayed within their walls until the end of the seventeenth century. They were not endowed with Gothic or Renaissance masterpieces, nor were they designed around squares or vistas. They were designed instead around the ordinary house and the canal that served it. The towns were compact and the houses were two to five storeys high and narrow-fronted, but each house had its garden (if a narrow one) and was famous for its large windows. Houses were built in long terraces but not as part of a set piece. Their windows were not graded in size like an English Georgian terrace for the sake of the total effect. Each window was designed only for its function of providing light.

In praising Dutch domestic building during the Renaissance it is not necessary to denigrate all housing in the rest of Europe. Because London was not constrained in the way that Paris was by the danger of building outside the old fortifications, the terraces of Bloomsbury and Mayfair were built within a short carriage-ride of the City as the middle classes became more prosperous. They were not architecture in the Renaissance sense: they were pattern-book buildings, simply designed for mass production by landowners of taste who wished to profit by selling to purchasers of taste. But they were designed around squares and vistas, and it was the appearance of the whole estate that 'sold' the house rather than the merits of any particular building. These speculative housing estates represented an interesting compromise between the grandeur of an Italian Renaissance city and the more egalitarian housing-for-housing's-sake of the Dutch towns. In London, as well as in Edinburgh, Nancy and Dublin, where similar expansion took place, a compromise between Renaissance and vernacular styles was considered good enough for the middle classes. As a result, building throughout Europe was enriched by national variations on classical style. This was particularly marked in Holland and England where ample supplies of suitable clay made brick available where stone was not (see Figures 3 and 4).

Completely different from either the city-states of Italy or the capital cities and trading towns of northern Europe was the late flowering of Renaissance town planning in the form of the eighteenth-century spa towns. Built mainly for the pleasure of the very small proportion of the population rich enough to enjoy them, they nevertheless provided scope for the planning and architectural talents of people like the Woods at Bath, who were given the opportunity to design new towns virtually from scratch, applying the familiar Renaissance principle of eschewing the individuality of each building for the sake of the concept as a whole.

Looked at from the late twentieth century, Renaissance town building seems to divide into two halves: the Italianate grandeur of

Fig. 3 Renaissance vernacular – Amsterdam

the early period, which carries right through to the end of the nineteenth century in its French form, and the more homely style of Holland and Georgian England. Examples of the former we admire as works of art rather than as buildings for living in, whereas we sneakingly admire the latter as providing an environment better than anything that has been designed since. Even our ubiquitous mid-nineteenth-century housing, shorn of the carefully planned squares and vistas of the previous century, is admired by Mumford in its modest form. He describes it as bringing order, decency and good manners from Boston and Baltimore to Geneva and Munich: '. . . drab and depressing in the old Brownstone section of New York or the duller parts of South Kensington and Pimlico, but usually a happy contrast to the romantic suburb.'

Privacy and Public Open Space

It would be wrong to see building styles as the only Renaissance influence on our towns and cities. There are two aspects of

Fig. 4 Renaissance vernacular – Bedford Square, London

Renaissance culture that have probably had a bigger influence on our environment. One is privacy and the other is the specially set-aside open space. The former is an asset acquired by the aristocracy during the Renaissance and gradually filtered down to everyone. The latter, like the Royal Parks in London or the Bois de Boulogne in Paris, we have inherited by acquiring a right of use that once belonged exclusively to the sovereign.

Privacy and the development of the private house were just as much manifestations of the Renaissance as were the more obvious squares and vistas. In the Middle Ages the home and place of work were not only in the same building, they were virtually in the same room. During the Renaissance they were gradually separated and from 1600 onwards eating and cooking were separated from sleeping – at least for the middle classes. When houses were first divided into separate rooms each room was reached by passing through other rooms, but by the seventeenth century rooms were placed along corridors like houses along streets.

Hygiene was generally even worse during the Renaissance period than it had been during the Middle Ages, if only on account of overcrowding. The WC was invented in 1596, but until the sanitary engineers of the nineteenth century found a way of sealing off the sewer smells the WCs were considerably less hygienic than the portable commode or outside privy and only a marginal improvement on simply 'using the yard'.

When comparing Renaissance towns with their precursors of the Middle Ages it is difficult not to deplore the concentration of power and the loss of corporate and individual freedom. On the other hand it was this centralized power that gave the patrons of fifteenth-century Italy the opportunity to sponsor great artists and thinkers, who in their turn gave birth not only to famous works of art and town planning but also to the beginnings of modern science.

We may laugh at the eighteenth-century notion of putting a church at each end of a street for reasons of symmetry rather than of religion, but it is no more absurd than the nineteenth-century custom of ruining a residential square by filling it with a church to accommodate those following the latest religious schism. The Renaissance aristocrat may not have jostled in the market place with the lower orders in the manner of the medieval merchant, but many of his kind were well-educated and well-intentioned; others may have had good intentions thrust upon them by ambitious architects. Whatever the cause, and whatever the shortcomings in other directions during the Renaissance period, when it came to building, a unity of purpose subordinated individual aspirations to the concept of the town as a whole: to great effect.

1 (iv) TRADING, MANUFACTURING AND FARMING

Systems of Manufacturing

This section is largely about the development of trading towns before the Industrial Revolution. However, in considering towns and their commerce it needs to be borne in mind that, regardless of any excellent siting on natural trade routes, such towns would never have existed in the first place if they had not been supported by a well-developed agricultural hinterland.

Some exchange of goods between primitive communities must have gone on before settled agriculture had been established, and therefore before there was any chance of urban settlement. Furthermore, enterprising traders of this distant past seem to have carried their wares a long way. How else is it that we can find Phoenician pottery in Cornish burial mounds which we know predate settled life in the British Isles? And it is not only trading that started before the existence of towns. Manufacturing, the *sine qua non* of urbanism until the latter half of the twentieth century, also preceded urban life.

We can easily imagine the primitive hunter shaping his own flint, and this can reasonably be described as the beginning of manufacturing. But it did not involve a division of labour. Hunting could not possibly provide a sufficient surplus of food for the hunter to be able to feed not only his own family but also a specialist weapon-maker and *his* family. However, when it came to manufacturing iron tools for a settled agricultural community it is reasonable to suppose that some form of specialization took place – both in the manufacturing of the tools and the mining and smelting of the ore. This did not lead immediately to the establishing of towns and markets; more likely it led to the bartering of food for tools and the establishing of a few specialist craftsmen in each agricultural village to meet the needs of that village only, not for the purpose of trading with the outside world. The development of the town and its guilds of craftsmen came later.

Lipson in his book *The Economic History of England* (A. and C. Black, 1931) divides the administration of manufacturing into four different systems: Household, Guild, Domestic and Factory. The order is chronologically correct but there was considerable overlapping, and the first three survived in one form or another until well into the nineteenth century, by which time the 'Factory system' was dominant and industry was concentrated in the large towns.

The term 'Household system' describes the earliest form of manufacturing: the making at home of articles used by the family or the local community. It may be that in the early stages of settled agriculture the serf-farmer made his own tools, but the Household system is more generally understood to describe the spinning of wool or the making-up of clothing by women and children.

The term 'Guild system' is used to describe the state of affairs reached when the craftsmen were no longer part-time farm labourers but instead worked exclusively at their specialist skills: first within their own village but more usually in the town as members of one of the town's craft guilds (see Chapter 1(ii)). Eventually, by the end of the sixteenth century, the power of the guilds became such that it bred moves to bypass their authority, and the most common effect of this development was for work to be taken away from the towns and returned to the rural cottage.

This revival of cottage industry, the 'Domestic system', was very different from the Household system. The work itself may have been similar, in that it was the old cottage crafts of spinning wool, weaving cloth and making clothing that most lent themselves to a return to work at home, but the Domestic system describes a completely changed way of organizing industry and marks an important stage in the early development of capitalism. It was no longer the cottager who bought the raw materials and sold the finished products but the entrepreneur from the town, who often owned the cottager's loom and could make a profit on its hire as well as on the products of its use. Not only did the new system undermine (perhaps deservedly) the status of the town and its craftsmen but eventually it also impoverished the cottage artisan who, unlike his urban counterpart, had no guild to protect his interests and who, in bad times, found that the payment received did not even cover the hire of the loom.

The development of power from water and steam in the eighteenth century made possible great reductions in manufacturing costs through labour-saving mechanization. However, the machines could be operated only where there was power and this meant that eventually the majority of artisans, male and female, were obliged to work in the factory rather than have work farmed out to them in their own cottages. The Factory system led first to the concentration of jobs in smallish communities which sprang up round the factory or mill, in the valleys of the fast-flowing rivers that provided the power. But as coal superseded water as the source of power, and as the canals and railways provided a cheap means of carrying coal to the centres of population, so the town regained its importance as the workplace.

Markets and Fairs

Many of us, nurtured on school-book history, know a little about the kings and queens of England and about the battles they fought. We may also know a bit about the history of London, at least as a capital city if not as a centre of commerce, but few of us appreciate how much of our early history revolved around medieval towns.

Towns came into being because of the rural community's need for manufactured goods, which were more efficiently produced in a craft-orientated urban community. In the Middle Ages there was no permanent retail outlet for such goods. Instead there was in each town a periodic market which was closely regulated to prevent fraud and the passing-on of stolen goods. A tenth-century law of King Canute laid down that any transaction worth four pence or more had to be in the presence of four witnesses independent of both buyer and seller: a requirement that it would be impossible to meet except on a market day.

Every town had its market but it dealt only in country produce and goods of everyday life for local people. Fairs were different. They provided the opportunity to trade in general goods, including luxuries from abroad, but they were usually confined to a few cathedral cities. They were held on holy days and attracted people from a much wider area, amongst whom it is easy to imagine gullible pilgrims of Chaucer's time being relieved of their money in time-honoured fashion.

In theory visitors were protected either by Church or monarch for the period of the fair's duration, which could be four weeks or more. In *The Economic History of England* Lipson quotes a proclamation of William the Conqueror to the effect that 'There shall be no market or fair save in the cities of our realm and in boroughs enclosed and fortified by a wall, and in castles and in very safe places where the custom of our realm and our common law and the royalties of our Crown . . . may not be defrauded or impinged but where all things may be done rightfully and in public and by judgement and justice.' In other words, the King got his royalties, the boroughs got their trade and the traders were protected from vagabonds. It was to ensure the reputation of the fair that the detention of debtors until they had paid their bills was initiated. But it was also understood that no one should be arrested during fair-time for any offence that was not connected with the fair itself.

After the end of the sixteenth century, trade (and especially international trade) tended to become concentrated on the capital city at the expense of provincial towns, but until the Tudor period international trade was carried out almost exclusively at the fairs in or just outside the large towns fortunate enough or prosperous enough to have obtained a royal licence.

The Wool Trade

After Magna Carta defence was no longer a major consideration for English towns and they came to thrive, as the rural community thrived, on the high quality of English wool. In 1312 one-fifth of the townspeople of Bristol were employed in the wool industry, and as early as 1265 cloth manufactured in Stamford was being sold in Venice. The importance attached to the manufacturing towns may have been partly due to their role as financiers to the monarch. Whatever the reason for it, the fact is that the Assize of Cloth, established by royal statute in 1197 to regulate the wool trade, was actually administered not by the monarch but by the towns.

When in the thirteenth century the making-up of cloth was threatened by the export of wool – which was the trade's raw material – attempts were made to prevent such exports. In 1337, to strengthen the towns and their cloth industries, Edward III banned the import of foreign cloth and gave franchises to immigrant cloth-workers from Flanders, allowing them to work in England. After the recovery of the cloth trade when the export of wool was resumed, the taxes raised on the export of staple materials (wool, leather, lead, etc.) were regulated and collected not directly by the state, for whose coffers they were destined, but by the mayor, constables and alien assessors of the Staple Towns of Newcastle, York, Lincoln, Norwich, Westminster (not London), Canterbury, Chichester, Winchester, Exeter and Bristol.

By the sixteenth century cloth manufacturing, which was still England's major industry, was controlled by the merchants from the towns but, perhaps to circumvent the power of the guilds, much of the actual manufacturing was carried out in rural cottages under the Domestic system described above, with the raw material and the cottager's loom owned by the merchant and financed by his capital. Under this system capitalism grew but the towns did not, and the depopulation of corporate boroughs like Norwich, Oxford, York and Nottingham was a cause for concern (in spite of the consequent growth of small market towns) as more and more manufacturing was carried out in rural areas where labour was cheaper. Skilled immigrant weavers were again brought into the boroughs, and one of the burghers of Norwich wrote that, 'By their means our city is well inhabited and decayed houses re-edified.' However, it was not until the development of the mechanical loom and similar labour-saving machinery at the end of the eighteenth century that the productivity of mechanized manufacturing under one roof outweighed the advantages of cheap rural labour which provided its own accommodation. Only then did the towns regain their ascendancy.

The Growth of European Trade

Law, order and political stability are generally regarded as essential to the development of trade. It is at first sight surprising therefore to find European trade at its strongest where, in national terms, there was a power vacuum. Fisher, writing about Germany in the thirteenth century, says, 'The vigorous and intelligent Teutonic stock which had overrun the Roman Empire and given dynasties to

Italy, Spain, France, England and even Russia, was stricken by palsy at the heart and deprived of all weight and initiative in the affairs of Europe.' Germany was not so much a state as a collection of minor nobles (the electors of the Holy Roman Empire) who 'pursued their separate ambitions with just so much political combination as might furnish the illusion of greatness and just too little sacrifice of personal convenience to enable the illusion to become a reality'.

War was endemic, and no convoy of merchandise could travel without an armed escort. During the fourteenth century, to counter this state of anarchy, the merchants of the Hanse (or Guild) in Hamburg and Lübeck established the Hanseatic League to provide through self-help the law and order that the Holy Roman Empire was incapable of providing. They were described as 'politicians by accident', but so effective were their policies that it was once said that every northern town of note from Bruges to Novgorod was a member of the League. When the Danish king was rash enough to dispute their authority he was actually defeated by force of arms and obliged to sign the treaty of Stralsund, giving the victorious merchant cities not only control of the Baltic fisheries but also a say in the selection of the Danish monarch!

In London the members of the Hanseatic League were given privileges denied to other foreign traders, including the right to their own Hanse, or guildhall. They were commonly referred to as the 'Easterlings' and Fisher comments that they were 'so important as a factor in the foreign trade of the island that Easterling in its shortened form of sterling came to denote the standard coin of the realm'.

Although the Italian city-states had a head start over their rivals because of the comparative order of the Byzantine Empire, in the long run it was the weakness of the Holy Roman Empire in northern Europe that led to the strength and independence of individual towns and provided the spur to trade and innovation which developed in northern Europe and eventually usurped the influence of Italy.

Agriculture

Since the earliest urban settlements arose in areas where there was a thriving agricultural community to support them it comes as no surprise to find that the expansion of European towns from about 1000 AD to the Black Death in the fourteenth century was accompanied by a minor revolution in agriculture.

Trevelyan in his *English Social History* says that this revolution broke the mould of the static feudal world and 'liberated mobile forces of capital, labour and personal enterprise which in the course of time made a richer and more varied life in town and village and opened out new possibilities to trade and manufacture as well as to agriculture'. Writing of the same period he also points out, in a sentence which seems to encapsulate the recurring dichotomy of progress, that 'the ever increasing wealth of the country was accompanied by greater inequalities of income'.

The open field system inherited from the earliest Saxon settlers worked well enough so long as the aim of the agricultural village community was simply to feed its own inhabitants. Although those who worked the land were serfs in relation to the lord of the manor, in relation to each other they were a self-governing community. According to Trevelyan, the system 'combined the advantages of individual labour and public control; it saved the expense of fencing; it gave each farmer a fair share in the better and worse land; it bound the villagers together as a community and gave the humblest his own land and his voice in the agricultural policy to be followed year by year by the whole village'.

Until the Black Death the population of England (and of Europe as a whole) grew steadily, and coincidental with the need to feed the expanded communities in both towns and rural villages there were great changes brought about in agricultural technology. The rotation of crops (to prevent land becoming stale) became more universal; water power and wind power for milling corn were used for the first time; and the iron horseshoe was developed as well as the horse collar, which greatly improved the harnessing of horses to ploughs.

One might have expected the advent of the Black Death to halt the development of agriculture, but it did not. The population of the towns was reduced by a half, and the rural community suffered almost as much. The result was that there were fewer people to feed, but there were also fewer people to grow the food. Labour became scarce, and the lord of the manor found it better to employ independent labourers than to make use of the grudging labour of his serfs, while the serfs now preferred to pay rent for their land rather than waste precious days working on their lord's land. Many lords gave up the attempt to cultivate their estates under the old system and instead let off farms to a new breed of yeoman farmer, not dissimilar to the tenant farmer of today. The serfs finally won their freedom from the lord of the manor in the reign of Queen Elizabeth I who, according to Trevelyan, 'characteristically compelled all the villeins she could find on her royal estates to purchase their freedom at a swingeing rate'. But although the serfs gained their freedom they gradually lost their rights to the land. By fair means or foul the Tudor sheep farmers (lords and yeomen whose prosperity was closely linked to that of the weavers and cloth merchants in the towns) often found ways of appropriating the village's open fields and commons and enclosing them for pasture – bequeathing the patchwork pattern of hedgerows so familiar to us until the 'prairie' farmers got going in the last few decades of the twentieth century. Some of the land enclosed was genuinely unused and some of the open fields were in desperate need of a rest from arable farming, but in the name of individual and national wealth the freed serfs were slowly forced off the land as the enclosures, which started in the southeast in Tudor times, spread by the nineteenth century to include almost all farmable land.

The upshot was the gradual breaking up of the feudal communities in which everyone had had the right to use the land even if they did not actually own it. The new system was undoubtedly less fair, but it provided the landlords and yeomen farmers with an incentive to improve agricultural productivity in a manner uncalled for during the age of feudal subsistence farming. Sir Thomas More, writing of the enclosures of 1517, commented that 'noblemen and gentlemen, yea, and certain Abbots, holy men God wot, not contenting themselves with the yearly revenues and profits that were wont to grow to their forefathers . . . leave no ground for tillage; they enclose all pastures; they throw down houses . . . and leave nothing standing but only the church to make of it a sheepcote'.

But the enclosing of land at the expense of the peasant led to the prosperous wool trade and the prosperous nation of Tudor times. It also led eventually to the ability to feed the growing towns as they gave birth to the Industrial Revolution, out of which grew the later advances of science. Whether all this could have happened without the injustices that went with it is outside the scope of this book, but it is a reflection of similar questions arising out of the development of towns, which are examined later.

2 THE INDUSTRIAL REVOLUTION

The modern man with Watt's steam-engine as burden upon his back, with Smith's *Wealth of Individuals* clasped to his bosom, is essentially the citizen of eighteenth-century Glasgow though he be now housed in one of its distant manufacturing suburbs called Birmingham, Bermondsey or Brooklyn . . . [which have like Glasgow] all the conditions of civic and national decadence on one hand, all the resources for recuperation on the other.

Patrick Geddes
Cities in Evolution

2 (i) INDUSTRY AND TRANSPORT

Rural Changes

It is rash to claim that a particular reign (or century even) marks the end of one stage of social development and the beginning of another, but there does seem some justification for regarding the Tudor period in England as a milestone. Not only did it mark the end of the Wars of the Roses and the beginning of a more stable political era, it also marked the age in which the Renaissance could be said to have properly arrived at last in this country. The growth of towns (which no longer needed fortifications), the increase in trade, and the flourishing of the arts were all interconnected. The permanent theatre of Shakespeare's day took the place of the medieval strolling players because urban populations were large enough and prosperous enough to provide an audience.

It was in Tudor times that the descendants of the feudal villein were being separated from their land as the large landowners and yeomen farmers enclosed the old communal fields. Although towns and cities of the time enjoyed more power than ever, this very power was leading the town-based merchants to avoid the well-organized urban craftsmen and rely instead on the Domestic system and its cheaper labour – often provided by those dispossessed of their land and keen to earn a living working with their families in their own cottages on the looms hired out by the merchants. For approximately the 200 years between the mid-sixteenth century and the mid-eighteenth century the face of England changed slowly as more and more fields were enclosed with hedges and the country-side became more prosperous. London steadily expanded at the expense of the provincial cities and, although new towns developed (like Birmingham and Bath), rural prosperity was at the expense of the towns.

The name 'Turnip' Townshend might conjure up a horny-handed son of the soil who, from a life of toiling on the land, came up with some innovative ways of increasing its fertility. In fact he was a second-generation viscount and former ambassador to the Netherlands who, having fallen out with Sir Robert Walpole, the Prime Minister, retired from public life to his estate in Norfolk where he applied Dutch methods of improving poor-quality land, during the middle of the eighteenth century. Instead of growing crops for two years and then leaving the land fallow for one year, in the fashion inherited from Saxon times, he worked on a four-year cycle: growing corn, root crops and grass in turn and then leaving the land fallow for a year. He used deep ploughing and harrowing, and the machinery that went with such operations, including the all-iron plough and the seed drill. It was only the likes of Lord Townshend who could afford the capital outlay involved in the new farming methods. The small yeomen farmers were driven out of business because they could not pay the rents now demanded when the large landowners realized how potentially valuable their land was.

The enclosures of the Tudor period, which first gave us the hedgerows of southern England, converted the land from communal arable farming to more profitable sheep grazing. The enclosures of the eighteenth century caused a change to even more profitable mixed farming. Not only did they almost destroy the yeoman farmer, they also took away much of the common land on which villagers had surviving rights to grazing and to wood and turf cutting.

The effects of this second rural upheaval were not dissimilar to the effects of sheep farming noted by Thomas More in Tudor times. The rich got richer and the poor got poorer. But the increased productivity of the land throughout Europe made it possible to feed the ever-growing population. For centuries production had been more or less stable. Between 1700 and 1800 it doubled. Bairoch points out that 'the Industrial Revolution was above all an agricultural revolution . . . that permitted and even generated unprecedented development in the industrial and mining sectors'.

Iron and Coal

The forests of England were decimated first for agriculture, then for shipbuilding, and finally for the smelting of iron. Smelting with charcoal involved burning many tons of timber to make one ton of iron. When the Sussex woods had been denuded, followed quickly by those of Shropshire and the Forest of Dean, England had no alternative but to import iron from Sweden and Russia where the forests were virtually inexhaustible.

Coal had been used domestically since the Middle Ages and was transported by coastal shipping from mines near the sea to centres of population that could also be reached by ship (e.g. Tyne coal to London). It was not until the seventeenth century that experiments were made with the use of coal for iron smelting, and it was not until a hundred years later in the 1750s that the Darby family's ironworks at Coalbrookdale used coal on a commercial basis. Instead of having to import iron from abroad it was now only the high-quality ore that needed to be imported, and this was brought to coal-mining areas like Tyneside and South Wales which were accessible from the sea.

Until the eighteenth century iron-making had been a local affair because trees (until they ran out) were available almost anywhere in England. On the other hand iron-making from coal had to be carried out near a coalfield (until the railways made the movement of coal easier), and this became a major factor in the siting of the new industrial towns.

The first iron bridge was built over the River Severn near Darby's Coalbrookdale works, and the first serviceable iron ship was launched in 1790. However, iron's greatest contribution to the Industrial Revolution was that it facilitated the introduction of accurately made, interchangeable machine parts, without which the machinery of mass production could never have been developed.

Textiles

As international trade expanded, it generated both competition and new markets in the textile industry. In 1700 the importation of Indian cotton was banned for its likely effect on England's wool and cloth industries, and for fear that their employees might become 'excessively burdensome and chargeable to their respective parishes', according to A.L. Morton in *A People's History of England* (Victor Gollancz, 1948). This led not only to a revival of the wool industry but also to the birth of Britain's cotton manufacturing: a new industry which was receptive to new ideas.

Although Kay's flying shuttle was introduced to the wool industry in the 1730s it was Hargreaves' spinning jenny, and more particularly Arkwright's water frame, introduced to the cotton industry in the 1760s, that revolutionized manufacturing. The spinning jenny, like the flying shuttle, was originally a piece of manual equipment. It allowed eight spindles instead of one to be controlled by one operator. But the water frame was in effect a spinning jenny operated by water power.

The use of water power had far-reaching effects on manufacturing. Although, like wind power, it had been used since the fourteenth century in corn-grinding mills, this use was to serve local needs only. Water power for cotton manufacturing was the means of mechanizing a growing industry which supplied the whole country as well as overseas markets.

Cotton manufacture had been established in Lancashire because the Pennine valleys were damp, and a damp atmosphere was important to the manufacturing process. They were also conveniently placed to receive shipments of American cotton as well as being close to the Yorkshire wool industry (wool was needed in the early days to strengthen the warp of the cotton fabric). Lastly, and becoming more important as time went on, there was fast-running water to provide power. It was not until steam-powered machinery was introduced in 1775 that factories could be set up in the great conurbations independent of water power, but the water-powered factories were the death knell of the cottage industries and of the rural communities which had gradually become more dependent on them as agricultural methods changed.

Rural Poverty

The feudal subsistence farming of ten to twenty acres per family gave way to the grazing enclosures and 'yeoman' farming of Tudor times, which in turn gave way to the largescale, scientific farming of Lord 'Turnip' Townshend. This second agricultural revolution increased production enormously but led to fewer people being employed on the land. For a time cottage industry kept the rural community from starvation but, with the beginning of the Napoleonic Wars in 1793, and with the wildly fluctuating wheat prices that followed, rural poverty became acute. Poverty relief from the Poor Rate was payable only at 'the parish of birth'. This was a sensible enough way of administering relief in the static rural communities that existed before the Industrial Revolution, but it became inappropriate when a large proportion of employment was not in the parish but in the towns. To meet their obligation to provide poverty relief the authorities either had to revert to the sixteenth-century practice of tying wages by statute to the cost of living or, much more acceptable to the landowners, they had to subsidize the family's earnings from the Poor Rate to bring them up to subsistence level. This was the course adopted by the magistrates of Speenhamland in Berkshire in 1795, and taken up universally.

The so-called Speenhamland Act had two side effects. Because payments were related to the number of children in the family, it encouraged an increase in the birth rate at a time when, thanks to medical advances, the death rate was already declining and, thanks to agricultural efficiency, employment was also declining. The result in the long term was increasing poverty, as more families became dependent entirely on the Poor Rate. This, in turn, led to an increase in the levy raised from employers which drove many of the surviving small farmers out of business.

Those small farmers who survived the increased cost of the Poor Rate were mostly put out of business by the fluctuating price of their products during the Napoleonic Wars. The large landowners had the resources to weather the bad years and make fortunes in the good ones, but the overall effect was again to reduce the number of jobs available on the land. This meant that in 1815 the returning servicemen had no alternative but to seek work in the towns, where they were joined by more than half of the rural population.

The sad postscript to the Speenhamland experiment (which had been administered with mixed motives in the countryside) was that it was replaced eventually in 1834 by the workhouses in the cities, where the clearly avowed motives were to punish people back into some sort of employment. Although it cannot have been what the Speenhamland magistrates intended, by making the Poor Rate unsupportable by the agricultural community they contributed to the general urbanization of Britain by the end of the Napoleonic Wars. A.L. Morton made the point, while admitting it to be an over-simplification, that 'Britain entered these wars as an agricultural country and emerged from them an industrial country'.

The Steam-engine

The steam-engine, or fire-engine as it was originally called, had its origin in the need to pump large quantities of water from mine-workings. Newcomen's steam pumps reigned supreme for about fifty years between 1720 and 1770. They worked not through steam pressure on a piston but through the atmospheric pressure generated in a closed tank when a vacuum is created by turning steam into water (which takes up less space).

Thomas Savery had invented and demonstrated a steam pump as early as 1698 which used both atmospheric pressure and steam pressure on a piston. But it appears never to have been used commercially, and it was not until James Watt installed his steam-pressure piston-engine at Boulton's Soho factory just outside Birmingham in 1774 that Newcomen's atmospheric-pressure engine was superseded.

Watt's steam-engine at Soho was still only a pump, but instead of pumping water out of a mine it pumped water to the top of a hill so that Boulton's factory machinery could be driven by water power. Watt first developed an engine to provide rotary motion in 1780, and the first spinning mill to use a steam-engine rather than fast-flowing water for its primary source of power was built in 1785. The effects were far-reaching. Whereas a water-powered mill before Soho had to be in the valley of a fast-flowing river, the steam-powered mill, or factory, could be built anywhere provided that there was a means of carrying coal to it.

Roads, Canals and Railways

The steam-engine itself, in its locomotive form, was ultimately to become the means of moving coal all over the country. But as early as 1759 the Duke of Bridgewater, who owned coal mines at Worsley, had commissioned James Brindley to build a canal to carry his coal to Manchester. The Bridgewater Canal reduced the cost of transporting coal to Manchester by half. By 1777 the Grand Junction Canal, which connected the Thames, Severn, Trent and Mersey, had reduced the cost of transporting clay, flint and coal to the pottery towns by three-quarters.

The canals may seem a slow way of transporting goods, but it has to be remembered that major attempts to improve the roads came after the first canals. Until the first Turnpike Act in the reign of Charles II, roads had been the responsibility of the local parish and had existed mainly for local journeys and the movement of cattle. Freight was generally carried by packhorse, and as late as 1750 it took a cart on average five hours to cover ten miles (see *The Industrial Revolution in the Eighteenth Century* by P. Mantoux, Jonathan Cape, 1928). After the 1745 rebellion in Scotland a national programme of road improvement was undertaken for primarily military reasons, and it was not until the end of the eighteenth century that Metcalf, Telford and McAdam were given the opportunity of improving the road network on a large scale. Before 1750 it took two days by coach from London to Oxford and there was no regular service at all to Scotland, but by the end of the century the stagecoach from London to Glasgow took only sixty-three hours, packhorses had been superseded by waggons, and the commercial traveller (carrying only samples) had replaced the merchant leading a string of packhorses carrying his wares for sale at the fair.

The turnpikes were unpopular with road users but the attempt to rebuild the Great North Road with public money was even more unpopular. Telford's Northern Road Bill of 1830 was thrown out, according to Hansard, on the grounds that it was 'a Scotch job to enable Scotchmen to mend their own road with English money'.

The railways, which were to replace both roads and canals as the principal means of long-distance transport, had their origins in the wooden 'tramways' which provided a comparatively friction-free 'road' for horse-drawn vehicles and guided their wheels with a vertical flange. According to Clapham's *An Economic History of Modern Britain* (Cambridge University Press, 1926), the first recorded tramway was one installed unsuccessfully in a Newcastle colliery in the reign of Charles I, but it was not until the middle of the eighteenth century, and the introduction of iron plates to protect the wooden rails from rapid wear, that the horse-drawn 'mineral lines' became popular. One of the few lines built to carry general traffic was the double-tracked Surrey Iron Railway, opened between Wandsworth and Croydon in 1805. Another was that from Glouces-ter to Cheltenham which, its promoters claimed, was not just to serve the coal market at Cheltenham but also 'to relieve the roads from the carriage of heavy articles'.

The first locomotive steam-engine to run on rails was built by Trevithick for an ironworks near Merthyr Tydfil in 1804. By 1808 he had built a circular track in London for demonstration purposes. One of George Stephenson's locomotives, Blucher, was working in Kellingworth colliery by 1814. In 1825 the first public railway (between Stockton and Darlington) was opened; and in 1830 the first passenger-carrying railway was opened between Liverpool and Manchester.

The railway-building boom in the 1830s and 1840s was still mainly concerned with the movement of coal from the mines to the factories. It ensured that industry could now be located at the centres of population rather than adjacent to its power supply, and it thus put the seal on urbanization at the expense of rural industry. Its second concern was the movement of people between cities. The movement of commuters to and within cities came later, as is illustrated by the fact that when the London-to-Birmingham railway was opened in 1834 there was no station between the London terminus at Euston and Harrow, some twelve miles distant. Never-theless, even at this early stage, the railways had an enormous influence on the current and future development of the towns and cities they served. For example, Stamford's success in repelling the Great Northern Railway ensured that the London-to-Edinburgh main line went through Peterborough instead. The result is that of

the two towns, once of similar size, Stamford now has a population
of 16,000 while Peterborough's population is more than seven times
that: 115,000. Both are pleasant towns, but they owe their very
different characters almost entirely to their respective positions on
the railway map.

The second boom in railway building in the 1860s began to take
the railway to almost every village in the land, and not just to serve
the suburbs of the cities but to provide a much quicker means of
transport within the city than could be provided by horse-buses.

Until the Railway Age London had expanded much more in
population than it had in geographical area. Bairoch points out that
at 350 people per hectare (140 per acre) a city of 100,000 people
would have its periphery less than one kilometre from the centre
(twelve to fifteen minutes' walk). Even a city of one million people
would have its periphery only an hour's walk from the centre.
London was unusual in that, with Westminster, it formed a linear
city along the Thames and used the river as its chief mode of
transport for both passengers and freight. It was a three-mile walk
from Westminster to the Tower of London, but few people lived
more than half a mile from a boat (see Figure 5).

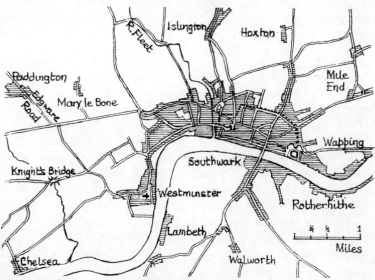

Fig. 5 The Thames as seventeenth-century transport corridor

With the benefit of hindsight it can be seen what an advantage it would have been if the steam-age cities of the nineteenth century had expanded in a similar (linear) manner to any length along the transport 'spine' but not beyond walking distance in width. This was not to be, for obvious historical reasons. By the latter half of the eighteenth century, London and all the other big cities were surrounded by villages on the coaching roads that radiated out from the centre. When the railways of the nineteenth century allowed cities to expand, they expanded in all directions, the steam trains usually running along the same valleys that the horse-drawn vehicles had travelled before them.

In the early days of railway-led expansion, however, the transport corridors in and out of the cities were, in effect, linear cities in their own right. In London's case ten of these linear cities radiated from the centre like the spokes of a wheel. Each 'spoke' had the centre of the metropolis at one end, the country at the other end, with a series of small centres in between. These suburban centres, more often than not, sprang up round the railway station built to serve the villages that survived from stagecoach days. As they expanded, they provided homes for the influx of clerks who commuted to the metropolis. At the same time local industries provided jobs for the indigenous population. Many of these expanded villages became

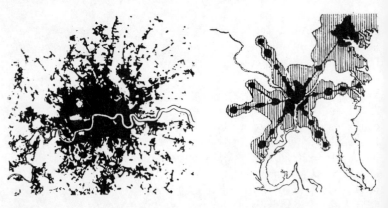

London 1914   *Washington Plan 1950*

Fig. 6 Radial cities

important towns in their own right, accessible to the population along the railway corridor which provided fast transport to the city at one end and to the countryside (in some cases the seaside) at the other end. In London's case the undeveloped countryside in between some of the radial corridors is clearly visible in contemporary maps up to about 1920. It is interesting to note that the most favoured option for the expansion of Washington DC after World War II was a similar system of radial corridors separated by green 'fingers' stretching towards the centre (see Figure 6).

At first sight it seems surprising that nineteenth-century London, having developed (albeit haphazardly) a promising overall plan and transport system, should have become a place of misery for those obliged to live and work there and a place to be escaped from as quickly as possible for those who could not afford a house in Mayfair but who could afford a suburban house and a railway season ticket.

Laissez-faire

It has to be remembered that the Industrial Revolution brought a change in the world more dramatic than anything since the collapse of Roman rule in Europe. The age dominated by a leisured and enlightened élite came to an abrupt end. The aristocracy, prepared in architectural terms to sacrifice personal aggrandizement to the achievement of a work of art, was gradually replaced by a new ruling class whose power derived from industry rather than ownership of land. These members of the new 'establishment' were less inhibited than their predecessors and set out to create wealth regardless of the cost in human terms. They obtained moral support from the Whig reformers, who went along with the theories expounded in Adam Smith's *Wealth of Nations* to the effect that interference in commerce by the state was a hindrance to the creation of wealth. From the Middle Ages it had been customary for the Government to intervene in trade in order to encourage the growth of home industries. Two examples are Edward III's ban on the import of foreign cloth in 1337 to encourage the weaving industry and the Corn Law of 1815 banning the import of cheap grain to encourage agriculture. The former probably served its purpose and the latter was probably pure protectionism, but the argument of those who advocated *laissez-faire* policies was that, however worthy the motive, in the long run such protectionist measures were inimical to free trade and national prosperity.

The medieval world in which the major part of the population was engaged in subsistence farming may have been insecure and impoverished but it was a good deal more fair than anything that followed. In the world of the Industrial Revolution new jobs were being created but they were more than offset by mechanization and the enormous expansion of the population: an opportunity for a combination of wealth creation and exploitation which the new industrialists grasped with both hands. It is difficult to blame them entirely for the social consequences. They were operating in completely new circumstances where it was every man for himself, and there was no legislation to guide or restrain them.

The Napoleonic Wars marked the end of the era when most people were employed on the land or worked in small, independent-minded towns serving the rural community; when agriculture had of necessity to be in balance with nature, and people, however poor and however exploited, could see that their work was of use to society; when lack of transport kept people in self-supporting communities; and when patriarchal responsibility usually ensured that the lord of the manor or the squire did not allow his villeins or tenants to starve, even if he often did treat them with scorn.

The new era of wealth creation saw to it that, in the name of economy, as many people as possible were crammed into one factory, the machines of which could be operated by one steam-engine; that the surplus of labour enabled hours to be long and wages short; and that, because there were as yet no public-health acts, housing could be cramped, insanitary and in the shadow of the smoking factory chimneys.

Although reform was on the way it was a long time coming. In *The Culture of Cities* Lewis Mumford describes *laissez-faire* as an attempt to break through outdated privileges: the result of which was to supplement the old privileged class with a new one. Of the Industrial Revolution generally he says that 'in an age of rapid technical progress the city as a social unit lay outside the circle of invention'.

2 (ii) URBAN REFORM

Reform before 1700

In *Urban Change and Planning* (G.T. Foulis and Co., 1972), Gordon Cherry draws attention to the fact that the English tradition of building towns to a conscious pattern goes back to the reign of Edward I in the thirteenth century. But until the latter half of the eighteenth century the urban population remained more or less constant, and the population of the country as a whole grew only slowly. There was seldom cause therefore for extending towns or founding new settlements. Consequently there was little opportunity for urban reform through town planning in the modern sense of the phrase. At the time of the Black Death in the fourteenth century, some villages were deserted in favour of new sites about a mile away, but this was done in a hurry to avoid infection and gave little time or opportunity for thought about the form that the new settlements might take.

We have already seen that the Great Fire of London in 1666 provided a splendid opportunity for rebuilding the city, and that this opportunity was not taken. Christopher Wren was successful in getting his new churches built, which was to our advantage, and the city's new roads were laid out to his design, which was rather less to our advantage. Otherwise the city reverted to its essentially medieval form. Nevertheless the Fire of London did lead in the end to reforms in building practice. They had no effect on the buildings erected in the immediate aftermath of the fire, but had a profound effect on the safety and appearance of eighteenth- and nineteenth-century domestic building. It is to the post-Fire of London legislators that we owe the ubiquitous party wall, which in pre-twentieth-century terraces projects through the roof to prevent the spread of fire from house to house (often at the expense of letting in the rain). And it is to them, legislating more than fifty years after the fire, that we owe our general ability to differentiate between a Queen Anne terrace (with its timber window frames more or less flush with the outside face of the wall) and a Georgian terrace (with its window frames set back from the face of the wall to minimize the risk of fire spread).

Georgian Estates and Spa Towns

Opportunity for reform in the layout of towns generally presented itself only when new building took place on a large scale under either a paternalistic industrialist or an enlightened landowner. Although at the time of the Fire of London Sir John Lowther was already laying out his Whitehaven estate as a coal and shipbuilding port it was not until a hundred years later that his descendant, the Earl of Lonsdale, completed the spacious grid layout of the new town. By this time towns were beginning to expand rapidly. In Bristol, Queens Square was built between 1700 and 1727 and St James's Square between 1707 and 1716. Cherry cites both as examples of a landlord achieving overall uniformity through conditions in leases which prevented householders making unsuitable alterations to their properties. In giving further examples he goes on to say, 'Georgian taste in architecture had a widespread impact, and there are many examples all over the country, ranging from high streets in country towns like Henley-on-Thames, to market places such as Newark, collegiate squares at Oxford and Cambridge, Inns of Court in London, and town design as at Blandford Forum where rebuilding followed destruction by fire in 1731.'

Mention has already been made in Chapter 1 (iii) of the benefit to London derived from the fact that, within the limitations of the transport available, it was free to expand – unlike Paris, which was hemmed in by fortifications. From the planning point of view it also benefited from the tendency for land to be owned in large blocks which could be developed as a whole. The first half of the eighteenth century saw the completion of Grosvenor and Blooms-bury Squares which were to be the precursors of many developments by the Dukes of Westminster and Bedford respectively.

The first half of the eighteenth century also saw the early development of the spa towns, many of which, like Bath, can be regarded as new towns in their own right, since their size and function swamped the small settlements on which they were founded. It is true that Bath owed its name to its Roman predecessor, but the new Bath Spa of the John Woods (father and son) had nothing else in common with the tiny English town that it replaced.

The spa towns were a phenomenon that belonged very much to the Renaissance life. Although Bath and Buxton and, later,

Brighton and Cheltenham had a homely 'English' look, they were nevertheless built entirely for the benefit of the leisured class. If health was their justification, pleasure was their real purpose (and pleasure they still give). The nearest equivalent to modern town planning was probably the New Town in Edinburgh. If the spa towns were for the good of the established gentry, and the new squares on the peripheries of London and Bristol were for the good of the up-and-coming middle classes, Edinburgh's New Town was for the good of the city as a whole. It may have housed the Scottish version of the merchants who came to live in the London squares, but it was conceived not just as a piece of enlightened real-estate development but as a means of extending rationally a city which had reached the geographical limits of its natural medieval site. The idea of Edinburgh's New Town was first mooted in 1752, and in 1765 'Architects and others' were invited to 'give in plans of a New Town marking out streets of proper breadth, and by-lanes, and the best situation for a reservoir, and any other public buildings that may be thought necessary'. James Craig's proposals were accepted and used as the master plan until the New Town conceived in 1752 had been completed in 1820. The city magistrates enforced compliance with the master plan when necessary to ensure that the original concept was not lost, and the only substantial variation from Craig's plan was in the case of Charlotte Square, which was designed by Robert Adam.

Development control for the overall good of the whole city, like that at Edinburgh, was rare in the eighteenth century. It was more common for the landowner-developer to be thinking only in terms of the increased value of the particular piece of land being developed. However, since it was customary to sell only a lease on the new property, the landowner who retained the freehold was more concerned with the long-term value of his land than with the short-term profit to be made simply from the selling of the houses on it. Furthermore the aristocratic landowner was generally well-educated and well-travelled, as well as being well-versed in Renaissance architecture and keen to show it. Hence the carefully laid-out squares and crescents, in a domestic English adaptation of the classical style, planned in a comparatively stable world, with long-term interests in mind.

Growth of the Urban Population

Development in the new or rapidly expanding towns and cities of the Industrial Revolution was carried out in very different circumstances from those of the mid-eighteenth century described above. By the time of Napoleon's defeat at Waterloo in 1815 the concentration of jobs in the large steam-powered factories, combined with the effects of rural poverty, had turned the drift to the towns into a headlong rush. Although the building of housing estates for the middle classes increased, it represented only a small part of the total volume of building. There was more money to be made by developing around factories, on land never thought of as building land, and letting the so-called housing to poor immigrants from the countryside. Gordon Cherry describes the scene thus: 'Speculative building and the virtual absence of building regulations produced housing of a very low standard. In Bradford one reads of superficial dwellings, rapidly erected, with no cellars or foundations, with walls only half a brick thick; and houses built back-to-back without ventilation or drainage, double rows forming courts with common pumps and privies.' Donald Osen, writing in *The Victorian City – . Images and Reality* (Routledge and Kegan Paul, 1973), describes the attitude of both the very poor and the better-off artisan, and says of both: 'Their chief requirement as to housing was that it be cheap and that it be densely enough built so that everyone could live within walking distance of his work.' It also has to be borne in mind that to the newly arrived bumpkin the city's mixture of brightly lit streets, music halls, crime, long hours of work for little pay, and squalid housing was better than stagnating in the country without either work or entertainment.

Because the cotton industry was the first to be mechanized, Manchester demonstrates one of the earliest and most sudden explosions of the urban population. In 1774 its population was 24,000 but within twenty-seven years (by the time of the first national census in 1801) it had almost trebled to 70,000. Cherry points out that Birmingham was rather different because the Black Country had a reputation for manufacturing before the Industrial Revolution and had since about 1600 consisted of scattered interdependent communities of miners and metalworkers. Nevertheless Birmingham's population increased from about 30,000 in 1760 to

60,000 in 1801. It was in the next half-century, however, when the steam-powered factory had become universal, that population growth in the industrial towns turned them into the overcrowded dens of despair described by Charles Dickens. The fact that these conurbations could be supplied by railway had the effect of making those who lived in the centre more remote than ever from the outside world. Milk supplies from nearby farms were made redundant by 'train milk', and the problems of sanitation were made worse by the fact that it was no longer economical for farmers to collect human excreta from the town for farm manure. Even London, which had already grown from 674,000 in 1700 to 900,000 in 1801, more than doubled its population in the first half of the nineteenth century (to two million). Furthermore it has to be remembered that it was not until about 1850 that the railways provided extensive suburban services (as opposed to inter-city services) sufficient to allow any significant decentralization. In other words London at the time of the Great Exhibition of 1851 was made up of two million people closely packed together so that most were within walking distance of the centre.

Salubrious Suburbs

Once steam power had superseded water power and factories could be sited in the towns where there was a plentiful supply of labour, not only were labourers drawn to the centres of the towns where the factories were but people who could afford to get away from the smoke of the factory chimneys were driven out: thus reversing the old order of things, whereby the wealthier members of the urban community had lived within the city's protective walls and the poor had been left outside.

From about 1820 to 1840 there was a boom in the building of large houses for well-to-do merchants within a carriage-ride of our city centres. In London's case prosperous new suburbs grew up around existing villages at places like Camberwell, Brixton and Islington, and the roads which led to them through open countryside were quickly lined with ribbon development. (The phrase 'ribbon development' was not coined until the 1920s and few people would use it now to describe the late-Georgian terraces of the 1820s, but it is nevertheless apt in many cases.)

The prosperity of these new suburbs was, however, short-lived. The development of the old village of Islington is typical of London and no doubt typical of other cities as well. Situated on a hill less than two miles from the City but separated from it by fields, its tea gardens in Samuel Pepys's time had been the object of many a Sunday-afternoon jaunt. From 1820 onwards the village was swamped by elegant Georgian squares and terraces built for the 'carriage folk' who wanted to escape the increasing pollution in London, but by 1860 the railways enabled such people to move out further to the 'real' country. In many cases these new houses survived as single dwellings for little more than ten years before they were divided up into small tenements for artisans.

Urban Transport and Geographical Expansion

Until the middle of the nineteenth century most of Britain's urban population lived within walking distance of both their work and the town centre. Even London with its two million inhabitants and expanding middle-class suburbs was still contained within a three-mile radius. However, from 1850 onwards towns and cities began to expand in geographical area on the same sort of scale that they had expanded in numbers of people at the beginning of the century. The suburban population of the capital grew by almost fifty per cent between *each* ten-year census from 1861 to 1901. As the capital city London was still the greatest magnet for the inflow of population but, unlike the situation before the end of the eighteenth century, the industrial cities of Birmingham, Glasgow, Manchester, Leeds, Newcastle, Liverpool, etc., were also attracting increasing numbers of people to them; and as the new immigrants arrived at the centre, so the original inhabitants tended to move out to the suburbs.

The outward expansion of cities was made possible first by the railways, then by the electric tram and Underground railway. The first (steam-operated) Underground was opened from the City of London (Farringdon) to Paddington in 1864, and it is interesting to note that Paddington was one of the first London suburbs to be colonized by artisans who would earlier have lived close to their places of work.

There had been extensive services of horse-trams in Leeds, Plymouth, Hull, Glasgow, Liverpool and Bolton, and there were

horse-buses in London, but it was not until the first complete
electric tram service in Bradford that there was any serious rival to
the railways for transporting people *en masse*. According to Bairoch,
horse-buses of a sort were first introduced in Paris as early as 1662,
but it seems that the authorities saw them as dangerously egalitarian
and therefore ruined them financially by banning their use by
'people of low estate'. The first 'modern' service of horse-buses was
also introduced in Paris (in 1828), but if the horse-tram was not a
serious rival to the railways as a mass transit system, the horse-buses
were even less so. They tended to be used only by 'respectable'
people, and then only for short journeys.

The 1880s, however, saw not only the introduction of the electric
tram but also the Cheap Trains Act of 1883 which brought in the
'workman's fare' for travel before 7 A.M. (a facility that was not
withdrawn until after World War II). Thus the labouring classes,
particularly the city clerks, joined the throng of people living in the
suburbs but working in the city centre. The City of London's
night-time population fell by 32.5 per cent – from 74,900 in 1871 to
50,500 in 1881 – while its daytime population rose 53.4 per cent in
only five years – from 170,000 in 1876 to 261,000 in 1881 (Cherry –
Urban Change and Planning). This trend was stimulated by the
opening of the first deep Underground (the City and South London
Electric Railway from the Bank to Stockwell) in 1890, the Liverpool
Overhead Railway between 1893 and 1896, and the Glasgow
Underground (originally cable-drawn) in 1896. Similar if less spectacular developments elsewhere ensured that during the 1890s,
when there was no planning legislation to prevent it, the central
areas of our cities were dominated by commercial development, and
housing was driven out. This outward movement was made possible
by the expansion of the transport system and led, in turn, to
demands for its further expansion.

2 (iii) NINETEENTH-CENTURY REFORM

Parliamentary and Municipal Representation

In the 1860s the Great Northern Railway displayed an advertise-
ment which posed the question, 'Why live in London when you

could live in the countryside at Muswell Hill?' However, as soon as people took the hint in large numbers, the countryside moved itself to Potters Bar, and the attempts of citizens to escape from the city by moving a little bit further out proved futile as a long-term answer to the question – and has done so ever since.

The fact that everyone who could afford to do so moved out of central London demonstrated that the city was not a place one lived in by choice. But there were so many injustices in nineteenth-century cities that it is hardly surprising that the politicians and reformers put improvements to the physical environment at the bottom of their list of priorities. Even Ruskin made the point that it was futile to have 'Art' until there was clean air and pure water. The result was that although the city worked as an economic unit, with goods and people carried probably more efficiently than they are today, the dreary streets in which people lived, overshadowed by the smoky factories in which they worked, represented even worse living conditions than the more primitive but less crowded conditions of town and country in the eighteenth century.

The first significant move to put right the injustices brought about by urbanization was the campaign that culminated in the Great Reform Bill of 1832. It had little to do with urban reform and dealt with electoral anomalies that predated the Industrial Revolution. Nevertheless, just as the Duke of Wellington feared, it made reform respectable and thus accelerated it. Having recognized the absurdity of two parliamentary seats for 'rotten boroughs' (which were in many cases only tiny hamlets) and none at all for the new, thriving industrial cities like Birmingham, and having consequently rationalized its own representation, it was only a matter of time before Parliament was obliged to turn its attention to the reform of local government.

Parliamentary reform had followed the economic slump in the years immediately after the Napoleonic Wars. It had been stimulated by a combination of unrest amongst the labouring classes, a fear of revolution amongst the middle classes and a demand for power amongst the new captains of industry, who felt ignored by the 'establishment'. Similar alliances brought about the Municipal Corporation Act of 1835. As Trevelyan describes it in his *History of England*, 'The fall of Parliamentary rotten boroughs involved the fall of the municipal rotten boroughs, analogous sister bodies in the field of local government. The Act of 1835 was more democratic than the Reform Bill for it gave all rate-payers the right to vote for the new municipalities.' The Act certainly made corporations more open and less corrupt, but their powers were constrained by the lack of control over their expanding peripheral areas, which were still administered as if they were part of the rural countryside. The situation in London was absurd. Only the old city (or square mile) was affected by the Act, as a result of which the capital as a whole was, according to Cherry, 'governed by 300 local bodies including seven Commissioners of Sewers, 172 vestries (based on the ecclesiastical parishes) and almost one hundred paving, lighting and cleansing boards'. In 1837 the Royal Commission on Municipal Corporations recommended that London should have a uniform authority. However, it was not until 1855 that the Metropolitan Board of Works enabled the capital to have an integrated drainage system, and not until the Local Government Act of 1888 that urban administration throughout the country was rationalized and the capital's administration was taken over by the London County Council.

Public Health Acts

Although it was representation in Parliament that brought about the early reforms, it was concern for health and public sanitation that maintained the reforming momentum through the mid-nineteenth century. Adam Smith's *Wealth of Nations* had been published in 1776 and its theories of *laissez-faire* had been adopted enthusiastically by the reform-minded Whig intelligentsia, who saw it as a means of destroying the power of the land-owning Tory establishment. It is hardly surprising, therefore, to find that at the beginning of the century there was a general suspicion of any reform that involved Government intervention on a large scale; but the worst of the speculative housing for those on low wages was built in the 1830s and 1840s, by which time the secretary to the Poor Law Commissioners, Chadwick, had demonstrated by his campaign for better sanitation that one landowner's cesspools could be polluting another's water supply, and that overall regulation could therefore no longer be avoided. In 1839 the Bishop of London proposed an inquiry into the sanitary conditions of the working classes, and 1840 saw the publication of the report of the Select Committee on the Health of Towns.

It was not until 1848, however, that the first Public Health Act gave new powers and responsibilities to local authorities on such matters as sewers, water supplies, refuse and the ventilation of dwellings. According to Cherry, the deep-seated resistance to public intervention had resulted in the rejection of the Act in 1847, and it was only a timely outbreak of cholera that led to its being passed the following year. It was not until the second Public Health Act in 1875 that local authorities were compelled to build sewage works, rather than discharge their drainage systems into existing watercourses, and it was then that smallpox, typhus and cholera were more or less eliminated.

Housing by Paternalist Employers

Bad sanitation in our towns and cities had demonstrably been a cause of death. Overcrowding had not. The reformers cannot be blamed therefore for tackling sanitation first. Nevertheless individual philanthropic manufacturers had perceived the advantages, both moral and economic, of a contented workforce, and provided good-quality housing adjacent to their factories with this in mind. The last thing they wanted to do was to oblige their workers to live amongst the dark, satanic mills of the existing townships, so these Utopian communities tended to be on cheap, greenfield sites served by canal or railway, and had little influence on the form of the towns themselves. The first of them was the exception that proves the rule. New Lanark needed neither canal nor railway, having been established in 1784 as a cotton manufacturing village on the Falls of Clyde at a time when water power was still king. It was taken over by that prophet of the co-operative movement, Robert Owen, in 1799 and run subsequently on paternalistic lines, as part of a wider scheme envisaged by Owen (but never realized) for 'agricultural and manufacturing villages of unity and mutual co-operation'.

In the 1850s Titus Salt developed his new town of Saltaire around his textile mill in the Yorkshire countryside not far from Bradford; while in the 1880s William Lever, of soap fame, developed Port Sunlight near Birkenhead and, most famous of all, George Cadbury built Bournville outside Birmingham.

Housing Trusts and Bye-laws

In established towns the main preoccupation was rightly still with sanitation. But with no building bye-laws, and most of the cheap housing being built by small builders, it was difficult to set any standards for housing itself. Once reforms in sanitation were under way, however, the reformers do seem to have turned their attention to housing, even if their influence was only slight. The Metropolitan Association for Improving the Dwellings of the Industrious Classes was established in 1841, and the Society for the Improvement of Conditions of the Labouring Classes was established in 1844.

Henry Roberts, with backing from Prince Albert, built a two-storey block of four small flats for the Great Exhibition of 1851 in Hyde Park. When the Crystal Palace, which housed the exhibition, was moved to south London, Roberts's 'Model Homes for the Working Classes' were re-erected in Kennington Park. Charming, simple, little dwellings they are, but even if a way could have been found of financing them, it must be doubtful whether they could have provided a sufficient density of population to solve London's housing problem – especially at a time when nearly everyone had to be housed within walking distance of a town centre.

Fig. 7 'Model Homes for the Working Classes'

It was not until the setting up of the Housing Trusts (of which the Peabody Trust, established in 1863, is the best known) that there were any significant improvements in urban housing for the less well-off. Apart from rules related to drainage and the prevention of fire spread, there were in effect no building regulations until the Public Health Act of 1875. However, it seems that the Peabody Trust set its own rules and erected the many solidly built, five-storey blocks of flats that are still, with modernization, serviceable today. It has to be admitted, though, that they hardly made much of an improvement to the appearance of the urban environment; and while they provided profit-free housing for some artisans they could only nibble at the housing problem as a whole, and they were certainly not able to help those most in need.

The bye-laws incorporated in the 1875 Public Health Act covered not only drainage but also ventilation, space at the rear of buildings, thickness of walls, etc. It is from these bye-laws that we have inherited the ubiquitous and monotonous two-storey housing, with large back additions and small back yards, which make up the housing of the latter part of the nineteenth century. They are generally well-built (although damp-proof courses did not appear until the turn of the century), and infinitely healthier than what went before. Even if the back yards were only small as 'gardens', they were sufficient to provide proper daylighting at the rear and cross-ventilation.

A popular image of the nineteenth century is of Dickensian squalor in housing (ironically often mistakenly associated with bye-law housing) contrasted with the civic splendour of Grainger's central Newcastle, Birmingham's Corporation Street, and countless town halls, trade halls and railway stations in London, Manchester, Liverpool, Glasgow, Leeds and Sheffield. The real blot on the nineteenth century, however, was not its housing nor its working conditions – bad though they were – but the appalling contrast between those who made their fortunes in the city and lived outside, and those, poorly paid or unemployed, who were forced to live in the city half starved because anywhere else they would have starved completely.

In the social sense the nineteenth-century city represented many steps backwards from the towns that gained their charters from Edward I 600 years earlier, and which represented the forefront of the common man's escape from feudalism.

PART II The Present Impasse

3   FAILURES IN PLANNING AND HOUSING

Ebenezer Howard . . . hated the city and thought it an outright evil and an affront to nature that so many people should get themselves into an agglomeration. His prescription for saving the people was doing the city in.

Jane Jacobs
The Death and Life of
Great American Cities

3 (i) SUBURBS, GARDEN CITIES AND TOWER BLOCKS

Ebenezer Howard, Patrick Geddes and Raymond Unwin

From 1850 onwards, John Ruskin, through his books and pamphlets, attacked the evils of the *laissez-faire* capitalism that had been born of Adam Smith's *Wealth of Nations* a century earlier, and which was then giving rise to the squalor and degradation rife in all large cities. Until the Railway Age the middle classes had been well aware of urban poverty because they had lived adjacent to it. In the mid-nineteenth century it was less obvious to them, except perhaps from the train window as they travelled from leafy suburb to the prosperous business centre. As a result Ruskin's voice was for some time an isolated one, but by the end of the century his ideas based on intellect had been supplemented by facts based on surveys: in particular by Charles Booth's survey of London which showed that thirty per cent of the capital's population lived on or below a poverty line which we in the 1990s would regard as distress indeed, and by Seebohm Rowntree's survey of York which showed that those in

smaller cities fared much the same. In the meantime the radical
Christians, William Booth of Salvation Army fame and Congrega-
tional minister Andrew Mearns, had added to the clamour for reform
which eventually reached sympathetic ears in both the Liberal and
Conservative parties. No doubt largely as a result of such influences,
the Housing of the Working Classes Act of 1890 gave local authorities the power to close and, if necessary, to demolish unhealthy
dwellings. It also gave powers to use public funds to build new
dwellings.

Although any concerted effort at clearing the slums and rebuilding cities was still a long way off, the reformers' pressure for
something to be done was echoed by a search amongst architects for
new forms in mass housing, which they had previously regarded as
outside their professional concern. They had responded to William
Morris's call for a return to an English vernacular style of house
building and they must have been influenced by the Viennese
architect, Camillo Sitte, whose book *The Art of Building Cities* (1889)
deplored the loss of the enclosed character of the street and its
reduction 'to a mere traffic utility'.

Henry George, an American who deplored the concentration of so
many people in cities at the expense of rural areas, had started
people thinking about decentralization, but it was not until 1898
when Ebenezer Howard published his *Garden Cities of Tomorrow*
(new edition, Attic Books, 1985) that serious thought was given
to the form of the city of the future. William Morris, who with
Ruskin had founded the Arts and Crafts Movement, published his
Utopian *News from Nowhere* in 1892. It was socially radical and
called, in effect, for the abolition of cities and the industrialization
that went with them. It was a plea for a return to the countryside
and to a rural life of social equality but shorn of mechanization.
Ebenezer Howard, on the other hand, combined idealism
with practicality, and a large part of his book deals with
the method of financing the building of the new cities that he
proposed.

Howard's garden cities were not intended to be the low-density,
middle-class garden suburbs that were built at the beginning of the
twentieth century and hailed as examples of his theories. His
treatise had proposed the dispersal of population and jobs from our
overcrowded cities to a series of planned garden cities located

beyond a green belt surrounding the parent city. These new towns would thereby relieve the overcrowding of the parent city and allow it, in turn, to be redeveloped gradually along more spacious lines. He argued that reducing the excessively high density that prevailed at the time would lead to a reduction in land values and hence make redevelopment cheaper. In the long term he envisaged a cluster of garden cities surrounding a larger central garden city but separated from it, and from each other, by countryside.

Howard imagined that the central city of his cluster would have a population of about 60,000 and that the population of each satellite city would be 30,000. Housing in the garden cities would be built to a net residential density (as described in Chapter 7 (i)) of eighty people per acre, but it would be separated from the shopping and administrative centre by generous public gardens. Similarly it would be separated by gardens from the industrial belt which would be on the periphery. Both the central city and the satellite cities would each have their own orbital railway serving the industrial estates on the periphery and linked to an intermunicipal railway, while radial and orbital transport within each city would be by electric tram. Thus the transport system for each city of the cluster echoed the system for the cluster as a whole (see Figure 8).

An important element of Ebenezer Howard's garden-city concept was the reform of land ownership. He envisaged each city being built by a company that would own the land and that, by virtue of the increase in land value generated by the development of the city, would be able to charge economic rents which would help pay for community services and amenities. This idea was far ahead of its time and it was not fully implemented at either Letchworth (1903) or Welwyn (1919), although the present Letchworth comes near to achieving it. Howard's other important concept – the balanced town with its own industries – was realized through the establishment of household names such as Spirella at Letchworth and Welgar Shredded Wheat at Welwyn.

The 'garden' part of the garden-city concept was also successful at Letchworth and Welwyn, where the principles of tree-lined streets and ample public open space were adhered to throughout the building process. The same principles were also applied successfully at Hampstead Garden Suburb in London, designed in 1905 by Raymond Unwin and Barry Parker (who had been the architects at Letchworth), and at Wythenshawe in Manchester (designed by Parker in 1930). Wythenshawe was half suburb, in that it was intended to provide some local employment and also living accommodation for people with jobs in Manchester. Hampstead Garden Suburb was nothing more nor less than a dormitory: much criticized for that reason, but much admired for its landscaping and for its original social mix, which had been one of the aims of the Garden Suburb Trust.

Although the number of people housed in any sort of garden city before World War II was pathetically small, Government approval of universal standards of housing along garden-city lines came in 1918 with the Tudor Walters Report on 'The Provision of Dwellings for

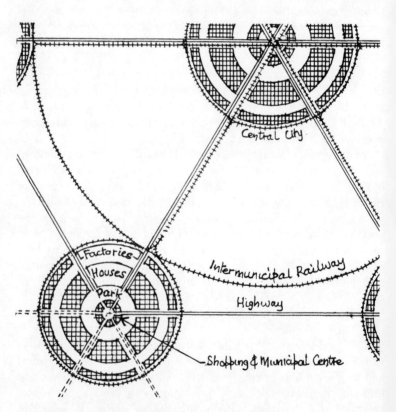

Fig. 8 Ebenezer Howard's Slumless, Smokeless Cities

the Working Classes in England, Wales and Scotland'. The Report's recommendations bore fruit in the form of local-authority housing estates in the 1920s and 1930s.

Parallel with these developments in the design and layout of housing was the pursuit of Howard's original concerns about the overall form of the whole city. Howard himself founded the Garden City Association in 1899, which is still active today as the Town and Country Planning Association, but the two most influential figures of the decade immediately after World War I were the geographer (and mentor of Lewis Mumford) Patrick Geddes, and the architect of Letchworth, Raymond Unwin. Geddes too had been involved in the surveys for Letchworth but his *Cities in Evolution* (Williams and Norgate, 1949), although largely written in 1910, was not published until 1915. It was concerned with the tendency for large industrial towns to coalesce into huge, continuous urban sprawls, which he christened 'conurbations'. Unwin translated this concern into practical terms and, in reports to the Greater London Regional Planning Committee in 1929 and 1933, pressed the need for a green belt round London to contain the built-up area. He argued that if further development in the city region were needed it had to be in the form of satellite towns beyond the green belt. His recommendations for London resulted eventually in the 1938 Green Belt (London and Home Counties) Act, but his reports to similar regional planning committees throughout England and Wales did not bear fruit until after World War II.

'Private' Suburban Sprawl and 'Public' Cottage Estates

It is one thing to look at the early twentieth century through the thoughts and deeds of the seers, as Peter Hall aptly describes them in his book *Urban and Regional Planning* (Allen and Unwin, 1985), but it is an altogether different and much more depressing experience to observe what generally happened. For the most part private suburban development was concerned with making money out of people's desire to move out of towns and cities at as little cost as possible. There was no question of planning in the garden-city sense, let alone in the Renaissance sense. Developers were not concerned with increasing the value of their land in the long term but with a quick profit from buying vacant land cheap, putting houses on it, and selling it dear. Whenever possible, buildings were simply strung along existing roads – a process that inevitably led to suburban sprawl as towns and villages were joined together and thus lost their individual characteristics. Such housing could be served by motorbuses, and later by cars, but, unlike the railway-served suburbs of the nineteenth century which were developed in depth around the station, the 'ribbon developments' of the early twentieth century were too scattered to support local facilities like shops and pubs within walking distance of everyone's front door, let alone to provide the identifiable community of traditional rural village or urban neighbourhood.

But if the 'private sector' had its pioneers in the Garden City Movement, the 'public sector' – after the Tudor Walters Report – had the resources and the idealism to adopt many of the movement's ideas, as exemplified by Wythenshawe and by the cottage estates in London. The latter were part of the London County Council's rolling programme of slum clearance between the two World Wars. They were not garden cities, because they were not designed as balanced communities with jobs as well as houses. They were simply well-designed dormitory suburbs, but they did adopt the garden-city principle of closely grouped buildings and generous open space (see Figure 9).

The LCC's cottage estates at Acton, Becontree, Dagenham, St Helier (near Morden), etc., together housed about 100,000 people (at least the equivalent of a new town) and it is surprising that they are so little talked about. But it has to be admitted that, although they accommodated many more people to the acre in far more pleasant surroundings than the speculative builders' ribbon developments, they were still too spread out to provide basic facilities within walking distance, and they used up too much land to be the pattern for a general solution to the overall housing problems of large cities. Perhaps their most important contribution to the history of urban housing is that they kept alive Ebenezer Howard's concept of the garden city until it finally flowered into something approaching its creator's ideal, in the programme of new-town construction after World War II.

The dilemma of housing reform in the 1920s and 1930s was nicely demonstrated by a series of contemporary documentary films on 'the housing problem' reshown fifty years later by the British Film

Institute. The earliest films from the mid-1920s showed small, cottage-style developments on isolated sites, reminiscent of Henry Roberts's 'Model Homes', but with more generous accommodation. They appeared as charmingly rural oases in the heart of industrial slums, but it was clear from the introduction to the films of the late 1930s (shown on the same evening instead of fifteen years apart) that the pair-of-pretty-cottages approach had done nothing more than scratch the surface of urban squalor. One of the later films then went on to extol the virtues of the Quarry Hill Estate in Leeds which, although popular while it was properly maintained, was demolished in disgrace in the mid-1980s because it provided such an unfriendly external environment.

It is very easy to be wise after the event, especially when it is possible to see propaganda from two decades in one evening, but it has to be borne in mind that even the worst of the 1930s multi-storey flat blocks were, for those living in them, infinitely preferable

Fig. 9 LCC cottage estate at Acton

to the bug-infested slums that they replaced. Furthermore, with the revival of the traditional urban street ruled out because of its association with such slums, the problem seemed insuperable: either one built 'small' and only nibbled at the problem, or one built 'large' and achieved a considerably less satisfactory environment.

New Towns after World War II

In 1939 seven and a half per cent of Britain's population were living at two or more people per room, and over half a million houses were still scheduled for slum clearance; but after two decades of house building since World War I, almost forty per cent of Britain's population was living in accommodation that was less than twenty years old: a third of them in council housing and two-thirds as owner-occupiers in the new outer suburbs (Cherry – *Urban Change and Planning*). The suburban housing of the 1930s, however, suffered from the same defects of leap-frogging as had been suffered in the nineteenth century. Every new suburb separated an existing suburb from the very countryside that had been the reason for the latter's existence. Furthermore, the internal-combustion engine made it no longer necessary to be within walking distance of a railway station and thus led to low-density sprawl. Gordon Cherry, describing the attitude of the 1930s visionaries, says, 'Suburbia was decried visually and from the point of view of its social sterility. Formless urban sprawl was abhorred and with it the economic waste associated with lengthy journeys to work.' Cherry clearly regarded this attitude as somewhat exaggerated, as did many others in the reaction against urbanism in the 1970s and early 1980s. However, with the advent of concern for the effects on the environment of excessive travel, the attitude of the 1930s visionaries now seems remarkably up to date.

As a result of fears about the effects of both uncontrolled industrial growth and suburban sprawl, a Royal Commission was appointed in 1937 under the chairmanship of Sir Anderson Montague-Barlow, 'first to inquire into the *causes* of the geographical distribution of industry and population, and possible changes in the causatory factors in the future; secondly to consider the *disadvantages* – social, economic and strategic – of the concentration of industry into large centres; and thirdly to report on *remedies* that were necessary in the national interest'. Due to the political crises that preceded World War II, and the outbreak of war itself, the Barlow Commission did not report until 1940, by which time the need for a planned economy to make the most of the 'war effort' had removed the last vestiges of support for *laissez-faire* as a form of geographical planning. Cherry describes the Commission's proposals for national action as threefold: 'the continued further redevelopment of congested urban areas where necessary; the decentralization or dispersal, both of industries and industrial population, from such areas; and the encouragement of a reasonable balance of industrial development, so far as possible, throughout the various regions of the country, coupled with appropriate diversification of industry in each region'.

Thomas Sharp's book *Town Planning* (Penguin Books, 1940) reached a wide readership and helped to generate interest not only in the Barlow Report but more importantly in the general possibilities of post-War planning; and F.J. Osborn's *New Towns After The War*, originally published in 1918, was reissued with amendments in 1942. The latter sought to rehouse two million people in fifty new towns throughout Britain. Each town of 40,000 people was to be (a) large enough to allow for efficient industrial organization and full social activity, (b) surrounded by a zone of land sufficient to possess a distinctively rural and agricultural character, and (c) owned and administered in the interests of the community.

The towns established under the New Towns Act of 1946 generally followed the principles expounded by Osborn, which had themselves followed those put forward originally by Howard and the Town and Country Planning Association. The Act established development corporations for each new town whose powers included the right to buy land in defined areas at agricultural values, to borrow money from the Government, and to act as their own planning authority. The Mark I towns, like Stevenage, Harlow and Crawley, were designed primarily as overspill accommodation for Londoners; the Mark II towns, like Redditch, Runcorn, Washington and Telford, were primarily to revitalize depressed areas of the country; while Milton Keynes (Mark III) was a conscious experiment in living with the motorcar.

There seem to be four main reasons why the new towns did less than was expected of them to solve the problems of our existing cities. First, the continued growth of London was not anticipated, and the likely effect of the new towns was therefore overestimated; secondly, there were not enough of them; thirdly, they failed to attract sufficient industry to provide jobs for all their inhabitants, many of whom continued to commute to the conurbations; and lastly, they were insufficiently compact to provide the vitality associated with urban living in the European tradition. These are harsh criticisms considering that the new towns were the bright stars of Britain's efforts at post-War planning. It would, in any case, have been impossible to justify a reliance solely on new towns to solve all our urban problems. Neither can the new towns themselves be blamed for failing to attract sufficient industry. They did their best, and if they had been more successful it would probably have been at the expense of the jobs of those left in the cities. They can, however, be blamed for failure to follow Howard's (and Osborn's) concept of the *compact* garden city. Although even here the Mark I towns were doing no more than following their brief to provide overspill accommodation, their opting for a form of development that was generally scattered and consumed a lot of land confirmed their role as a sort of urban safety valve rather than as Howard's provider of a more radical and more universal replacement of existing cities.

Nevertheless, in spite of its shortcomings, the post-War pro-gramme of new-town building did provide a greatly improved environment for a large number of people. Harlow worked particu-larly well in its early days, with its town centre and lively market square easily reached by an excellent bus service from compact neighbourhoods laid out around intimate green spaces. But as cars took over from buses as the primary means of transport the centre became less accessible and the environment deteriorated. Some of the later new towns were able to take more account of rising car ownership, but the Mark I variety suffered from the fact that their early growing pains were quickly followed by a constant erosion of the maturing environment, as they (like existing towns) tried to cope with more traffic than they could accommodate. In particular their town centres, which were supposed to be surroun-ded by public parks, were surrounded instead by multi-storey car parks.

Milton Keynes was designed as a car-oriented city to overcome the transport problems of the Mark I towns. Through careful planning and detailed design it goes a long way towards solving the problems of car-oriented living, but even in the 1960s and 1970s, when it was being designed and built, it represented a burying of heads in the sand so far as an alternative to existing cities was concerned. If the population of London were to be rehoused at the density of Milton Keynes the capital's built-up area would be increased by two and a half times (see Chapter 7 (i)) and finding space for it in the southeast of England would certainly not be possible without intolerable damage to the rest of the region. This suggests that we can live in a car-oriented society only if we are prepared to forgo the countryside, or that, if we retain our country-side, some people can live at Milton Keynes densities provided that others are prepared to live in high-density cities.

Milton Keynes demonstrates that if enough is spent on roads, planting and careful design of housing, low-density neighbourhoods can be designed to accommodate the car without destroying the environment. Some of its grid-layout neighbourhoods are truly appalling, but at its best it can be described as a group of well-designed neighbourhoods surrounding a well-designed out-of-town shopping centre. By no stretch of the imagination, however, is it a city in the usual sense of the word. Spread out as it is, it is not only extravagant of land, it is also extravagant of fuel, because every 'local' journey is a comparatively long one. Therefore, although it is an interesting experiment and liked by many of its inhabitants, Milton Keynes cannot be seen as a prototype for the cities of an environmentally conscious twenty-first century.

Abercrombie's Greater London Plan

We have seen that almost forty per cent of Britain's population was rehoused in the 1920s and 1930s. In fact, four million homes were built during that period, almost a third of them by local authorities as low-cost housing for rent. But a large proportion even of these were built in the suburbs. Apart from the commercial centres, the inner areas of our towns and cities remained much as they had been since the nineteenth century.

World War II, however, provided another boost to the reformers. Not only was much of our urban fabric destroyed by bombs but, as

Gordon Cherry puts it, 'the debate as to whether planning was necessary belonged to the past.' Since planning the economy had been found necessary to ensure maximum efficiency during the war, it seemed obvious to everyone that planning ahead while the war was still going on would be the safest way of ensuring a successful programme of reconstruction when the war was over. Lord Reith, founder of the BBC, was appointed Minister of Works, and as early as 1941 he had asked the London County Council to prepare a plan for post-War London. The result was the County of London Plan, by Foreshaw and Abercrombie, published in 1943, which was followed in 1944 by Abercrombie's Greater London Plan.

Abercrombie saw the need and the opportunity to provide a strategic plan for Greater London which at the time was governed by 143 local authorities, all working on plans independently of each other. His plan combined the decentralization called for in the Barlow Report with the principles of Osborn's *New Towns After The War*. It called for a reduction of densities in the inner area, a stable suburban ring, a green belt beyond, and ten satellite towns beyond the green belt. However, while the LCC was one of the most enthusiastic supporters of new towns, the new-town development corporations were outside its control. Furthermore the LCC had a well-established housing department only too keen to tackle London's war damage – at a time when London had one-sixth of the nation's housing stock. Not surprisingly, post-War rebuilding got under way in London before most of the new towns had been designated or their development corporations had been appointed. A similar situation prevailed in the provinces, exacerbated by the fact that most provincial cities, unlike London, were positively hostile to the idea of satellite towns. During the 1930s there had already been a considerable drift of people and jobs to London and the southeast, and provincial urban authorities saw new towns, even in their own area, as a further threat to their prosperity.

The builders of the Brave New Britain faced not only a post-War shortage of building materials and severe restrictions on costs but also the same dilemma as the slum-clearers of the 1930s: whether to build 'small' and house a few people well, or build 'large' and solve the housing problem at the expense of the environment. Just as in the 1930s, new, intimate, streetscale, three- or four-storey housing (or the better streets rehabilitated) could have provided the answer but, as in the 1930s, this solution was spurned because of the traditional street's association with slum houses and bad drainage. Furthermore, there were some dreadful, well-documented examples of nineteenth-century houses not only built to a very high density of population but also occupied by three or four times the number of people they were designed to accommodate. Smallscale housing was therefore synonymous in most people's minds with overcrowding, and it was erroneously concluded that the only way to retain the existing population and the jobs that went with it was to build upwards.

The *Ville Radieuse* and the Demise of the Street

It seemed fortunate to the young idealists who flooded into the newly established LCC Architects' Department in 1950 that, while we in Britain in the 1930s had been arguing the toss between 'cottages' and 'five-storey walk-ups', Le Corbusier in France had been developing his ideas for a vertical garden city or *ville radieuse*.

The concept of the *ville radieuse* was one of tall, slender blocks built on stilts above parkland which flowed around and under them. Instead of shops, primary schools and community centres being allowed to clutter up the park, it was proposed that they should be built halfway up the blocks. In other words, each block (perhaps a kilometre high) would be a self-contained village with its own shopping centre. One such block, L'Unité d'Habitation, was built outside Marseilles as a sort of prototype. But it was at Roehampton in London during the 1950s that something approaching Le Corbusier's ideas was first tried on a large scale: by the architects of the London County Council.

The site chosen for this first experiment was in many ways ideal. It consisted of a large area of private park with trees and shrubs already established, and it adjoined an even larger area of mature public space in the form of Richmond Park. Its disadvantage was that Roehampton is a suburb remote from any substantial centre and from any possible sources of employment. Furthermore, although a shopping centre was provided at ground level it was a long way from some of the blocks, none of which was large enough to support shops within itself. Nevertheless, the visual impact of towers growing out of trees and grassy slopes was breathtaking, both to the new inhabitants, who came from the bomb-scarred slums of London, and to the representatives of other housing authorities from Britain and abroad who were shown round the estate in large numbers (see Figure 10).

At last the LCC architects had broken away from the familiar and dreary street patterns of the nineteenth century. It seemed that a new age had dawned, and every housing authority in Europe wanted to get in on the act. Alas, there were few sites like Roehampton, and when similar schemes were tried in inner-city areas they were a failure. The economic impracticality of providing shops and play facilities within the blocks led to clutter at ground level. At Roehampton this was hardly noticeable because of the grandeur of the adjacent Richmond Park, but without an established park nearby which could remain untouched, the cluttered space between the buildings was all too dominant, and not as friendly as the old nineteenth-century streets.

By this time the urge to build upwards had become unstoppable. The only debate now was about style. The LCC Architects' Department divided itself between 'Brutes' and 'Swedes': the former calling a spade a spade and claiming that a concrete building

Fig. 10 Roehampton's Ville Radieuse

must look like a concrete building, the latter following the Swedish tendency to soften the impact of concrete. The bow-tie-wearing architects who had built the 1930s cottage estates and flat blocks in an English vernacular style were banished to the County Hall attic, where they were relegated to repair work on their pre-War estates.

In spite of the Cassandra-like warnings of Osborn and the Town and Country Planning Association, the tower-block solution to the nation's housing problem was Government policy during the 1950s and 1960s. Grants to housing authorities were massively increased to make up for the fact that tall buildings were very much more expensive than more traditional housing. In 1965 Richard Crossman, the Minister for Housing and Local Government, was persuaded that the only way to restrain costs and maintain the housing programme was to use industrialized (prefabricated) building methods. Use of the new systems was virtually forced on housing authorities by a form of grant application for new building projects which asked whether industrialized building methods were to be used, and followed up with an if-not-why-not question which made it difficult to answer in the negative.

For the most part, local housing authorities followed Government policy willingly. There was some demurring from sociologists during the 1960s, but it was not until the safety of prefabricated tower blocks was called into question by the collapse of Ronan Point in 1967 that the public woke up to the fact that they did not really want families living in tower blocks, for social reasons.

3 (ii) THE DESTRUCTION OF COMMUNITIES

Comprehensive Redevelopment

The safety of tower blocks was really a red herring. It was generally only those built by certain industrialized building methods that were unsafe. But once the received wisdom about the necessity for tall buildings was questioned, all sorts of other fundamental issues were raised.

Because of the obvious impossibility of building large blocks on very small sites within the existing street pattern, it had become accepted that comprehensive redevelopment was a good thing and that piecemeal development was bad. However, if ways could be found of rehousing people without building tall, was the comprehensive redevelopment of large urban areas any longer necessary? Would it not be possible to develop only those areas that needed developing, rather than destroying comparatively sound buildings for the sake of 'tidying up' the site? Could not whole streets in some areas be rehabilitated rather than demolished and rebuilt?

These arguments rumbled on for a long time and the concept of comprehensive redevelopment outlived the *ville radieuse* by at least a decade. A major reason for this was the desire of local authorities to solve their housing problems and their traffic problems at one blow, using the opportunity provided by a large housing development to incorporate new roads for the benefit of the town as a whole. Another reason was a desire to separate vehicles and pedestrians on the housing estates themselves by providing access at two levels – something that could be achieved only in a large project. A third reason was the desire to separate industry and housing.

We shall see the futility of most urban road building in Chapter 6 and of pedestrian segregation in Chapter 7. On the other hand it seems difficult to condemn the desire to remove obnoxious industries from sites close to where people live. Such industries had been a cause for concern, mostly connected with health, since the nineteenth century, and once public transport had made it no longer necessary for workers in such factories to live close at hand, the case for moving either housing or factory seemed overwhelming. But the local authorities' ability, through comprehensive redevelopment, to separate such incompatible land uses often coincided with the industry's ability, through improved industrial techniques, to become more compatible; and both coincided with an increasing concern, not about people living too close to their work, but too far away.

The case against comprehensive redevelopment, however, went beyond its effect on any particular site. What had not been foreseen in the 1950s and 1960s was that the demolition of a large area of housing at any one time would not only break up the communities being rehoused – at least in the short term – but would also lead to the failure through lack of custom of shops, pubs, and other local facilities in the surrounding areas, and thence to a general decline of

the whole neighbourhood: a decline from which many neighbourhoods were destined not to recover, and which was to be responsible
for an increasing dissatisfaction with living in cities.

Planning Blight

Appreciation of the damage that could be done to an area by the
dereliction that went with comprehensive redevelopment drew
attention to a more insidious form of damage that had been going on
for a long time. Immediately after the war many large sites had
already been cleared by Hitler's bombs, but as time went on
development sites took longer to assemble, as compulsory-purchase
notices had to be served, businesses relocated and residents
rehoused. In the meantime building on small derelict sites within
the development area (and repairs to existing buildings) had to be
discouraged in order to keep down the ultimate cost of land
purchase. 'Planning blight' was the generally accepted term used to
describe the dereliction that gradually overtook an area once it was
rumoured that redevelopment was to take place. The effect was a
catastrophe for the local inhabitants, even if the rumour soon proved
true and they knew that they would eventually be rehoused. It was
much worse when the future remained uncertain and people were
left living in streets where there was no incentive to carry out
running repairs, let alone to embark on the renewal of property.

Rumoured redevelopment was not the only cause of blight. A
more common cause was the safeguarding of road-widening lines.
Whether or not any particular piece of road needed to be widened,
there could be no statutory objection to it if the highway authority
concerned had gone through the proper democratic procedures and
had published the widening line in its development plan. The cause
for complaint was that many of the safeguarding lines were neither
debated nor published, but came to light only as and when planning
applications were referred to the highway authority for its comments. In the early 1970s Christopher Booker, in the magazine
Private Eye, was able to show that if all of the relevant bottom-
drawer road-widening lines were to be implemented, virtually the
whole of the newly designated conservation area in London's Soho
would be demolished.

The Department of the Environment published a circular in 1978 asking local authorities to abandon all safeguardings other than those that had been formally approved and made public. In London it was not until 1982 that this policy was adopted wholeheartedly.

Demolition, Gentrification and Suburbanization

In the meantime, the questioning of the need for so much demolition had bred campaigns to save the better of our nineteenth-century urban streets. By the 1960s much of the worst slum housing had been replaced, but the procedure of condemning buildings as unfit for human habitation so that housing authorities could purchase them at 'site value' continued. In 1970 the Packington Estate in the London Borough of Islington became a national *cause célèbre*. The estate's tenants lost the battle to save their dilapidated homes but they won a reprieve for many similar areas, as subsequent events showed that the replacement of Packington's eminently convertible Victorian houses by six-storey flats created no additional dwellings and a considerably less satisfactory environment. (The successful rehabilitation of housing for rent in the 1970s and 1980s is described in Chapter 7.)

Unfortunately the campaigns to save dilapidated buildings of character were often followed by the purchase of such buildings by estate agents and developers with the aim of moving out the existing tenants, by fair means or foul, and rehabilitating the properties for owner-occupiers. That our cities were divided into areas of either exclusive owner-occupation or exclusively rented accommodation was due largely to historical accident and to the fact that the land had originally been owned in very large blocks (see Chapter 2 (ii)). To the extent that 'gentrification' began to break up such ghettos it was to be welcomed; but gentrification was rarely reciprocated by council purchases in owner-occupied areas, and in popular locations it usually went too far: in saving the original buildings it often destroyed the original community, rather than adding vitality to it.

Nevertheless, public reaction against comprehensive redevelopment and unnecessary demolition undoubtedly led to changes of planning policy which were of long-term benefit. But the changes of policy that followed public reaction against tower blocks were a very mixed blessing. It was right that tall buildings should have been discouraged as a means of housing people with children, but it was wrong that they should have been seen as a consequence of planning to high densities, when they were really just a consequence of the battle of building styles. Chapter 7 demonstrates that streetscale housing could have been built instead of tower blocks and the same density achieved in most cases, but since traditional urban densities were mistakenly equated with tower blocks they were rejected. The result was a reduction of densities in local-authority development plans in the 1980s to a level below that which would support facilities like shops, pubs and primary schools within walking distance of everyone's front door. If inner-city housing had been given the same priority in the 1980s that it had in the 1960s we would, through decentralization, have begun to lose the local facilities that are the *raison d'être* of urban living.

The housing illustrated in Figure 11 was built in an early-Victorian square in the 1950s to fill a gap caused by war damage, but the dilemma that it illustrates is typical of the problems faced during the 1980s by many housing associations, who found not only that low-density housing was now fashionable but that the building-cost yardstick laid down by the Government via the Housing Corporation permitted precious little else. This made it difficult for the

Fig. 11 Incongruous low-density housing, Wilton Square, Islington

scale of existing streets to be maintained, and it also limited the number of people who could be rehoused. Applied on a large scale it would lead inevitably to a loss of people from the inner-city areas and would threaten the viability of local services for those who remained.

The process seems to have already started in Liverpool which, having suffered more than its fair share of deprivation and mismanagement, was given special treatment by the Government after the Toxteth riots in 1981. The city has seen some interesting experiments in co-operative housing carried out in conjunction with the Council and various housing associations. However, the wish to give people what they want has led in some cases to the abandoning not only of the hated tower block but also of the city street – in favour of a suburban style of development even more incongruous than that illustrated in Figure 11. Because it was assumed to be popular, some semi-detached housing has been built in inner-city areas at a density of population that seems to be too low either to bring back local shops or to support a good public transport system. It is difficult to see how the city of Liverpool can recover its former vitality if this is to be the building pattern of the future. Indeed it must be doubtful whether anyone would have opted for this sort of urban housing if they had appreciated the social, transport and environmental problems it is likely to pose in the long run.

During the 1980s, when so much money was being spent on commercial development, few resources (public or private) were devoted to housing in inner-city areas. The Government starved local housing authorities of funds although it invested directly in housing in particular areas through Housing Action Trusts. However, this was a device designed primarily to bypass the local authorities and, however justified it might have been in particular cases, it inevitably led to a loss of local accountability. The resources allocated in this way were only a fraction of the resources withdrawn. The result has been a disgraceful deterioration in the environment of our cities. The enforced breathing space could, however, be used to ensure that the next round of urban reform does not hasten the decline of our cities in the way that the last one did. Suburbanization would be as horrid as the word that describes it, and could be as damaging to the urban areas as were the tower blocks of the 1960s: not just because of the sort of aesthetic disfigurement illustrated in Figure 11 but, more importantly, because depopulation would lead to the collapse of the local facilities that we expect in cities but that are viable only where there are high concentrations of people.

3 (iii) THE RISE AND FALL OF STRATEGIC PLANNING

The Town and Country Planning Act 1947

At the end of World War II planning powers were needed to give effect to the principles expounded by Unwin, Osborn and Abercrombie which had been generally accepted by the War-time Coalition Government. The new post-War Labour Government introduced in quick succession the 1945 Town and Country Planning Act, the 1946 New Towns Act (which authorized the Mark I new towns around London), the 1947 Town and Country Planning Act and the 1949 National Parks and Access to the Countryside Act. The first controlled the location of industry through the issue or denial of industrial development certificates, and the last gave birth to the National Parks Commission. The cornerstone of all post-War planning, however, was the 1947 Act which, while leaving landowners free to enjoy their land under its existing use, denied them the right to change that use without planning permission. In *Urban and Regional Planning* Peter Hall comments about the 1947 Act: 'Without it effective control of land use and of new development would have been impossible. Green belts, for instance, could not have been drawn around the bigger urban areas in order to contain and regulate their growth; a plan like Abercrombie's would therefore not have been enforceable.'

Not only did the 1947 Act give the state control over changes in the use of land, it also reduced the number of statutory authorities responsible for planning matters in England and Wales from 1,441 to 145, which consisted of the counties and the independent county boroughs (large towns). These new planning authorities were made responsible for drawing up surveys and development plans for their areas which would provide them with the necessary land-use guidelines for their new role in administering development control.

As well as making any change in the use of land subject to planning permission, the Act also (via a 'development charge') denied the landowner the profit resulting from any change of use permitted, on the not unreasonable grounds that the profit arose from the decision of the planning authority, not from any effort on the part of the landowner. It was recognized that in some cases land might have been purchased with development in mind, and so a system of compensation was established. However, the landowner's hope that a future government might make the development charge more modest led to a lack of incentive to develop, and the charge was eventually abolished by the Conservative Government in 1953.

The first generation of post-War new towns had been designated at a time when the birth rate was stable and expected to remain so. Instead there was a 'baby boom', followed by pressure for new housing – in the provinces as well as in Greater London – which led to a return to the suburban house building of the inter-War period. This threatened the generally agreed policy of curbing urban growth and encouraging development in new towns. As a result a second generation of new towns was designated by both the Conservative and Labour governments of the 1960s. This time there was a greater emphasis on metropolitan areas other than London, partly in the hope that people might be enticed away from the over-populated southeast.

The Local Government Act 1972

A total of almost thirty new and expanded towns had been designated by the mid-1960s but they accounted for only three per cent of the national housing programme. Although the inner-city areas were losing population, expansion just inside and just outside the green belts of the large cities was getting out of control, and the long-distance commuting that resulted was straining the transport system of virtually every town. The situation in London was rationalized to some extent by the creation of the Greater London Council, under the London Government Act of 1963, but outside London the influence of the core cities now spread well into their surrounding counties, although their authority did not.

In 1965 the Government's Planning Advisory Group recommended a two-tier system of planning: with regional, county or city councils drawing up strategic 'structure' plans for their areas, and with the local councils within each area drawing up their own local plans. In 1969 the Royal Commission on Local Government for England, under Sir Redcliffe Maude, endorsed the two-tier system for the provincial metropolitan areas (bringing them into line with London), but suggested a single medium-sized authority (smaller than a county but much larger than a local district council) elsewhere. The Commission seems to have assumed that it was in the national interest to put administrative convenience before the convenience of those being administered, and proposed only fifty large local authorities for England outside the metropolitan areas of London, Birmingham, Manchester and Merseyside. The area covered by these authorities would have approximated to the average-sized county, and the services expected of a local town hall would often have been up to forty miles away from where people lived.

In the Local Government Act of 1972 the Conservative Government wisely rejected the Redcliffe Maude proposals (except for those appertaining to the metropolitan areas, to which were added South Yorkshire and Tyne and Wear) and opted for a two-tier system throughout the whole of the United Kingdom. In the meantime the previous Labour Government, conscious of the urgent need for the co-ordination of public transport services in the large provincial cities, had set up Passenger Transport Authorities for each metropolitan county (Transport Act 1968), and it is ironic that these survived the Thatcher Government's axe, while the metropolitan counties brought into being by the Conservatives' 1972 Act did not.

The object of the Local Government Act of 1985, which abolished the metropolitan counties, was ostensibly to simplify the administration of urban planning, and the White Paper of 1984 which preceded the Act was entitled 'Streamlining the Cities'. It is true that the two-tier system did involve a great many overlapping responsibilities, especially in London. Under the 1963 Act, the new GLC had retained the old LCC's responsibilities for housing and parks, in spite of the fact that the London boroughs also had responsibilities in those spheres which were, in any case, probably better administered at a local level. But much the greater cause for complaint about the GLC was that it *lacked* power where power was most needed: to co-ordinate London's strategic planning. It took over the old LCC's role as the authority responsible for maintaining and updating the Development Plan for London, and responsibility for metropolitan (main) roads. But it had no control over London Transport until 1974 and it never did have any say in policy over British Rail's suburban services. As a result there was never a properly integrated planning and transport policy in the capital.

For a short time the large provincial cities fared better. As well as being responsible for strategic planning, each metropolitan county also became its own Passenger Transport Authority. By abolishing the metropolitan counties the 1985 Act, far from reforming strategic planning, in effect abandoned it: at least so far as cities were concerned. The Passenger Transport Authorities survived and continued their important task of co-ordinating public transport, but they now had no control over strategic planning.

The Abolition of Metropolitan Counties

The abolition of the metropolitan counties also meant the abolition of the strategic 'structure' plans, which had been prepared by the counties and had been made statutory once they had been approved by the Secretary of State for the Environment. Instead, under the 1985 Act the development plans prepared by local district and borough councils were made statutory and had to include strategic guidance handed down from the Secretary of State. They were named *Unitary* Development Plans to distinguish the new system from the two-tier system that it replaced and which, after much debate, still survives in the shire counties.

To provide local input to the Secretary of State's strategic guidance, powers were established under the 1985 Act for him to obtain advice from the district councils that made up the metropolitan area. But because the people involved in giving such advice were not directly elected or appointed for that purpose, they carried little clout; moreover they did not have the technical back-up available to the old counties. Under the Act, London alone was given a quango to co-ordinate the advice from its constituent boroughs (the London Planning Advisory Committee), but when the LPAC presented its advice to the Secretary of State in 1988 it was almost completely ignored – in spite of the fact that it had been presented, most remarkably, with the blessing of all three main political parties. The result was that the Secretary of State's strategic guidance, given to the London boroughs in 1989 for incorporation into their new Unitary Development Plans, contained virtually none of the policies suggested unanimously by London's local politicians.

To criticize the abolition of strategic planning is not necessarily to claim that where there has been some form of strategic planning it has worked satisfactorily. Even when county councils have had a say on strategic issues they have often acted ineffectively. There are far too many cases of the poor siting of large developments affecting more than one local authority which could have been prevented by the county council concerned. The most obvious examples are large shopping centres, hospitals, schools and public offices sited outside urban areas and remote from public transport, thus increasing traffic and putting them out of the easy reach of those without cars. Some London boroughs (in co-operation with the GLC, which was then the strategic planning authority) were allowing planning permission for out-of-centre developments which they knew would prejudice their existing centres, apparently on the grounds that the developers would otherwise build in an adjoining borough and take the trade with them. In the shire counties, district councils seem to have taken similar decisions where county structure plans have not addressed the issue.

Nevertheless, the failure of strategic planning in the past should have led to its reform rather than to its abolition. Without it, the problems of urban transport and land use will never be solved, and as a result, urban living is likely to become even more unattractive. If people are driven out of urban areas, many urban problems, including traffic congestion, will spread to the surrounding countryside.

3 (iv) THE CONSEQUENCES OF DISPERSAL

Central Decay and Peripheral Expansion

One of the immediate effects of the Industrial Revolution had been to draw the manufacturing workforce from its hand-operated cottage workshop to the machine-operated factory. In turn, more factories had been drawn to the new concentrations of people and industry, and thus our cities had become centralized and overcrowded. Towards the end of the nineteenth and the beginning of the twentieth century, the workforce began to live further from its work, but the place of work remained at the focus of the typical radial transport system which was geared entirely to getting people in and out of the town centre.

Ebenezer Howard had proposed something rather different: places of work on the periphery and administrative and cultural activities at the centre, with housing and public gardens in between. But Howard's ideal garden city, although intended to be one of a cluster of its own kind, was limited to 30,000 people, and both the centre and places of work were intended to be within easy walking or cycling distance of the residential area. It was not therefore in pursuit of Howard's ideals that commercial developments on the periphery of large cities became popular in the 1960s and 1970s.

The apparent advantage of commercial developments in the outer suburbs was that they would not only relieve pressure on the centre but would also enable public transport to be used in both directions during the rush hour – a sort of reverse commuting. The disadvantage was that in an essentially radial city, with public transport geared to carrying people to and from the centre, a suburban development could be served only by the single radial transport corridor on which it was located, whereas the established commercial areas at the centre of the city (where all the radial transport corridors meet) could be served from all points of the compass. Developments on the periphery therefore made very little use of the railways' spare capacity for reverse commuting, and they were usually too small or too scattered even to justify new bus services. The result was a switch from public to private transport and the spreading of congestion from the centre to the outer suburbs.

Where jobs were transferred to a suburban town centre (rather than simply to a site close to a suburban railway station) the problems were less acute. Not only were ancillary services available but there was usually some form of local radial public transport. But even in the case of Croydon, one of London's better-endowed suburban centres so far as public transport is concerned, it is only since 1987 that serious attention has at last been given to coping with the transport problems caused by the office-building boom of the 1960s and 1970s.

The Location-of-Offices Bureau

In central London, firms moving out to the suburbs were quickly replaced by others. Furthermore, the 1961 census showed that although there had been a decline in inner London's residential population (as called for in Abercrombie's Greater London Plan of 1944), the area within a fifty-mile radius of London had actually experienced an increase of half a million people in ten years. As a result, in 1963 the Government established the Location-of-Offices Bureau with the purpose of persuading businesses to move out – preferably to cities in the less prosperous 'Development Areas', but certainly out of London. So far as the latter was concerned, the Bureau was enormously successful, and by the end of the 1960s 10,000 jobs a year were being moved. But firms moving out were still being replaced by other firms moving in. Furthermore the Bureau's successful advertisements, mostly on the Underground and at mainline stations where they would catch the businessman's eye, tended to show a new office block in idyllic countryside rather than in the centre of a provincial city. Most relocations, therefore, were to places only just outside London's green belt. Worse still, they tended to be on greenfield sites, poorly served by public transport. They thus added a further turn to the screw of road congestion in the Home Counties.

The moving of heavy industry from city-centre locations to the urban periphery had some merit in planning terms, and it was made almost inevitable with the general switch of freight transport from rail to road. On the other hand the dispersal of offices to peripheral locations turned out to be a transport nightmare, as described above, and the more recent trend for light industry to move out could become a threat to the prosperity of the central area that it serves (see Chapter 5 (i)). Moreover, although the movement of residents from central areas was once considered imperative because of overcrowding, by the end of the 1960s poor living conditions were no longer the consequence of overcrowding but of poorly designed or poorly maintained housing.

In London, post-War dispersal was certainly deliberate and some of it was necessary. In the other major cities of Britain the outward movement of people and commerce happened almost willy-nilly. The result was decay in the centre and only limited growth on the outside: like a dying tree. Public transport designed for a radial city with a strong centre was poorly placed to serve either dispersed commercial areas or outlying housing estates (and some of the latter had very low levels of car ownership). The once-efficient services in the inner areas were run down through lack of patronage. Worse still, in a mistaken belief that new roads would bring back prosperity (see Chapter 4 (ii)), an environment impoverished by neglect was further eroded by positive action in the form of destructive road building. It seems that the only cities and large towns to escape the worst of such urban destruction (although they have suffered enough) were Oxford, Cambridge, Edinburgh and London. All four have prosperous centres. Perhaps they also had the greatest number of prosperous people living or working centrally who had the foresight or the influence to hold road building at bay.

Shops: Bigger, Fewer and Further Away

The abolition of Retail Price Maintenance in 1960 may seem to have little to do with the development of urban planning, but in fact it had a profound effect. RPM allowed manufacturers and whole-salers, rather than retailers, to determine the retail price of goods. Its enforcement was effective in large shops but almost impossible in small ones. As a result, small shops with low overheads were able to undercut the large shops with impunity. With the abolition of RPM the position was reversed. Large shops could, for the first time, benefit from their economies of scale and so undercut the small shops.

From the customer's point of view this seemed an unmixed blessing. Not only were prices reduced but the larger supermarkets that sprang up often offered a wider choice of food than the traditional grocer. So long as the supermarkets were in the local shopping centre all was well. But a combination of aggressive pleading by large retailers and weak planning control on the part of some local authorities quickly led to an expanding number of out-of-centre superstores, which impoverished the shopping facilities in the old centres where more people lived.

As the concentration of retailing into larger and fewer outlets progressed, the motives of the retailers became less clear. Prices at hypermarkets were not cheaper than those at supermarkets. It seemed that the battle for out-of-centre sites was more of a power struggle between the major retailers than a genuine attempt to provide a better service for their customers.

In its initial stages, however, the 'retail revolution' did lead to a reduction in costs so far as the retailer was concerned – if only because, instead of having to distribute to a number of small shops near where the customers lived, the superstore operator obliged customers to come and collect their purchases themselves. This was reflected in reduced prices at the large stores, but it must be doubtful in the long term whether the customers benefited from such a big switch from many small retail outlets close at hand to a few large ones further away. They paid not only in inconvenience and lost time but also in the cost of travelling to the larger outlet.

In some parts of the country, people who had a car themselves and did not live on roads suffering from traffic generated by superstores may still have had the best of both worlds: a superstore they could drive to for one-stop shopping plus a local shop for emergencies. But even they were worse off than their forebears in the 1930s who would have had their weekly shopping delivered to their homes. Those without the use of a car were much worse off. Even where local centres survived, their shops declined dramatically in quantity and quality, and prices increased because wholesalers were no longer interested in delivering to a large number of small outlets.

The Government could not be blamed for abolishing Retail Price Maintenance. It was a reform that benefited too many people in the short term for it to be resisted in a democratic society and, linked with sensible planning policies, it should have been of long-term benefit. But in the same way as the Government saw in 1961 that increased car ownership (of which it approved) could have a detrimental effect on towns if it were not properly controlled (see Chapter 4 (i)), so the Government in the 1970s should have been concerned about the long-term effects of superstores, and about the adverse effects of increased mobility of which they were an expression.

I took a great deal o' pains with his eddication, sir; let him run in the
streets when he was very young, and shift for hisself. It's the only way
to make a boy sharp, sir.

Sam Weller's father

Charles Dickens

Pickwick Papers

4 (i) 'UNIVERSAL' CAR OWNERSHIP

Tarmacadam, Motor Vehicles and Ribbon Development

The theory of education propounded by Mr Weller senior in 1837
could still be applied (if one agreed with it) one hundred and fifty
years later, but for rather different reasons. The urban streets of Mr
Weller's day, however unsalubrious, were primarily places where
people lived, whereas those of today are primarily traffic routes.
This chapter is an attempt at assessing why this change has come
about (mostly during the last fifty years) and whether it need have
done so.

'Universal car ownership' is a misleading phrase. First, there will
always be some families who do not own a car. Second, even in a
car-owning, or even a two-car-owning family, a car is not necessarily
available to each member of the family at any one time. Third, there
will always be some people unable to drive because they are too
young, too old, disabled, ill or inebriated. Nevertheless, the phrase
has been used to describe the difference between the limited car
ownership of the 1930s and the substantial car ownership that has
existed in Britain since about 1970. At the time of the last National

Travel Survey in 1985–86 thirty-two per cent of individuals and sixty-one per cent of families had regular use of a car (Department of Transport National Travel Survey Report, 1988). Bearing in mind these qualifications about what it really means, 'universal car ownership' is used here in its generally accepted sense.

John McAdam revolutionized road building during the heyday of the stagecoaches at the end of the eighteenth century, but when the steam-engine enabled mechanized transport to replace the horse, the railways superseded the roads for journeys of any distance and the trunk roads fell into disrepair. In the first decade of the twentieth century, however, the addition of tar to McAdam's road-topping of small stones, and the development of the internal combustion engine, brought transport back to the roads. Petrol-driven buses not only took over from horse-buses in the towns but they also enabled large numbers of those commuting from the suburbs to live further from the railway station. The private car, however, remained the preserve of the rich: either as a means of making short journeys (chauffeur-driven), or as a toy (self-driven).

The 1920s saw the spread of ribbon development along the roads leading out of the towns. The same decade also saw the spread of car ownership, but the two were not directly connected. Ribbon development along existing roads took place originally because it was cheaper than development that was dependent on new estate roads; and it was made possible by the bus which, by carrying a large number of people per vehicle, made little difference to the number of vehicles on the roads.

Early developments of this sort were therefore not dependent on the car, and few of the houses built along bus routes in the 1920s had garages. When car ownership began to spread, however, and those living in the ribbon developments themselves had cars, the extra traffic made the existing roads unsuitable for housing. By this time it had also become apparent that the merging of towns and villages and their consequent loss of identity was neither conducive to a satisfactory environment nor was it necessary. The nuclear expansion of each settlement into its own hinterland would have provided much more housing, without destroying the countryside in between.

There was already considerable agitation for the establishment of 'green belts' round our larger cities and the retention of some countryside between the villages engulfed by commuterdom. The trouble was that, although local authorities had powers to acquire land up to 203 metres' depth on each side of a highway, they were reluctant to use such powers until the 1935 Restriction of Ribbon Development Act obliged them positively to approve any development within 68 metres of the centre of a classified road, without the obligation to purchase any land if they did not approve it.

The 1930s saw a rapid growth in concern about the design and administration of the highway system. Trunk roads were brought under the general administration of the Ministry of Transport in 1934 and local highway authorities started to build bypasses round their towns to prevent long-distance traffic from clogging their commercial centres. In 1938 Alker Tripp, one of the Metropolitan Police Commissioners concerned with traffic, published *Road Traffic and Its Control*. He suggested a hierarchy of roads: arterial, sub-arterial and local or minor roads. Arterial roads were to exclude all but motor traffic (equivalent to post-War motorways); sub-arterial roads were to cater predominantly for the interests of vehicular traffic (including horse-drawn vehicles, of which there were still a great many); and local roads were to cater for local traffic only and provide access to premises. Tripp later turned his attention to the more directly urban problems of traffic and, in 1942, published *Town Planning and Road Traffic*, which suggested that main roads should be largely sealed off from local streets by the creation of 'precincts' – partly to improve the flow of heavy traffic on the main roads and partly to protect residential streets from the adverse environmental effects of through-traffic.

In terms of planning and housing, the 1943 County of London Plan (see Chapter 3 (i)) set the tone for attitudes to post-War reconstruction. It played a similar role in transport. Not only did it apply Alker Tripp's hierarchy to the capital's roads (including a series of proposed new orbital routes), it also recommended his system of precincts and gave examples of how they might be achieved. For example it showed a north–south arterial road, or motorway, running under the Bloomsbury precinct, with Gower Street reduced to the status of a local access road. However, it is clear that its general rule was that all through-traffic should be canalized on to the existing main roads. In the event, it was not London that gave birth to the 'precinct' but Coventry, where the war-time destruction of the central area provided the opportunity to build Britain's first traffic-free shopping centre.

Neither the Foreshaw and Abercrombie plan for London nor Gibson's plan for Coventry – imaginative though they were when compared with the contemporary state-of-the-art – came anywhere near to providing a blueprint for a city capable of coping with the not unnatural desire of motorists to drive to the city centre. This was due not so much to the fact that no such city was possible with universal car ownership as to the fact that nobody seems to have anticipated universal car ownership in the foreseeable future.

This twin failure of the imagination – to foresee either the likelihood or the effects of universal car ownership – bedevilled much of Britain's post-War thinking about planning, housing and transport. There seems to have been an assumption that car ownership might spread to the families of white-collar workers (then very much a minority) but no further, and that council tenants would never become car owners in large numbers. The consequence was a failure to grasp the implications of increasing car ownership for either new towns or new housing estates, or for the environment generally. Students of architecture and planning in the late 1940s and early 1950s were happy to show new motorways serving their make-believe developments without the slightest idea of what would happen to the imaginary traffic when it reached its central destination. Their mentors were equally uninformed. They praised the fantastic shapes created by the proposed motorways but were unable to comment on them as anything other than urban sculpture.

In the contemporary real world no such projects existed. Abercrombie's plans had been put on the back burner because there were more pressing post-War problems to be solved and there was an economic crisis. Furthermore, petrol rationing had lasted until 1950 and was to be reintroduced again at the time of the Suez crisis of 1956. But by the end of the decade the increased use of cars and the shift of freight from rail to road were beginning to make the pre-War congestion on the Kingston bypass look like a golden age. Long-distance journeys by car were becoming slower than ever, and in town centres life was becoming impossible for everyone, not just for the motorist. It was expected that the programme of motorway building would overcome the problems of long-distance journeys by bypassing the congested towns. But it was appreciated that this would do little for the towns themselves, especially for the large ones, where most of the traffic was not simply passing through but was destined for the town centre.

The Buchanan Report
and The Greater London Development Plan

The Government realized that something had to be done and, on the advice of a steering committee under Sir Geoffrey Crowther, it set up the Buchanan Committee which reported in 1963. The Buchanan Report examined the sort of infrastructure required and the restrictions on traffic necessary to provide free-flowing urban roads. It also suggested, for the first time, environmental standards around which urban roads should be planned. One of the Report's most significant concepts was that of the environmental area: an area set aside for family housing, from which through-traffic should be excluded and within which vehicles would be limited to twenty miles per hour or less and would be subservient to pedestrians: a development of Alker Tripp's residential precinct which, unlike the shopping precinct, had not yet captured the public's imagination.

Above all, the Buchanan Report demonstrated what needed to be done if the car were to be accommodated without destroying the environment of the very people it was intended to serve. The Report also made clear its authors' view that if, because of the need to save historic buildings or to save money, the infrastructure needed was not attainable, then traffic entering the town would have to be restricted. In other words traffic was to be limited to a level that was consistent with a decent environment.

However, Professor Colin Buchanan and his co-authors were strongly 'pro-car'. They anticipated acceptance of the principle that most towns should be completely rebuilt around a new network of roads, with pedestrians, moving traffic and parked vehicles all at different levels, at least in the central areas (see Figure 12). It was only if the nation were not prepared to accept this concept that the Report envisaged comprehensive traffic restraint as the alternative.

In a nutshell, the Report's message to the Government was: 'Rebuild our cities or restrain urban traffic.' The Government and Opposition changed roles in 1964, but in 1963 both had hailed the

Report and, like Professor Buchanan, seemed to assume that the 'rebuild' solution would be the alternative chosen. But when a combination of public doubt and financial restriction effectively ruled out rebuilding, neither Government nor Opposition had the courage to countenance the alternative of traffic restraint which they had both implicitly endorsed.

A further opportunity for serious debate about urban transport occurred in 1970 when the GLC published its Greater London Development Plan. The transport section of the GLDP showed an obsession with orbital movement, as opposed to radial movement to the centre (which is the movement that most people want to make in a radial city like London). The result was a proposal to spend billions on new motorways running round central London, and comparatively little on the public transport system that served the central area itself. At the GLDP Layfield Inquiry Michael Thomson, who was at the time Research Fellow in Transport at the London School of Economics, gave evidence which poured scorn on the inner orbital roads. Although the Layfield Report suggested that one should be built, both of them were eventually abandoned. (The outer orbital became the M25.) Neither the GLC nor London

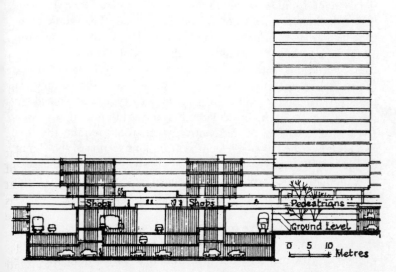

Fig. 12 The Buchanan Report – Three-level local shopping street

Transport was persuaded of the need to invest in the modernization of the capital's public transport system. It is true that the long-overdue Victoria Line had only just been opened, and that a truncated version of the Fleet Line (renamed Jubilee Line) was in the planning stage, but the failure to plan for general improvements in the late 1960s, together with the loss of bus passengers because of congested roads, led to the serious crisis of overcrowding on the Underground in the late 1980s.

This failure to appreciate the importance of public transport is particularly surprising in the light of the GLC's own evidence to the GLDP Inquiry, which showed that in 1967 only ten per cent of commuters to central London arrived by private car – although their cars accounted for sixty-seven per cent of central-area traffic. Since they also accounted for a large part of the traffic outside the central area, it would have made more sense for the GLC to propose improvements to public transport instead of proposing, as they did, a massively expensive road-building programme that was bound to encourage the use of cars and exacerbate congestion.

It is also surprising that the GLDP took little cognizance of the Buchanan Report so far as the central area was concerned. As one of its examples of a typical inner-city problem the Report had taken the area of London bounded by Oxford Street, Great Portland Street, Euston Road and Tottenham Court Road. It had come to the conclusion that even if the area were completely rebuilt (including all the roads leading to it) only twenty per cent of those wishing to commute to jobs in the area would be able to do so by private car (given that proper provision was made for essential commercial traffic). Furthermore, as part of its study of a typical provincial city (Leeds) the Report had calculated that the road building necessary to carry all travellers to the centre by car would require the total demolition of the 2,000-acre central area. This section of the Report concluded: 'There is no possibility, in a town of this size and nature, of planning for the level of traffic induced by the unrestricted use of the motorcar for the journey to work in conditions of full car ownership.'

It is difficult to believe that the authors of the GLDP had not read the Buchanan Report. It is almost as difficult to believe that they disagreed with the Report's main findings, since there was little criticism of them by transport planners at the time. The inevitable conclusion must be that those responsible for the transport section of the GLDP ignored Buchanan's principles because they felt that the alternatives of wholesale rebuilding or the strict restraint of commuting by car would be politically unacceptable: an attitude that is typical of the timid approach to transport planning that has prevailed in Britain ever since, and has resulted in piecemeal urban road building or road widening that was designed to give the appearance of doing something to ease congestion but in fact made it worse.

4 (ii) FREIGHT

The Switch from Railways to Roads

The development of railways during the Victorian era revolutionized the movement of freight over long distances but had little effect on the final mode of delivery to the consumer. The horse and cart that delivered goods from the railway station in the nineteenth century was almost indistinguishable from the horse and cart that had delivered from the local market town a hundred years earlier. British society changed during that hundred years from one that was predominantly rural to one that was predominantly urban; but in both town and country neither the roads nor the transport that used them changed significantly (for that matter neither did the buildings that lined the roads). The transport revolution, in effect, kept itself to itself and did not impinge physically beyond the boundaries of railway land.

Even the dramatic changes in road transport associated with the twentieth century were by no means universal until well into the second half of the century. Certainly the combination of tarmac roads and the internal-combustion engine had led to the extensive development of buses and lorries for local use, and there was some trunk haulage on the roads before World War II, but long-distance freight was rail-dominated until the 1950s. More surprisingly, much local delivery of freight from goods yards was made by horse-drawn vehicles: hay apparently proved a more economical fuel than diesel for short journeys in heavily congested urban streets. Even the long-distance road hauliers used horse-drawn vehicles for local

deliveries from their distribution centres. Horses were used at
Carter Patterson's depot in London's City Road until about 1950
and were famous for their knowledge of regular customers. This
enabled them to move slowly to the next point of collection or
delivery while the driver dealt with documentation at the previous
point of call, and the driver's dog guarded the back of the open van.
The railways mechanized their local delivery services in the 1950s,
introducing independent driving units and trailers so that the
loading of the trailers did not keep the expensive driving units 'off
the road'. It is interesting to note that this innovative system and its
sophisticated, quick-coupling device was introduced as 'The New
Mechanical Horse and Trailer'!

These quaint goings-on of the mid-twentieth century are, however, of more than sentimental interest. They mark the end of the
railways' domination of freight and, more importantly, the regrettable end of the railways' ability to deliver to the heart of our large
cities. They also mark the end of the era when it was accepted that
the vehicle that was used for local deliveries was a different beast
from that used for the long-distance part of the journey. Although
the trunk haul was traditionally by rail, even when it was by road
there was no question of the long-distance vehicle being used for
the final delivery in urban streets. Hence Carter Patterson's London
depot in City Road from which the local deliveries were made: a
procedure now known as 'breaking bulk' to which all sorts of
objections are raised by the very section of the transport industry
which once operated it as a matter of course.

It is difficult to understand why in the 1950s and 1960s there
should have been so little co-ordination between the railway
industry (then in decline) and the road-haulage industry (which was
expanding rapidly). To put it down to 'politics' is correct but facile.
Both industries were nationalized in 1946 but there was apparently
no attempt to integrate the two. Instead of concentrating the
railways' energies on long-distance freight and the road-haulage
industry's energies on medium- and short-haul journeys, British
Railways and British Road Services were treated as separate and
competing businesses. The railways even kept their comprehensive
system of local deliveries and their legal obligation to carry anything
they were asked to carry between any two addresses in Britain,
however remote they were from stations or goods yards.

The denationalization of BRS in 1952 and the opening of the Yorkshire Motorway (M1) as far as Birmingham in 1958 hastened the decline of the railways as carriers of freight. Although the railway modernization programme of 1954 did something to redress the balance, it was short-lived and was superseded by the cutback of the railways as a result of the Beeching Report of 1958. It was not until Barbara Castle's 1967 Transport Bill that any serious attempt was made to integrate road and rail transport, by encouraging long-distance freight back on to the railways. The Bill originally envisaged a system of 'quantity licensing' for lorries similar to the system in West Germany. Licences would be granted for trunk hauls of over 200 miles only if the railways decided that they could not handle the traffic. The quid pro quo was the lifting of the restriction on the number of general road hauliers and allowing them access to railway freight depots, which had previously been served exclusively by the railways' own collection and delivery lorries. The railway unions' bitter opposition to the loss of their monopoly within the railway depots was exceeded only by the even more bitter opposition of the road-haulage industry's 'Kill the Bill' campaign. The latter was also supported by the lorry drivers' Transport and General Workers' Union, whose general secretary was Frank Cousins. It led to Barbara Castle's famous remark that Frank Cousins's socialism stopped at the door of the lorry cab. It also led to the emasculation of the Transport Bill so that, when it became the 1968 Transport Act, the limit on the number of lorry operators' licences was relaxed without the compensating quantity licensing which could have encouraged long-distance freight back to the railways. The only significant railway-oriented measure to survive was the Public Service Obligation grant for socially necessary but unremunerative passenger services. Although the Act established the National Freight Corporation, which was encouraged to use a combination of road and rail transport, the attempt to reverse the drift of freight from rail to road, through the Freight Integration Council, was abandoned.

The Cost of Lorries to the Community

Rail freight has always had to carry the cost of maintaining its share of the track it uses, whereas until recently road freight has made only a token contribution to the cost of building and maintaining the roads that it uses. So long as lorries were small and trunk roads were congested the railways could survive in spite of this handicap, because a train crew of one to three people could do the work of up to 100 lorry drivers. As motorways were built and lorries increased in size, road haulage became more competitive, in spite of the fact that it remained inherently labour-intensive and now has to pay its 'track costs'. But hauliers are still not obliged to pay for the damage that they do to the community in terms of the environment in which people have to live. This is partly because much of the damage, though considerable, is difficult to evaluate. The result is that the more environmentally friendly railways have continued to operate under a financial disadvantage.

Lorry operators are certainly not charged for the delay and inconvenience they cause by bringing excessively large vehicles into the small streets that are typical of many urban environments and an important part of their character. Figure 13 is an accurate interpretation of the photographic evidence of an incident in London's Soho, when a lorry too large for the street it was using got stuck for half an hour. If the time wasted by everyone affected by this incident had been charged to the operator of the vehicle concerned, the bill would have been enormous. It would almost certainly have been sufficient to ensure that there was no repetition of such anti-social behaviour. Indeed, such a 'polluter pays' policy would have made it clear to road hauliers that, in real terms, it would be more economic for them to return to the use of special vehicles for local delivery. After all, the sort of vehicle designed primarily for delivery in Soho must have very different characteristics from a vehicle designed primarily to carry freight in bulk from Scotland to London.

So far as residents were concerned, it had been recognized in the early 1970s that the very many people who lived on main roads were suffering from intolerable traffic noise at night. The Department of the Environment decided that all new housing for which it was responsible (i.e. local-authority housing) should be properly insulated from any such noise that exceeded decibel level 70(A), measured inside bedrooms at night with the windows shut. As this level was reached on most roads used regularly by lorries at night, the effect was that almost all new local-authority housing on urban main roads received the allowance: an additional seven per cent on the building cost, as defined by the Government's 'Housing Cost Yardstick'. Requests to extend this allowance to the rehabilitation of existing buildings and to make grants available to private owners were refused on grounds of cost (an estimated 250,000 dwellings would have been affected in London alone). But the cost had to be borne by someone, either in terms of inconvenience suffered or in terms of sound insulation that had to be paid for. Furthermore everyone, including those who benefited from the noise allowance for new buildings, still had to suffer the inconvenience of not being able to open windows in summer or talk to the milkman on the front doorstep. The costs of these nuisances should have been charged to those who caused them: the lorry operators. If they had been, necessity being the mother of invention, lorries would have been made quieter or the number of their journeys reduced. As it was, the

Fig. 13 A large lorry stuck in a small street

occupants of existing buildings were left to suffer and the taxpayer picked up the extra cost of new buildings, not via the Department of Transport but via the Department of the Environment. Lorries were in effect subsidized, and the standard of living for those in urban areas suffered as a consequence.

In order to reduce the number of London streets suffering from the noise of heavy lorries, the GLC suggested in 1975 a system of lorry routes to which such vehicles would be confined except for access to their destination. It was estimated that traffic on the lorry routes would increase by only one per cent; but 100,000 dwellings would still have been affected and the consequent furore led to the dropping of the proposal. In 1981, therefore, the GLC commissioned an independent panel of inquiry into 'The Effects of Bans on Heavy Lorries in London' under the chairmanship of Derek Wood QC. The Wood Report is dealt with more fully in Chapter 6 because its findings, if implemented, could have far-reaching effects on all urban environments. One of its more interesting side effects was to expose the exaggerated nature of the haulage industry's claim that restrictions on heavy lorries would have an adverse effect on the urban economy – a claim that had hitherto been treated with unwarranted respect.

Unfortunately only one of the Wood Report's recommendations could be put into effect before the abolition of the GLC in 1986, i.e. the interim banning of vehicles over 16.5 tonnes at night-time and at weekends. The ban had an immediately beneficial effect on roads carrying lorries to the Channel ports, by diverting to the M25 most of the heavy night-time traffic that had found the route through London to be quicker. The ban even survived its half-hearted enforcement after the abolition of the GLC, as road hauliers saw little advantage in using the shorter direct route if it were going to tarnish further their already discredited image with the general public.

The GLC's night-time ban, and similar exclusions on a smaller scale throughout the country, demonstrated that the heavy lorry could be tamed, but little has been done since to do so. Even the GLC was obliged to issue exemption permits to allow night-time deliveries to businesses within the area of the lorry ban; and nothing has been done to prevent incidents similar to the one illustrated in Figure 13, let alone to relieve the general damage done to both the

economy and the environment through the use of unsuitable lorries
in urban areas.

4 (iii) ANARCHY AS A POLICY FOR URBAN TRANSPORT

Political Timidity and the Freedom of the Motorist

It was due to a lack of political will that the recommendations of the
Buchanan Report were ignored in 1963, and feeble, duplicitous
government did not end there. During the 1960s and 1970s
politicians continued to ignore fundamental reforms like traffic
restraint and improved public transport. Instead, they pressed ahead
with urban road-building schemes, in spite of mounting evidence
that any additional road capacity would be quickly filled with extra
traffic. There was no better illustration of this than London's
elevated Westway (M40), opened in 1970, at the time of the GLDP
Inquiry. Its opening immediately clogged up the Marylebone Road,
which had only just been widened in a vain attempt to cope with the
anticipated increase in traffic. The result was chaos for this particular road and endless delays to delivery vehicles, buses and taxis, the
effects of which were felt throughout the West End.

The building of Westway had led to strong objections from
householders along the route, but it was argued that their loss would
be the gain of those living in parallel roads which would be relieved
of traffic. The upshot was the establishment of compensation for
householders affected by the construction of a new road, but not for
those affected by increased traffic on an existing road. In the event,
traffic on existing roads increased as morning rush-hour commuters
diverted back on to the old routes to avoid the congestion where
Westway traffic disgorged into Marylebone Road. Westway certainly
made it quicker to get into or out of London by night, but this
small advantage was far outweighed by the great disadvantage of
increased congestion in central London during the day, and by the
environmental damage caused. Stephen Plowden in his book
Taming Traffic (André Deutsch, 1980) showed that, as a result of the
building of Westway, the weekday accumulation of vehicles in

central London between 7 A.M. and 11 P.M. rose by twenty-one per cent. He also pointed out that the resulting chaos was a major contributor to the switch from buses to private cars and to the consequent vicious circle of declining bus services and increasing congestion (see Chapter 4 (iv) and Figure 16).

All towns and cities in Britain had suffered from 'Westways' of one sort or another by the end of the 1970s. It should have been clear from such practical experience, backed up by the well-publicized evidence of the Buchanan Report and the GLDP Inquiry, that only a tiny proportion of commuters to city centres could ever be accommodated by private car. It should also have been clear that without restrictions on the use of private cars, urban road building would never satisfy the demand for road space, any roads that were built would quickly be filled up, and congestion in central areas would increase. In spite of the availability of this knowledge, and in spite of the fact that congestion could be good for neither the economy nor the environment, politicians preferred to let traffic control itself by its own congestion rather than embark on a rational alternative which might have been seen as a curb on the motorist's freedom. Perhaps it was felt that congestion would be accepted as an act of God, whereas anything done to get rid of it would be regarded as something for which politicians could be blamed by a noisy, if misguided, minority.

Although it is easy to criticize political timidity, the championing of the motorist's freedom at first sounds more understandable. But what did freedom to cause congestion really amount to? It was little more than the right of motorists to cause inconvenience to themselves and everyone else. The fact that most motorists are responsible citizens, who are prepared to respect simple laws which keep civilization going, seemed to escape the notice of the politicians. Drivers accept their loss of freedom to ignore a red traffic light because they know that it is in everyone's interest, including their own, that they do so; they even, with reluctance, accept the need for parking controls. Similarly most drivers, who at present have to accept the loss of freedom due to traffic control by congestion, would apparently be only too pleased to try a more rational system of control if it could be demonstrated that it would enable everyone, including themselves, to get around more easily (see Chapter 6 (i)). But even socially responsible motorists can do nothing by themselves. One person driving on the left-hand side of the road does not make the roads safe unless everyone else does likewise. In the same way, one person leaving the car at home will not cure urban congestion unless there is legislation to oblige (or simply encourage) other people to do the same.

Company Cars

Perhaps the most curious expression of Government tolerance of anarchy in urban transport has been the uniquely British phenom-enon of condoning 'perks' for the users of company cars. The system first got out of control under a Labour Government in the mid-1970s when employers used perks to employees as a means of evading the Government's incomes policy, and the Government condoned them for fear of damaging the British motor industry. (In retrospect it seems that they simply made the industry less competi-tive.) The Conservative Government, ostensibly opposed to perks, allowed the abuse to increase during the 1980s – in spite of reductions in high-rate taxes which, it was assumed, would discour-age tax-avoidance schemes.

There is, of course, no objection to the use of a company car for business purposes being treated as a business expense. Any payment that the user receives for the costs incurred in making journeys on the company's behalf is, quite rightly, not treated as part of his or her income from which tax has to be deducted. The problem arises from the fact that the Inland Revenue assesses the benefits of the private use of the company car – and of petrol supplied for private use – by adding to the user's taxable income sums that are substantially lower than the true value of the benefit.

Stephen Potter and Peter Hughes, in their book *Vital Travel Statistics, 1990* (Transport 2000, 1990) demonstrate from the 1985–86 National Travel Survey that sixty-five per cent of new cars are company cars, that drivers of company cars average 129 miles per week more than the drivers of household-purchased cars, and that fifty-four per cent of this extra mileage is for private rather than business purposes. This is hardly surprising when one notes that the combined car and fuel benefit claimed by the Inland Revenue from the user of a 1300cc company car for the

year 1984–85 would have been £750, while the Automobile Association's estimate of total running costs for such a car covering a
typical 10,000 miles per annum was £2,640. This represents a
tax-free 'perk' to the company-car user of £1,890 which is, of
course, at the expense of those taxpayers who do not have the
benefit of a company car (Stephen Plowden, *Transport Reform,
Changing the Rules*, Policy Studies Institute, 1985).

The total loss to the Exchequer through tax concessions for the
private use of company cars in 1990 was £3,400 million ('Company Car Costs in the UK', Greenpeace and Earth Resources
Research, February 1991). Of this figure £1,500 million arose
from undervaluing the car itself, £750 million arose from not
taxing at all the benefits of subsidized fuel and workplace parking, and £1,120 million arose from failing to reflect the advantage
of those benefits in National Insurance Contributions. In the 1991
Budget the Treasury clawed back £200 million by increasing the
deemed value of the company car by twenty per cent, and £600
million by reflecting the benefit of subsidies on car and fuel in
National Insurance Contributions. But this still leaves the tax
subsidy to company car users at £2,600 million. (A report from
the National Economic Development Office ('Company Car Parking', March 1991) claimed that, as ninety per cent of cars entering
central London between 7A.M. and 1P.M. were company subsidized, the taxing of company car parking would be the most
effective way of easing urban congestion.)

The company car is an anachronism with many side effects. First,
it is unfair: there is no good reason why those with company cars
should have tax concessions that are not available to the private
motorist, nor to anyone else. Second, it leads to less fuel-efficient
cars: Swansea's figures show that over the years engine sizes have
been between twenty-five and thirty per cent larger for company
cars than for privately owned cars. The third and most disastrous
side effect has been the distortion of travel patterns brought about
by the fact that those with company cars are encouraged to live
further from their place of work and therefore to travel greater
distances. The consequence has been increased traffic congestion,
particularly in towns, followed by a switch from public to private
transport and a further increase in congestion.

In many European cities, such as Paris, the journey to work by public transport is subsidized by both national and local government and by the employer, but the journey by car is not. This encourages people to travel by public transport rather than on the congested roads. In Britain we perversely do the reverse and clog up our roads unnecessarily by encouraging journeys to work by company car.

Trend Planning, Cost-Benefit Analyses, Public Inquiries and Assessment Studies

We have seen that successive governments have fought shy of making difficult decisions in the fields of strategic planning and transport, particularly in cities. This has usually been because enabling everyone to enjoy a decent environment has meant a curb on certain anti-social activities, like driving cars unnecessarily into congested areas. Governments have, with some justification, feared the reaction of powerful vested interests which have put the greatest good for the greatest number well below the interests of their own members which they have often tried to present as the interests of the majority.

It is not unreasonable for particular groups of people to band together in organizations that can explain their point of view forthrightly. Neither is it unreasonable for an organization with such terms of reference to put its members' interests above the interests of similar groups and above the interests of society at large. But it is the duty of the Government, while avoiding unnecessary restriction, to ensure the well-being of *all* citizens, even if this means making decisions that are unpopular with some. It is in this duty that every British Government has failed so conspicuously since the advent of universal car ownership. They have preferred instead, so far as strategic planning and transport are concerned, to let things take their course. To the extent that long-term planning has happened at all it has taken the form of anticipating the current trend irrespective of the likely results.

Trend planning is most obviously exemplified by the attempts to anticipate not just increasing levels of car ownership but also increasing levels of car use: regardless of whether such increased use is sustainable by our limited resources of fuel and land, and regardless of its effect either on our local environment or on the long-term survival of the planet. It is true that the Government has now conceded that catering for projected traffic levels may be neither desirable nor achievable in all circumstances. For some time it had recognized the impossibility of increasing traffic in central London, but it has now assured the public that, although it wants where possible to cater for people's desire to use their cars, it is not necessarily committed to catering for the eighty-five to 140 per cent increase in general traffic that present trends would imply by the year 2015.

It is also true that since the 1960s the Department of Transport has used cost-benefit analysis as a means of making a choice between possible planning options. This was an improvement on the use of intuition, which Michael Thomson in his book *Modern Transport Economics* (Penguin Education, 1974) describes as the more usual way of arriving at a decision before 1970. But Peter Hall, commenting on cost-benefit analysis in *Urban and Regional Planning*, says that it is too arbitrary in character and 'conceals the very considerable value judgements that underpin it behind an appearance of value-free objectivity'. It is impossible at one end of the scale to put a cost on damage to the local environment, let alone on the long-term damage to our planet; and at the other end of the scale it is arbitrary, to say the least, to value time saved by a financier as more valuable than time saved by a teacher simply because one earns more per minute than the other.

It was in the aftermath of the planning and housing disasters of the 1960s that governments became anxious to improve their image by taking more account of public opinion. The Labour Government set up the Skeffington Committee in 1969 to investigate the possibilities of public consultation, and most of its recommendations were adopted. But almost from the start the consultation processes were generally seen as a cynical exercise in public brainwashing. Inquiries into road-building proposals became particularly notorious: often giving the public the choice of several options, none of which was likely to appeal to them. David Widdicombe QC, writing in his foreword to John Tyme's book *Motorways Versus Democracy* (Macmillan Press) in 1978, said, 'Our public inquiry system works well enough when the proposal under consideration is promoted by a local authority or a private developer – that is, someone other than the Government. But as applied to Government-sponsored projects like motorways it is thoroughly unsatisfactory. This is partly because the Government combines the roles of advocate for the scheme and judge of the objections to it, compounding this unfairness by appointing as inspectors at the inquiries persons such as ex-civil servants who do not strike the public as independent. Far more important though is the embargo placed at the inquiry on all discussion on the main thing everyone wants to discuss, namely whether the project should take place at all.'

David Widdicombe's foreword was written before the demise of the metropolitan counties, i.e. before the Government had taken even more power for itself. But ironically it was the Government's apparent desire in 1984 to avoid confrontation with the public at local road inquiries in London that led to the setting up of the Road Assessment Studies. It seemed that the studies were designed to speed up the consultation process but they actually had the opposite effect and provided a more genuine form of consultation which led, in 1990, to the abandonment of road building as a solution to the capital's traffic problems.

London's Road Assessment Studies were, however, fundamentally flawed. Any sane attempt to find a cure to a city's chronic congestion would surely have looked first at that city's strategic problems and, having settled on an overall policy for resolving them, would then have worked within such policies on each local area. Instead, the Government persisted with its cart-before-the-horse approach, and agreed that each assessment study should be as far-reaching as it could be within the constraints of a do-nothing option at the strategic level. The result was a series of local options, most of which involved environmental upheaval but which did little to relieve congestion, because traffic restraint on a London-wide basis was ruled out by the terms of reference. For the same reason the Priority Route Network, proposed for London in 1990, will also fail. If it does succeed in driving out shops and businesses and in turning London's high streets into mere traffic arteries, it will be self-defeating even in traffic terms because, with car restraint ruled out by the Government, the newly cleared roads are bound to fill up again.

The silver lining to this cloud of ill-conceived proposals is that, if the London Assessment Studies did nothing else, they made it clear that extensive urban road building was politically impossible; and they made many very unlikely people question for the first time the desirability of unlimited use of the motorcar.

Fragmented Responsibility

Apart from the politicians' natural desire to avoid grasping difficult nettles, there seem to be two main reasons for Britain's inability to get to grips with strategic transport planning in cities. First, transport planning and land-use planning are dealt with by two separate government departments (and they were still treated as separate departments even when, to make things look a bit more rational, transport was brought under the Secretary of State for the Environment from 1970 to 1976). This failure to co-ordinate at national level has led, hardly surprisingly, to a similar failure at local level, which has been greatly exacerbated by the loss of the metropolitan counties. In London's case trunk roads are now controlled by the Secretary of State for Transport; local roads by each of thirty-three boroughs; strategic planning by the Secretary of State for the Environment (advised by the London Planning Advisory Committee); local planning by each borough; and public transport by London Regional Transport (except for surface railways which are controlled by Network SouthEast) – not an efficient-looking tool for planning the future of a large city.

The second cause for the failure of strategic transport planning lies in the nature of the Department of Transport. So far as airways, railways and waterways are concerned, the Department is simply, and rightly, the regulating authority; but when it comes to roads it is also the building and operating authority. This, together with the lack of any strategic planning authorities for our cities, puts the Government at a grave disadvantage when it seeks advice on strategic planning and transport. Instead of objective, independent comment from a 'Department of Transport', it gets almost inevitably road-biased advice from a 'Department of Roads' (see *Wheels Within Wheels* by Mick Hamer, Routledge and Kegan Paul, 1987). With this flawed process of decision-making, it is hardly surprising that the country has fallen behind the rest of Europe in the provision of urban transport that not only moves people and freight efficiently but is also consistent with a decent environment. In Europe and America it is now recognized that better public transport is the main

THE PRESENT IMPASSE 133

practical solution to the problems of urban congestion, and that in high-density cities this usually involves some form of railway building. As a result of its unique failure to plan objectively, Britain, which used to have the best urban transport system in Europe, is now near the bottom of the league.

Divided responsibilities have not only contributed to the lack of coherent strategic planning, they have also led to poor management of the existing system and poor enforcement of the laws that are there to support the system. For example it is general knowledge that in central London alone more than a quarter of a million parking offences are committed every day, with only two in every 100 offences leading to prosecution. Not only does this bring the law itself into disrepute, it also undermines the policies that the laws were designed to make workable. So far as the police are concerned it is understandable that parking offences are low on their list of priorities; but so far as the highway authorities are concerned car-parking control may be the most effective instrument available to them for the implementation of their traffic policy. Because of this it has often been argued that local authorities should be made responsible for the traffic wardens in their area, but when this was suggested to the Home Office by the London Amenity and Transport Association in 1977 the response was that, although the police had insufficient resources to recruit the necessary number of wardens, they felt it inappropriate that they should relinquish control. In 1990 the Government's proposals for Priority Traffic Routes in London included the transfer of the administration of legal parking (meters, residents' bays, etc.) to local authorities while illegal parking remained the responsibility of traffic wardens controlled by the police.

Lack of funds could also, of course, make it impossible for the local authorities to do the job any better than their police forces; but the present system allows, by default, illegal parking in most streets in most towns. The result is that delivery vehicles cannot reach the kerb to off-load but park instead in the middle of the road and cause congestion, to the disadvantage of everyone – including those who, by parking illegally, are the primary cause of the obstruction.

Fragmented responsibility in Britain has led not only to a vacuum at the level of strategic planning but also, at the other end of the spectrum, to failure in the simplest tasks of road management.

Roads without Reason

It may well be assumed that the fragmentation of responsibilities described above should at least have the advantage of ensuring that, while nothing good might come of it, nothing bad should come of it either. To a limited extent this is true of London. Many American visitors to the capital have commented that although it has the worst public transport system in Europe it has also suffered less from the major road-building disasters that hit other European cities in the 1960s and 1970s.

The same can probably also be said of Edinburgh, but it certainly cannot be said of any other major British cities. In a misguided belief that new roads would bring back prosperity to areas threatened with decline, fine cities like Birmingham and Newcastle were torn apart in vain. By the mid-1970s there was evidence that road building often brought the reverse of prosperity, as no one wanted to live, work or do their shopping in the windswept deserts created by new roads. Furthermore the existence of the new roads did not lead to the more efficient movement of either goods or people. Outside urban areas it simply led to both being moved over greater distances; while within urban areas congestion remained constant or got worse.

	1968	1973	1978	1983	1988
(A) Freight lifted in Million tonnes	1,707	1,671	1,491	1,344	1,751
(B) Freight moved in Billion tonne/kilometres	79.0	90.4	99.3	95.1	129.8

Fig. 14 Road freight in the United Kingdom

The Department of Transport's statistics for Great Britain, from which Figure 14 is extracted, demonstrate that although the weight of freight being moved on our roads has fluctuated it did not increase significantly during the twenty-year period 1968 to 1988 (see (A)). What did increase – by almost fifty per cent – was the distance that the freight was carried (see (B)): more the sign of a fuel-extravagant policy towards the location of industry than an indication of increased economic prosperity. Indeed it was in 1977 that evidence

Fig. 15 Heritage damaged for a pointless road – St Benets, London

given to the Government's Leitch Committee on Trunk Road Assessment pointed out that a new road, designed to make it easier for traders to despatch their goods from a particular town, would also make it easier to supply the town with goods from outside the area, at the expense of local industry.

In London congestion is worse than ever, although there are now fewer people living there and the number of people travelling to work in the central area has remained more or less constant (see Figure 16). The level of freight moved nationally has also remained more or less constant, but since industry has tended to move out of inner-city areas the weight of freight lifted in such areas has actually fallen. It follows that urban road congestion is not due to increased activity in our cities but rather to our mismanagement of the transport system.

Where new roads have been built, in the mistaken belief that the problem was lack of capacity rather than lack of management, they have proved pointless. Traffic levels have increased to fill up the new road space available, and as a result congestion has returned almost immediately, but with a higher level of traffic. Figure 15 shows St Benets Church in London's St Paul's Conservation Area during road construction. It demonstrates all too clearly the costly and unnecessary destruction of the environment for the sake of a road that has left congestion much as it always was.

4 (iv) SIDE EFFECTS

Communities Dispersed and Industries Concentrated

Not only did successive governments believe that road building was good for the economy, they also assumed that the dispersed communities and out-of-town shopping centres that went with road building would lead everyone to a better life. And this outlook was not confined to governments, highway authorities and the road lobby. Like the escape to the suburbs made possible by the railways from 1860 onwards, it was seen as the answer to the prayers of a great many people. But just as the ideal suburb on the boundary between town and country was a Will-o'-the-Wisp which disappeared as soon as it was leap-frogged by the next suburb, so the easily accessible, out-of-town shopping centre slips from our grasp as more and more people try to get to it, and we are threatened with California-style suburban 'gridlock'. Similarly the dream of living where you want and working where you want regardless of distance travelled becomes a nightmare when large numbers of people try to realize it.

Even the dream of cheap goods transport has turned sour: not only because of the urban congestion and general environmental damage caused by large lorries but also because of the entirely unforeseen effect of cheap transport on local industries and the local crafts that go with them. When it is cheaper to transport bricks a hundred miles or more from Bedfordshire than it is to use local materials, local building traditions die out and local jobs are replaced by centralized jobs at the brickyards that supply the whole nation. Perhaps most seriously of all, parts of the country that were once proudly 'different' lose not only their livelihoods but also their unique character and their self-esteem.

The Decline of Public Transport

There can have been no greater side effect of universal car ownership than the decline of public transport, and nowhere has this been more damaging than in our cities. But it has taken us almost thirty years to grasp the full significance of Buchanan's warning that commuting by car was incompatible with a decent environment in existing cities, and there is still no sign of our acting upon that warning.

Britain is not alone in this. Some European cities, like Venice which never had any cars and Vienna which never had very many, have prevented their cities from being overrun by traffic (though they are in danger of being overrun by tourists). A very few others, like Florence, have in desperation excluded cars from their central area and not regretted it. The vast majority, including Paris, have allowed the car to overrun them; but in Paris and the other major European cities people have been provided, through improved public transport, with an adequate means for getting round. In Britain they have not (see Chapter 6 (iii) and Figure 27).

Mention has already been made of inadequate investment in London's public transport. The Victoria and Jubilee Lines and the Docklands Light Railway did not even make up for the decline in bus services, and Figure 16 demonstrates that no more people travelled to central London by public transport in 1988 than in 1956, in spite of increased overcrowding. The only positive attempt in the capital to relieve congestion by encouraging people to use public transport was made by the GLC in 1981. The Council's Fares Fair policy reduced congestion on the roads by ten per cent and might have achieved more if there had been the power and the will to restrain car traffic. As it was, the scheme was nipped in the bud by legal action over the Council's fiduciary duty to ratepayers who did not use public transport, and by the Government's unwillingness to introduce legislation that would have allowed the experiment to continue for the benefit of London as a whole. But even if the policy had continued it would have been overwhelmed eventually by the lack of investment in the public transport infrastructure.

Britain's most striking development in public transport since World War II, and the only one to bear comparison with similar developments in Europe, was Tyneside's Tyne and Wear Metro, opened in stages between 1975 and 1980. It took over a network of underused British Rail lines and connected it to the centre of Newcastle by a new section built under the central area. Furthermore, in order to reduce congestion in the central area, bus passengers from places not served by Metro were encouraged to switch to the Metro for the last stage of the journey at well-organized interchange stations. During the 1980s the other metropolitan counties (through their Passenger Transport Authorities, which survived the abolition of the counties themselves) made bold attempts to improve their public transport systems with limited resources: mostly by financing improvements to their local railway services and by limiting fare increases. The jewel in the crown is, of course, Manchester's Metrolink, at last under construction with financial assistance from the Government and due to be completed during 1991. Its two-car trains will run on BR rails to the north and south of the city and will run tram-like through the central streets between the railway terminals: a form of light-rail system popular throughout Europe but new to Britain (see Figure 28).

The city with a difference was Sheffield, whose Passenger Transport Authority, the Metropolitan County of South Yorkshire, pioneered cheap bus fares combined with frequent services throughout the day, including the off-peak and evening periods. The result was that the people of Sheffield really did leave their cars behind in large numbers and, with little congestion, the buses were fast as well as cheap. When a combination of Government-imposed financial restrictions and bus deregulation led to the break-up of the system, congestion returned and mobility was lost for car users and bus passengers alike. It would be surprising if the real cost to the economy of Sheffield did not greatly exceed the saving made by removing the bus subsidy.

Alas, the disaster of Sheffield is typical. The germ of possible success in Manchester is not. Even Newcastle's Metro has suffered from bus deregulation and the consequent break-up of a once integrated system.

Through a combination of road building and more sophisticated traffic management, the road capacity of our cities is now considerably greater than it was in the 1960s. Moreover, in the centre of London and most other cities the number of people to be moved and the weight of freight to be lifted are both below their peak levels. It follows that roads in our city centres should now be less congested than they once were. The fact that congestion is actually worse is due almost entirely to the inexorable switch of passengers from bus to car.

It will be seen from Figure 16 that the number of people travelling to work in central London in 1988, although twelve per cent higher than for the strikebound year of 1982, is eight per cent lower than the figure for the peak year of 1964 and almost identical to the figure for 1956. Because buses can carry a greater number of people on a given piece of road than can be carried by cars, roads to central London were carrying fewer people in 1988 (278,000) than they were in 1956 (404,000), in spite of greater road space and more sophisticated methods of traffic control. No wonder the Underground services were overcrowded in 1988.

We are caught in a vicious spiral of increasing congestion, poorer bus services, further use of private cars, increasing congestion, etc. In other words, we probably have as much vehicle-carrying capacity

People entering central London 7–10 A.M., measured in thousands, by mode of travel

	1956	1964	1970	1976	1982	1988
Car and cycle	144	176	171	187	236	177
Coach and minibus	x	x	10	10	22	21
Bus	260	191	152	151	99	80
Underground only	361	385	387	316	283	411
BR with Underground onwards	97	114	117	108	122	188
BR only	290	350	347	293	268	280
Total	1,152	1,216	1,184	1,065	1,030	1,157
Total by road	404	367	333	348	357	278
Total by public transport	1,008	1,040	1,013	878	794	980

x Before 1970 these were mostly LT Green Line coaches and are included under Bus.

Fig. 16 Rush-hour journeys to central London (abridged from LRT's 1989 statistics)

in our cities as we need, but the roads are congested because they are carrying people in cars who could, and used to, travel by public transport. The result is that there is no room for the efficient operation of either buses or commercial vehicles, let alone for the provision of a better environment for pedestrians and cyclists.

The failure of successive British governments either to restrain the use of the car in urban areas, or to invest in public transport, or to do both, contrasts with the policies of other European governments, which have consistently seen public transport as the key to solving the problem of urban mobility. By the end of 1987 congestion on the roads and overcrowding on the Underground in London had become so bad that none other than the Governor of the Bank of England took up cudgels on the commuters' behalf. Fearing that London's very future as a financial centre was threatened by the poverty of its public transport services, he set up the City Commuters' Group to press for public funds to improve the railways and Underground serving the City of London.

It was encouraging that such a move was made, but it was discouraging that it should have been necessary. It is ironic that at the time, instead of concentrating on improved public transport as a means of reducing congestion, the Department of Transport was busy trying to revive through its Road Assessment Studies sections of the old inner-orbital roads that had been so firmly rejected after the Layfield Inquiry. Even when the Secretary of State for Transport at last authorized the extension of London's Jubilee Line in 1989, his decision seems to have been aimed more at bailing out the Canary Wharf development in Docklands than at solving London's overall transport problems. The Government's own Central London Rail Study had put the east–west, cross-London rail link and the Chelsea–Hackney Line at the top of its priorities, and the Jubilee Line at the bottom. But in agreeing to go ahead with the latter, the Secretary of State again delayed a decision on the two more important lines (see Chapter 6 (iii)).

Treatment of Pedestrians and Cyclists

It is not only the impoverished state of public transport that has threatened London's future as a commercial centre; the impoverished environment for pedestrians is also a serious cause for concern. Whether people arrive in a city by car or by public transport, most of the journeys they make within the centre, before returning home in the evening, are on foot. Indeed, the 1985–86 National Travel Survey shows that forty-five per cent of journeys in high-density urban areas are made on foot, and this excludes the beginnings and ends of journeys otherwise made by mechanized transport (*Vital Travel Statistics, 1990* by Potter and Hughes). Nevertheless, pedestrians are shabbily treated. They are usually confined to narrow pavements, hemmed in by heavy traffic, unable to cross the street at the most convenient place and, where crossing is controlled by traffic lights, given very little time to do so. The final ignominy is being obliged to cross by a footbridge or subway, both of which involve a great many steps or circuitous ramps, and the latter of which usually involves not only dreariness but also a positive danger of assault. Even at London's main tourist attractions the pedestrian is treated as a second-class citizen. In spite of tourism's considerable contribution to the national economy, visitors to Buckingham Palace have to watch the Changing of the Guard from a traffic roundabout which they share with the statue of Queen Victoria. Although pedestrians outnumber other road users at Piccadilly Circus, the 'centre of the universe' still looks like a temporary traffic-management scheme, with endless 'safety' railings which are really there to stop visitors from getting in the way of traffic.

The tragedy of the post-1945 period is that, contrary to expectations, it has seen a deteriorating environment. This has been to everyone's disadvantage, but no one has suffered more than our children, who can no longer play spontaneously in their street or cycle to school. They may now live in more hygienic houses, but their peer community has been destroyed. If they want to visit a friend, they have to be escorted by an adult because increased traffic has made the street so dangerous.

The sacrifice both of our environment and of our children's freedom might have been justified if there had been a gain to show for it; but we have already seen that far from making it easier to get people and freight around our cities, the increased traffic that has driven the children indoors has actually made it more difficult. Furthermore, disregard for the interests of pedestrians and cyclists has led many people to make journeys by car which, given a decent environment, they would have preferred to make on foot. The journey to school is a good example. In an ideal world, and provided the journey was little more than the typical trip to the local inner-city primary school, most children would probably prefer to cycle to school with their friends (like previous generations of children) rather than be driven by an adult. Similarly many parents with small children like the idea of walking to school and meeting other people on the way. In present circumstances some of these feel obliged to take the car and forgo social intercourse rather than face the polluted air on the narrow pavements of congested streets. So strong is this feeling that the journey is often made by car even when, because of congestion, it would be quicker on foot.

Although the number of people cycling to work in British cities is now on the increase again, it is still less than fifty per cent of the number doing so in the 1950s, and well below the average figure for cities in Europe as a whole. This is not so much due to a lack of special facilities like cycle lanes, but rather because modern traffic-management practice in Britain, outside the new towns, takes little account of cyclists or their safety. This is best exemplified by the number of roundabouts and one-way gyratory road systems which still survive in our cities and which, because they demand frequent changes of traffic lane, make cyclists particularly vulnerable. Roundabouts are, in any case, an absurdity in heavily congested areas. If one route becomes blocked, traffic taking the other route is also blocked; whereas in similar circumstances at a crossroads controlled by traffic lights, the second route can be kept clear. But our failure to phase out anachronistic roundabouts and gyratory systems is not just a failure to protect the safety of the cyclists who already use the roads, it is probably the most important of the many discouragements to 'new' cyclists who could be forsaking their cars, thus reducing congestion and pollution, and at the same time improving their own health by taking more exercise.

From the Buchanan Report onwards there has been increasing awareness that the prosperity of a city, and the health of its inhabitants, does not depend on more roads, more cars and increasing congestion, but that it depends instead on a better urban environment brought about by greater use of public transport, walking and cycling. This message has been accepted in principle in most large European cities, but it has taken a long time to filter through to transport and highway authorities in Britain (where, ironically, the Buchanan Report is less quoted than it is in Germany). Since the abolition of the GLC and the other metropolitan counties, responsibility for seeing that the message is eventually accepted in this country rests with the Government. If the message is not heeded the Motor Age will be seen, retrospectively, not as a new dawn, but as the age that brought about the decline of British cities environmentally, socially and economically.

PART III   Urban Revival

STRATEGIC PLANNING

. . . the new town lacks the diversity, stimulation and serendipity associated with the jumble and congestion of old town and city centres.

Ray Thomas

5 (i) CONCENTRATION – v – DISPERSAL

Old Cities and New Towns

The quotation above is from Ray Thomas's introduction to the 1985 edition by Attic Books of Ebenezer Howard's *Garden Cities of Tomorrow*. In it, Thomas contrasts the order and logic of Britain's new towns with the vitality of the old cities, which he sees as a product of history, high density and unco-ordinated decision-making. Unlike Ebenezer Howard, he commends both, and looks for a balance between the two.

It may be that a new form of urbanism can strike a balance between the healthy garden-city logic of the new town and the brash vitality of the high-density city; but it seems more likely, and more practical, that both should continue to exist separately. If the density of new towns were raised to give them more vitality, they would lose their essentially garden-city character. If the density of our old towns and cities were lowered to make them garden cities, they would lose the very compactness that gives them their vitality. Without sacrificing the overall environment, we can no longer find greenfield sites for new settlements in the southeast. There is, however, sufficient derelict urban land to repopulate and reinvigo-rate our old cities: thus avoiding the need either to spoil the garden-city character of our new towns or to expand further into our dwindling countryside.

Professor Peter Hall, surely Britain's most prolific writer of books on planning, made the point in the 1970s that the post-War programme of new and expanded towns had contributed no more than about three per cent of the total housing programme – 'so the fond hope of Ebenezer Howard and the 1945 Reith Committee – that urban populations would decentralize to self-contained communities – was never fulfilled. But as car ownership produced greater mobility this seemed less necessary. Nevertheless the resulting pattern of movement created unprecedented new problems – above all for transportation planning.' Hall also outlined the frustrated attempts of the Redcliffe Maude Committee to establish regional planning authorities that might have solved the new problems, but he gave the impression that greater mobility and the dispersal of centralized cities are developments to be applauded.

Gordon Cherry also seems to welcome the breaking-down of traditional European urbanism. His book *Urban Change and Planning*, published in 1972, suggests that the radial transportation system that has supported the old compact city might well change to one based on a rectangular grid covering a whole region. 'In this way urban areas will not have a setting of a green belt surrounding a circular, compact area but will be loosely dispersed with belts of green between. Within this polyform type of area, not one but a number of central concentrations where specialist activities take place will be located at junctions of the circulation system.' This amounts to something not dissimilar to Ebenezer Howard's cluster of garden cities. But even though Howard's public-transport-oriented cities of 30,000 people that make up his clusters were designed to be compact (each city was less than one and a half miles across), he intended that each cluster should house only 250,000 people on 26,000 hectares (or 66,000 acres or 103 square miles). This enabled each city in the cluster to be separated from its neighbouring city by almost two miles, so that anyone travelling on the orbital inter-municipal railway (see Figure 8) would be travelling alternately through one and a half miles of garden city and two miles of countryside.

London rebuilt on the lines of Milton Keynes would take up two and a half times its present area, with open spaces separating each neighbourhood but with no genuine countryside within the giant conurbation, and with the existing green belt swallowed up (see Chapters 3 (i) and 7 (i)). This would clearly be unacceptable, so let us consider what would happen if we were to attempt to rebuild London along Howard's ideas of genuinely separated sub-cities grouped in clusters. Howard of course would not approve, but his system of clusters could in theory be extended endlessly because (unlike Milton Keynes which was designed as a single city) it contained areas of genuine countryside within it.

The area covered by the former Greater London Council was 616 square miles – six times the area of Howard's cluster of seven cities. But the population of London at the time of the 1981 census was 6,713,000 – twenty-seven times larger than the population of Howard's cluster. London rebuilt as twenty-seven clusters (or 184 garden cities) would therefore take up four and a half times its present area (twenty-seven divided by six). In fact, assuming that the new 'London cluster of cities' were designed to accommodate the motorcar, it would take up a very much larger area, because Howard's concept was based entirely on public transport, cycling and walking. But assuming that, by reducing the amount of countryside between each city, the new cluster of garden cities called London could be limited to only four and a half times its present size, it would still expand into an area of the Home Counties that at present houses another four million people. In order to accommodate them, in addition to its own 6.7 million, the new London would cover seven times its present area. The argument is endless, and enough to make poor Ebenezer Howard turn in his grave. At least in his calculations he did not have to contend with inflated outer suburban populations.

But if there is not room to restructure the southeast on the lines of Ebenezer Howard's comparatively compact garden cities, there certainly would not be room for the car-oriented rectangular grid foreseen by Gordon Cherry, nor for a series of Milton Keyneses with green belts between them. If the depopulation of the southeast is ruled out as a serious option, we have no alternative but to retain our public-transport-oriented, high-density cities and make the most of them.

There may be a case for new towns as a way of dealing with particular growth pressures in the southeast arising from massive isolated projects like Stansted Airport or the Channel Tunnel. They would be preferable to the swamping of existing towns, and to the small new dormitory villages so beloved of speculative developers and so destructive of the countryside. However, for the reason given above, they can never be seen collectively as an alternative to London.

We should clearly encourage people to move north where there is more space available and where, thanks to lower costs, the standard of living for those with jobs is higher. To this end it is vital to ensure that maximum use is made of rail links from Scotland (and Wales) to Europe via the Channel Tunnel. But incentives by themselves have proved poor persuaders in the past. To effect a better distribution of population in Britain we need to ensure strict planning control over development in the southeast to enable market forces to achieve the movement of people and jobs to the north.

In the meantime the southeast has to concentrate on preserving and enhancing its surviving countryside, on reinforcing the independence of the new towns, making use of London's twenty-five square miles of derelict land (see Chapter 5 (ii)) and, above all, on massively improving the existing urban areas along the lines outlined in Chapters 6 and 7. Furthermore, although it may be clear that we need some sort of restraint on growth in the southeast in order to encourage market-led growth elsewhere, it would be wrong to imagine that, as a corollary, *laissez-faire* planning policies can be applied in the provinces.

The great advantage enjoyed by cities like Manchester, Leeds and Sheffield is the proximity of the 'real' countryside. Dispersal has already eroded this advantage, but it has not yet destroyed it. Further dispersal could easily lead to the feeling of endlessness that already applies to London. If, however, contrary to expectations large numbers of people could be persuaded to move from the southeast to the north of England, and if that number were more than could be accommodated within the built-up areas of existing towns and cities, then it would be infinitely preferable to accommodate them in new settlements rather than imitate London's suburban sprawl. Always assuming that the north of England (or for that matter Wales and Scotland) were prepared to accept a large influx of people, it would provide an excellent opportunity to build another generation of new towns; but it is to be hoped that such towns would be closer to Ebenezer Howard's compact garden cities than to the dispersed, car-oriented precedent set by Milton Keynes.

Peter Hall was right to see the motorcar as both the solver of problems and the begetter of new ones. It makes possible the servicing of scattered communities but, in a country that has not got sufficient space for scattered communities without their being turned into a sort of endless suburbia, it creates more problems than it solves. We have seen that without the high-density cities to house some of the population there is not room for both the low-density communities that some people prefer and the countryside that is necessary to relieve the monotony and provide the space for environment-friendly agriculture. But are the people who continue to live in cities in the traditional European sense doing so only so that the rest of us can live more spaciously? Or is there a continuing case for the close-knit community that cannot easily accommodate the private car but that instead has all the pleasures and necessities of life close to hand?

Urban Communities

Professor Rayner Banham, the architectural critic, used to suggest that communities, in the generally accepted sense of the term, were a thing of the past. He maintained that the only community that counted was the dinner-party community of like-minded people who met by deliberate arrangement and who did not have to live in close proximity with one another so long as they were connected by a motorway – a surprisingly dull-sounding way of life to be commended by one whose lectures on planning may have been unorthodox but were never dull.

Banham's ideal was Los Angeles. But one man's meat is another man's poison. Even if some are content with driving long distances to meet socially, and some are content to do business without meeting face to face, there are others who want the stimulus of meeting people easily and of meeting accidentally people who are not their friends or business acquaintances. They are the people who like the jostle, the variety and the vitality of an urban environment. Take away the high concentration of people and activities, together with the diversity and vitality that go with them, and there is no longer any point in being in a city.

Although the concentration of people and activities is the *sine qua non* of the traditional city's existence, ever since the collapse of Ronan Point in 1967 there has been increasing pressure to dilute it, mainly due to the mistaken assumption that high densities are synonymous with tower blocks. More recently the case for low-density living for its own sake has been revived on the grounds that most people who have lived all their lives in an urban environment are pining to live in a suburban semi-detached house. This line of thought is little more than a revival of the old nineteenth-century Will-o'-the-Wisp based on the house conveniently situated between town and country, which never materialized because town and country never stood still. It ignores not only the fact that three- and four-storey houses in urban streets can have gardens (see Chapter 7 (ii)) but also the failure of the car-oriented suburbs of the 1930s, and the more recent failure of the California sprawl which has ended up with suburban gridlock in spite of all its road space.

There are plenty of people who want to live in cities and many who are prevented from doing so by a shortage of dwellings. The major part of Britain's housing stock lies outside the inner-city areas; so it makes better sense to enable those who wish to move out of the cities to do so, rather than to attempt the wholesale suburbanization of the central areas, which would deny everyone the option of urban living and the facilities that go with it.

Interdependence of Businesses

Not only can the concentrated city offer advantages to people who live in it, there are also advantages for people who work there. For those whose workplaces are near the centre of gravity of the public transport system, there is no need for the journey to work to be long or unpleasant. None of our cities is so dense that it cannot be well served by a properly planned public transport system.

The reason that office accommodation is so sought after in the City of London is surely that financiers either need to be, or want to be, where other financiers are; and this is possible only where offices are highly concentrated into a small area. In spite of the rundown state of London's transport system, and the lack of new investment in its infrastructure, the existing railways and Underground are well situated to serve the 'square mile', and once there, those who work in the City are within walking distance of everyone who does likewise. Furthermore, those who work in finance houses are not the only ones who want close proximity to one another and to the facilities that a central location can provide. London has the advertising and film industries in Soho, the jewellers and silversmiths in Clerkenwell, the lawyers and stationers in Holborn, and the politicians and civil servants in Westminster, to mention but a few in one city who are dependent on the central area generally and on one another. Moreover it is not just certain employers and self-employed who want to be in the central area of a town for business reasons; many employees also like to be centrally located – if only to be near the superior entertainment and shopping facilities, which are not available to those working in suburban factories or offices, and still less to those working in remote industrial parks.

A high concentration of commercial activities in a radial city certainly makes sense from a planning and transport point of view; it also makes sense environmentally. A city with a spectacular group of tall buildings at its centre is likely to make a far more interesting townscape than one in which building heights have been standardized.

Fig. 17 The City of London as townscape

New York's skyline is rightly famous. The view of the City of London from Waterloo Bridge deserves a similar fame, especially as it manages to symbolize simultaneously the City's modern and historic images (see Figure 17). But such a large secondary centre as that created by the Docklands development at Canary Wharf is a disaster, not just as a transport problem (see Chapter 6 (iii)) but also as a piece of townscape. It detracts from the historic commercial centre which should be visually pre-eminent.

A similar disaster befell the city of Stockholm in the 1950s. At the beginning of that decade Stockholm's new commercial centre, on its island site, was a striking contrast to everything around it. Although it dominated the old town it marked its position, and was a spectacular piece of townscape in its own right. By the end of the decade the tower blocks, instead of being concentrated spectacularly at the centre, stretched monotonously to the suburban centre of Vallingby, almost ten miles away – a classic case of a city's visual dilution.

Derelict Land

Since it is the high concentration of people and activities that gives the city its major advantage over other locations, it follows that derelict and underused land, which is the very antithesis of concentration, must have a debilitating effect on the city as a whole. Yet the Civic Trust's *Urban Wasteland Now*, published in 1988, showed that 3.4 per cent of all urban land was wasteland. By the Trust's own admission, this figure was conservative and excluded land in temporary use, operational land not fully used, and wasteland on the urban fringe that was not part of a green belt. When such land was taken into account the figure rose to five per cent. As the area of wasteland in London was above the national average it amounted to at least twenty-five square miles (five per cent of the built-up area). The Institute of Economic Affairs put the national figure even higher, at ten per cent of all urban land, or four times the area of Leeds.

The decline of some industries, as others expand, is to be expected, but it does not follow that land that has become derelict should remain so indefinitely. That it has is due largely to the fact that redevelopment is easier on a greenfield site. But short-term gain cannot be justified at the long-term cost of using up valuable rural land, especially when the non-use of urban land is so damaging to the concentration, and therefore the prosperity, of our cities.

Much wasteland is the result of economic changes that have caused unforeseen industrial dereliction, but much of it, especially in the all-important central areas of our cities, is the result of 'self-inflicted' planning blight. In the 1960s this was usually caused by the long-term assembly of sites for comprehensive redevelopment by local authorities. However, the cause for concern as we enter the 1990s is dereliction as a result of developers demolishing buildings before their new developments are ready to start. There are now many commercial sites in city centres where tenants have been evicted, the buildings demolished and the site then left empty. To prevent this version of blight, the planning laws need to be changed so that permission has to be sought for demolition as part of the permission for the development itself. In this way local authorities would be able to make it a condition that demolition could not proceed until developers could demonstrate that they were ready to commence rebuilding work.

It is often assumed that once a central site has become derelict it might as well be turned into a temporary car park. But this is likely to be a disaster on three counts: it will generate no activity, except perhaps for the employment of one car-park attendant; it will encourage people into the area by car instead of by public transport and thereby cause congestion; and 'temporary' is often a euphemism for indefinite. (There is at least one car park in central London, of all places, which in 1991 celebrates its fiftieth anniversary as a bombsite – complete with the original peeling bitumen on its retaining walls which, for the first three years of its life, allowed it to be used as an emergency water supply tank!)

Public Open Space

It is often argued that all urban wasteland should, where possible, be used as public open space, and this would certainly be preferable to continued dereliction. But such a policy would perpetuate urban dilution. In her book *The Death and Life of Great American Cities*, Jane Jacobs made a strong case against too much open space within towns for this very reason. She claimed that the idea of parks as lungs was 'science fiction'. It led to dispersal, which in turn led to the greater use of cars and therefore to a greater pollution of the atmosphere.

It is true, however, that every city needs some 'wilderness'; and every urban district, or borough, needs a substantial park of several hectares which has plenty of forest trees and areas of grass that are large enough to survive unrestricted use and therefore do not require protective fencing. It is also true that every neighbourhood needs its all-weather football pitch and its small supervised public garden for the quiet enjoyment of trees, grass and flowers, and for toddlers' play. However, many existing municipal parks consisting mostly of grass are too large to be properly supervised but not large enough to survive unlimited football. They are a waste of urban land, and they contribute to the dispersal scorned by Jane Jacobs and to the loss of local facilities, like shops, which depend for their survival on a high concentration of people.

To proclaim the uselessness of the typical small patch of public urban grass, however, is not to decry the need for verdure in our towns and cities, which are generally all too bleak. But outside parks, such greenness is best provided in urban areas by trees and shrubs in paving, be it in streets, in squares like London's Sloane Square, or in the haphazard spaces between buildings which can make or mar our surroundings (see Figure 18). Such trees and shrubs must be sufficiently robust or well-protected to be vandalproof, or they must be planted in such a position that it is in the interests of the nearest residents to protect them. Account should also be taken of the importance to the general environment of planting within private open space – although, except through Tree Preservation Orders, it is difficult to protect from unsympathetic owners.

From the environmental point of view, the greatest single failing of our towns and cities is that streets that used to be meeting places and areas where children could play have been taken over by traffic. The result has been increasing demands for playgrounds where children can play in safety. Although traditional playground equipment, like the swing, retains its popularity with the very young, children in general seem to prefer playing outside their own front doors rather than in fenced-off playgrounds to which they have to be escorted by adults (see *Housing as if People Mattered* by Clare Cooper

Fig. 18 A small urban open space, Copenhagen

Markus and Wendy Sarkissen, University of California Press, 1986).
If the speed and volume of traffic in residential streets were to be
drastically reduced, as suggested in Chapter 6 (iv), there would be
no need for many of the little-used formal playgrounds, nor for the
safety railings that go with them.

Instead of frittering away valuable urban land as a palliative to
those who suffer a poor environment, we should use our resources to
improve the appearance and safety of the whole urban environment
while, at the same time, maintaining the concentrated form of the
city.

Cities, Fuel Efficiency and Pollution

Scattered communities like Milton Keynes were described earlier as
extravagant of fuel. This needs some elaboration because it is often
assumed that low population density, free-flowing traffic and fuel
efficiency go together. It is well known that the fuel-efficient speed
for most cars lies between thirty-five and fifty-five miles per hour:
hence the speed limit of fifty-five miles per hour on American
freeways, which is imposed for reasons of fuel economy. It is also
well known that in congested streets, travelling largely in low gear,

cars are at their most inefficient in terms of fuel consumption per mile: hence the assumption that low-density sprawl, however disliked for other reasons, at least saves fuel. Nothing could be further from the truth. The more dense the city the less the need to travel and the more likely that walking, cycling or fuel-efficient public transport will be the mode of travel.

Per passenger/mile the 1.4 to 2.0 litre car at its national average occupancy of 1.5 people, uses more than twice the fuel of a single-decker bus, almost four times the fuel of a double-decker bus and four and a half times the fuel of a suburban electric train: assuming that the buses and train are also at their average occupancy of thirty-three per cent full and seventy per cent full respectively (*Vital Travel Statistics, 1990* by Potter and Hughes).

Whether cities as a whole are more fuel efficient than suburban areas depends, of course, on whether the reduced number of journeys, and the journeys made more efficiently by public transport, outweigh the more inefficient use of motorcars in congested streets. Clearly, the more dense the city and the greater the use of public transport, the more likely this is to be so. It is interesting therefore to find that the most comprehensive survey on the subject comes from Perth, Western Australia: a medium-sized city of 500,000 people with densities at the centre much lower than the typical European city. Even so, Newman and Kenworthy's survey in 1987 found that: 'In Perth, even though vehicles in central areas have 19 per cent lower fuel-efficiency than average due to congestion, the central-area residents still use 22 per cent less actual fuel on average due to their locational advantages. On the other hand, outer suburban traffic is 12 per cent more efficient than average but residents use 29 per cent more actual fuel.' The authors go on to point out that in New York the contrast between the less fuel-consuming central area and the more fuel-consuming outer area is more than double that in Perth – central New York using, per person, half the fuel of central Perth, and suburban New York using fifty per cent more per person than suburban Perth.

Commenting on their survey of thirty-two cities worldwide, Newman and Kenworthy concluded that: 'The general picture of an energy-conserving city is one where there is a good balance between automobiles, public transport, walking and bicycling; an intensive, more centralized land-use system; and high levels of traffic restraint.

The importance of rail systems is further confirmed, with cities in the poorest energy-conserving category having only 13 per cent of total public transport travel on trains, while the other more energy-conserving cities have an average of over 50 per cent on trains.'

It seems therefore that, in addition to the social and environmental advantages of retaining our high-density cities that were outlined in the earlier sections of this chapter, we can add the imperative advantage of saving fuel; and unless there is some unforeseen advance in fuel technology, the less fuel we use the less we pollute the atmosphere.

Even if the social and economic arguments for retaining compact communities were to be ignored we would need to save our cities in order to save our planet.

5 (ii) DIVERSITY AND MARKET FORCES

A Balance of Land Uses

The Monopolies and Mergers Commission exists because unrestrained market forces tend to lead to monopoly. Monopoly means, by definition, a lack of competition – and lack of competition is regarded as against the public interest. It could equally be said that unrestrained market forces tend to lead to a lack of diversity in land use – and such a lack of diversity means a lack of vitality in our towns and cities, which is also against the public interest both economically and socially.

The City of London is a dreary place in the evenings and at weekends, because there are no people about and nothing happens at these times (except at the Barbican which is too isolated from the rest of the City to redress the balance). During the late nineteenth and early twentieth centuries, when the 'square mile' became solely a financial centre at the expense of its other historical functions, there was no planning legislation to ensure that some housing, shopping and entertainment remained. The West End of London, on the other hand, retains its vitality outside business hours. Although there has been considerable pressure from landowners to turn every floor of every building into office accommodation, this pressure came much later than it did in the City and was predated by the Town and Country Planning Acts, which have been used to ensure that buildings other than offices remain in the area. Even in buildings mainly converted to office use, shops or restaurants have been retained at street level.

Recently, however, a serious blow has been struck against the fragile diversity of our city centres. The Town and Country Planning (Use Classes) Order of 1987 merged two very different categories of land use: 'commercial' (or offices) and 'light industry' – thus enabling owners to change the use of their buildings (or sites) from one category to the other without the need for planning permission. Needless to say, this makes it virtually impossible for local planning authorities to maintain control over the development of inner-city areas that abound with light industrial sites: some derelict, some underused, but some essential to maintaining central-area services, and all – especially in London – threatened by the spread of offices.

It seems that the Government's reason for merging these very different categories of land use was that some local planning authorities were keeping more land available for light industry than could conceivably be taken up in a time of changing employment patterns. The local authorities replied that they were simply protecting the jobs of local residents; but in many cases that attitude led to long-term dereliction, which was of no benefit to anyone, and so the Government felt that such a doctrinaire approach had to be ended. However, allowing every light industrial building to be turned into an office block is another case of throwing out the baby with the bathwater: the worthy aim of bringing derelict land into use is more than offset by the driving out of vital service industries as their leases come up for renewal. As a result, the prosperity of London's central commercial districts is threatened not only by declining public transport but also now by the loss of supporting industries which may not be able to afford 'office' rents although they provide a vital service to those that can. An important side effect is the loss of industries that have given their area its character. In London the threats to Soho's 'rag trade' and to Clerkenwell's craftsmen have brought strong pleas for a change to the 1987 Order from both Conservative Westminster and Labour Islington.

It is clear that the variety of activities in our city centres is under its greatest threat since everything except finance was driven out from the old City of London a hundred years ago. It could be argued that, however dreary London's 'square mile' may now be, its prosperity has not been affected, but there are signs that this may not be true for long. People are already suggesting that they would prefer to do business in more congenial places where back-up services are more readily available. Cities like Paris and Frankfurt which take trouble over their environment (and their public transport), and ensure that there is variety (including culture) in their central business districts, are increasingly likely to draw commerce from London. A much more serious threat, however, to the welfare of Britain as a whole is the situation outside London. Since we have insufficient space to do without cities and still retain a decent environment, we have no alternative but to make all our cities attractive to their inhabitants as well as to those who work in them.

Even dreary cities attract some people, and it is a good thing that they do, but among those attracted are inevitably some of the thugs of society who, if the streets have few people in them to observe their villainy, will prey upon any that they can find. Central areas that are half deserted are not only dull but downright dangerous – and there is nothing worse for a city's reputation than dangerous streets. On the other hand, nothing enhances a city's reputation more than friendly streets where there is plenty happening. It is therefore imperative that the central areas of our cities have a diversity of activities which, because they take place at different times, ensure that there is always something going on – a thesis first propounded by Jane Jacobs thirty years ago, and which has led to a lot of talk but little action.

Let us assume that within cities there are five basic uses of land: commercial, residential, retail, recreational and communal (the latter including education and health). It seems that every street, or group of streets, in the central areas of our cities needs at least two of these activities. Furthermore, if commerce is the major activity in any particular area, then shops that close when the offices close should not be the only alternative activity, as is the tendency in the City of London. Such an area should also contain either housing or leisure activities. At present there are two obstacles to housing as a use of land in a predominantly commercial area. One is the price of land; and the other is the right of landowners to refuse to change the use to which their land is put. In the short term, recreation is probably the alternative activity most easily combined with commerce in a central area. This already happens in the West End of London, but in many other cities there has been a tendency for leisure facilities to be moved, like shopping, out of the central area. The same fate has befallen many community facilities, like hospitals, which have been moved to greenfield sites, sometimes because there is no community left to serve (itself a tragedy for the town concerned), but sometimes to realize the asset of a valuable site. If our towns are to be reinvigorated, this process must be reversed.

If it is important to keep a balance of activities in the central area, the last thing a city needs is to have its theatres, concert halls and the like in a place specially set aside for them. Not only do such places tend to become cultural ghettos (like London's South Bank) which makes them disappointing in themselves, but they also deprive the central area of one of its major ingredients for success. It is true that sufficient restaurants, pubs, etc., may eventually be established on the South Bank, but it is taking a long time for this to happen. It is also true that the South Bank is slowly contributing to the revitalization of the Thames. But it seems to be due more to luck than good judgement that a sudden boom in the tourist trade saved the South Bank from killing entertainment in the West End. In any case London, with its history and its role as a capital city, is different from other towns and cities in Britain. Mistakes can be made in London which, because of its magnetism as a capital city, it can sometimes survive. Almost anywhere else such mistakes can easily lead to the complete collapse of the city centre as a place of social and cultural activity which, in turn, can threaten that city's economic activity.

Old Buildings for 'Downtown' Activities

Although variety of activity is the most important aspect of diversity in a city, variety in the city's fabric also has an important role to play. Old buildings are needed as much as new buildings, partly to express the city's identity and history, partly to provide the citizens with a sense of familiarity and of 'belonging' but more particularly to provide the venue for the many 'downtown' activities that are essential to the commercial vitality of the city but cannot support the market rent of new accommodation. One of the reasons that

London's West End succeeds and its South Bank fails is that the former has plenty of old buildings to accommodate pubs, clubs and restaurants, while the latter does not. It is beyond the scope of this book to examine the reasons why new developments have failed to provide for such facilities, but it is important to note the fact and in the meantime to draw attention to the need to keep the buildings that do provide for them (see Figure 19).

Ways therefore have to be found of extending the scope of planning legislation so that it becomes possible to retain particular buildings for no better reason than that they provide low-rented accommodation vital to the area. At the same time it has to be borne in mind that, while planning has to ensure that citizens have a say in preserving and enhancing their environment, too much planning control – and particularly planning control that is too detailed – may not only prevent the very diversity which we ought to be seeking, but also drive out initiative and enterprise, which are vital ingredients for a successful city. The very difficult task the planners have to perform is to ensure that diversity, initiative and enterprise are not squashed by the too successful invasion of an area by one particular use of land, to the exclusion of all others. Market forces need to be both encouraged and restrained. If possible, ground rules

Fig. 19 Old buildings for 'downtown' activities – Covent Garden

should be set so that market forces can then operate freely within them. Examples of such ground rules already operating with varying degrees of success are green belts, conservation areas and protected shopping frontages.

The Need for Housing in City Centres

We have seen that, in the short term, recreational activities are the easiest to mix with commercial activities in the central areas of our cities; but only in a few special cases will leisure activities survive in an area where no people live. Any long-term solution to the dreariness of central business districts must therefore involve the return of housing. Such housing is likely to be more attractive to single people than it is to families, but it is essential to the service industries that low-cost accommodation is available near the centre of a city, and some of those working in the service industries will need family accommodation.

In terms of housing in central areas, London's problem is probably more intractable than that of the provincial cities. As demand for offices spreads outwards, there is a steady erosion of residential land, in spite of attempts by planning authorities to resist it. A more serious obstacle to low-cost housing, applying not only to London, is the gradual selling off of council properties – first to sitting tenants but ultimately to the better-off. Either local-authority housing (or something like it provided by housing associations) has to be revived, or the private sector has to be invited to build subsidized housing. Cheap housing will never be built on expensive land within the generally accepted rules of the market. Without cheap housing, those who command low wages, but who are nonetheless vital to the central area, will have nowhere to live; and without housing, generally, our city centres will not regain their vitality.

5 (iii) CITY CENTRES FOR PEOPLE

The Urban Environment and Pedestrianization

If cities need a concentration of people and a diversity of activities it goes without saying that they also need a decent environment, without which people and their activities will eventually melt away. And a 'decent environment' does not mean simply pleasant buildings and plenty of trees. Important though these are, they are insufficient by themselves. It surely has to mean that our surroundings feel friendly, human in scale and, above all, safe.

Britain was the first country to feel the dehumanizing effects of the Industrial Revolution and it was in Britain that the first reforming antidotes were tried. Although it was Germany that first developed the replanning of towns, towards the end of the nineteenth century, and the United States that led the revolution caused by mass car ownership between the two World Wars, it was Britain – country of second highest car ownership until the 1950s – that gave birth not only to town and country planning on a national scale but also to many of the earliest ideas for lessening the adverse effects of the motorcar (see Tripp's shopping and residential precincts and Buchanan's environmental areas, both described in Chapter 4 (i)). From the 1970s onwards, however, these ideas were mostly pursued in Europe, and it is Europe that, for the most part, now has the more pleasant and prosperous cities.

Britain's planning system, set up under the 1947 Town and Country Planning Act, ended the spread of *laissez-faire* urban sprawl which until then had followed the American pattern. However, failure to follow the recommendations of the Buchanan Report in 1963, coupled with a partial rejection of planning and a reversion to *laissez-faire*, meant turning our back on European traditions and again following the American pattern: a pattern that worked – economically if not environmentally – in the wide spaces of North America but was completely inappropriate for a small, densely populated island.

In order to accommodate the motorcar, American cities were thinned out, and many central city (downtown) areas collapsed altogether. Few tears were shed for some of the smaller, newer and more brash cities, but the temporary demise of once-proud centres like Philadelphia had serious consequences for the local economy and for the population dependent on it. It seemed for a time that the 'land of the free' could live with the economic collapse of its cities, and with the endless suburban sprawl that its people chose and which seemed to work. But it now looks as if even low-density California is eventually going to grind to a halt in atmospheric pollution and suburban gridlock. As a result, while Britain is following the America of the 1950s and 1960s, America of the 1990s has rediscovered the virtues of strategic planning and is revitalizing its inner-city communities.

Urban Planning in Europe

In 1988 Transport and Environment Studies (TEST) published *Quality Streets*, a report edited by John Roberts on some of the more interesting and successful attempts in Europe to revive urban prosperity by improving the urban environment. The report's hypothesis is that 'a good physical environment is a good economic environment'; and it is clear from all the examples given from France, Germany, Italy, Holland, Denmark and Sweden that the key to success has been in giving the city back to the people. Cars have been forced out of the central streets, public transport has been improved and the central area has been pedestrianized. In many cases this has led to double the number of people walking in the main shopping streets and thus to an increase in trade.

London is actually included in the report only for the sake of projects that did not materialize; but London's problems, like those of Paris and Rome, are different from those of other cities, both in type and magnitude. Moreover it seems that transport-linked problems of very large cities are, in theoretical terms at least, more amenable to solution than those of smaller towns and cities. Draconian measures of, say, traffic restraint, which might be necessary for long-term improvements to a city's vitality, may in the short term cause inconvenience to some people. But the magnet effect of a large metropolis will probably persuade such people to retain their loyalty to the city, whereas in the case of the typical middle-sized British or European town, allegiance can be transferred to a neighbouring town or, so far as shopping is concerned, to an out-of-town centre. TEST's study of Stuttgart is therefore particularly interesting because it highlights problems (and possible solutions) typical of many towns in both Britain and mainland Europe that until the mid-1970s had been planned to accommodate the motorcar.

Stuttgart is a prosperous motor-manufacturing town of 550,000 people, and capital of Baden-Württemberg. It is a low-density city by European standards, surrounded by four smaller but prosperous towns with large centres of their own. Development in the 1950s and 1960s was hardly surprisingly car-oriented, and a great many underground car parks were built in the central area. The town could easily have destroyed itself through traffic congestion, and lost business to the satellite towns which were easier to reach by car. But, seeing the threat, the city council reversed its transport policy. Car traffic was restrained, while railway, tram and bus services were greatly extended and improved. At the same time the centre of the city was largely given over to pedestrians. The proportion of journeys made by car was reduced dramatically, and the proportion of those travelling on foot, by bicycle and by public transport increased accordingly. As they would have been in Britain, traders in the central shopping area were originally opposed to such extensive pedestrianization, but their opposition melted when it became clear that the new policy was bringing prosperity back to the central business district.

Improved public transport, together with restraint on out-of-centre development, also led to the continuing prosperity of Stuttgart's satellite towns, and allowed this whole area of low population density and high car ownership to avoid American-style suburban congestion. TEST estimates that in the central shopping area a ten to fifteen per cent increase in turnover in the last ten years can be attributed to traffic restraint. They also estimate that the figure would have been higher if more car parks had been closed and traffic reduced further.

Freiburg is a West German town with characteristics almost directly opposite to those of Stuttgart. It is smallish (population 175,000) and it is best known as a university town and cultural capital of the Black Forest. It has no nearby town to rival it but, unlike Stuttgart, has to compete with a large out-of-town centre, which was built before the introduction of legislation controlling such centres (see Chapter 5 (iv)). Like all cities during the 1960s it suffered from misguided attempts to accommodate the motorcar. However, a plan to close down the tram network was abandoned, and from the 1970s onwards the system was greatly expanded. At the same time pedestrians and trams were given priority in the whole of the central shopping and business area – most streets being completely closed to other vehicles but some allowing access for

Mode of travel	Walk	Cycle	M/cycle	Car	Tram	Bus	Train
Percentage	29.2	28.5	2.8	13.9	13.6	11.5	0.5

Fig. 20 Freiburg residents' mode of travel to shops

delivery outside peak shopping hours. It is apparently recognized by all, including the retailers, that the continuing prosperity of the central area is due almost entirely to its pedestrian-friendly environment: made possible by the fact that eighteen per cent of journeys within the town have been switched from private car to public transport (thirteen per cent if student travel is included). In spite of the proximity of the out-of-town shopping centre, a great many people from outside Freiburg still shop in the city, but the majority of shoppers come from within the built-up areas and their mode of travel is as shown in Figure 20.

Freiburg is in one of the areas of highest car ownership in Europe. The fact that well over half its citizens walk or cycle to the shops is a reflection on the quality of the urban environment and its success in attracting people back to the inner city. The fact that, of the remainder who travel by some form of mechanized transport, almost twice as many travel by public transport as travel by car is a reflection of improved services and of the political climate under which they have been introduced. The Freiburg area is dominated by the conservative CDU, but ever since 1962 the mayor (a much more important post in mainland Europe than it is in Britain) has been a Social Democrat. The result of this unusual enforced coalition is a consensus on strategic planning and transport, and a continuity of policy that is so often lacking in Britain.

Copenhagen, capital of Denmark, has a similar population to Stuttgart's and a similar recent conversion to public transport. In the 1950s it had been the city of bicycles, with plans for an ambitious new part-underground 'metro'. During the 1960s these plans were dropped in favour of road building, but the resulting congestion and decentralization threatened the prosperity of the central area, so in the 1970s the city introduced a new policy of traffic restraint, improved public transport and pedestrianization. Prosperity returned, car use – and even car ownership – declined, and Copenhagen is now one of the most attractive cities in Europe – for visitors, workers and residents alike. Figures 21 and 22 demonstrate

the size of Copenhagen's pedestrianized area by comparing it with
the West End of London, drawn to the same scale.

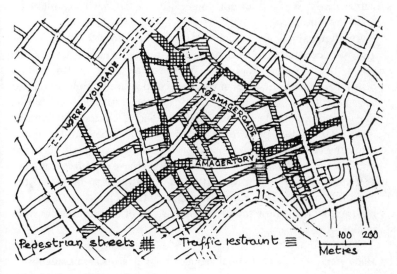

Fig. 21 Central Copenhagen

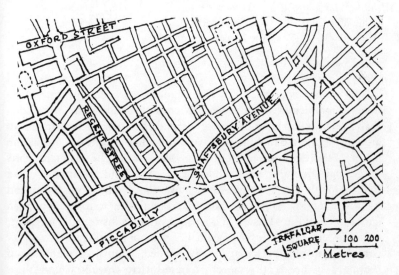

Fig. 22 The West End of London (same scale as Fig. 21)

To demonstrate the spirit of the time, TEST's *Quality Streets* quotes the description of a sign outside a Copenhagen bicycle shop which reads 'We will accept your car as partial down payment for your new bike.'

Another capital city much admired by visitors for the priority given to pedestrians in its main streets and for its easy-to-use public transport is Vienna, capital of Austria and home to 1.5 million people. Although the level of car ownership is similar to London and the use of suburban railways has declined, the use of public transport generally has increased enormously. Underground travel went up thirty-four per cent between 1978 and 1985, and bus travel went up fifty-three per cent between 1977 and 1985. It will be noted from Figure 23 that there is an unusually high use of public transport in the suburbs. For journeys within the central area, however, the use of both cars and public transport has declined in favour of walking, which is now the most popular way of getting to work or to school.

Mode of travel	Central Vienna	Vienna including suburbs
Car	24.9 per cent	34.8 per cent
Public Transport	34.6 per cent	46.2 per cent
Other Transport	2.6 per cent	3.0 per cent
Walking	37.9 per cent	16.0 per cent

Fig. 23 Vienna – journeys to work and school

The examples given above are not intended to demonstrate that cities in mainland Europe have reached some sort of perfection, nor that British cities have completely failed: far from it. Birmingham and Newcastle are making massive efforts to put right the mistakes of the 1960s; Wolverhampton has pedestrianized the major part of its central shopping area; while Leeds, Sheffield, Plymouth and Peterborough – to mention but a few – have embarked on more modest schemes. York has pedestrianized all the 'tourist' shopping streets around the Minster, and most of Britain's historic towns have either taken similar steps on a smaller scale or have been endowed with historic precincts that simply needed to be preserved. Furthermore it needs to be remembered that Coventry and the post-War new towns pioneered the principle of separating vehicles from pedestrians in shopping centres, although Edinburgh's 'one-sided' Princes Street (with its beautiful gardens and Castle on the other side) has followed that principle without thinking about it for about two hundred years.

During the 1960s disastrous decisions on strategic planning and transport were as common in Europe as they were in Britain. The examples given above of good practice from Europe are not typical, nor do they represent complete answers to the problems of the national and global environment. They do, however, represent a recognition of the fact that mistakes were made, and they show what can be done to make amends. They particularly demonstrate that the social, economic and environmental decline of cities can be reversed by improving conditions for pedestrians and cyclists, expanding public transport, discouraging the use of cars in central

Fig. 24 Princes Street, Edinburgh

areas, and curbing the development of out-of-centre retailing.

Changes along these lines are regarded in Britain as very difficult nettles to grasp, because they are seen mistakenly as threats both to individual liberty and to general economic well-being. It is therefore encouraging to find that they have been grasped in Denmark and Germany, which between them are known neither for their lack of liberty nor their lack of economic success. Furthermore, if it is possible to control the indiscriminate use of cars and the siting of shopping centres, it must be possible in the long term to develop a strategic land-use and transport policy that reduces the need to travel, and that benefits not just our towns but the nation as a whole. The effort and imagination required of politicians, local and national, to generate such action must not be minimized – strategic-planning authorities will have to be re-established for a start – but the importance of the experiments in Copenhagen, Stuttgart, etc., is that they provide precedents for taking the most difficult of the political decisions.

5 (iv) THE FUTURE OF RETAILING

Retailing in the Right Place

If a major object of land-use planning is to avoid the need for unnecessary travel it follows that the provision of shops that are easy to walk to is an important part of such planning. This can be achieved only if the density of population is sufficiently high to support such shops. In Freiburg, where people have been encouraged to move back into the city centre, fifty-eight per cent of shoppers now travel by bike or on foot. However, in Carlisle (population 100,000 as opposed to Freiburg's 170,000) only ten per cent walk to the central shopping area, and in Newcastle (population 750,000) the figure is only nine per cent. In both cases this is probably a reflection of the fact that few people live in the central area. In Newcastle's case, sixty-three per cent of central-area shoppers travel by public transport – most of them from within the city boundary – but in Carlisle those travelling by public transport amount to only twenty-five per cent, while sixty-five per cent travel by car – most of them from far away.

Carlisle in fact epitomizes one of the great dilemmas of the 1990s. It has an energetic planning department anxious to improve the quality of life in the city and to make the most of its history as an attraction for visitors. It has been remarkably successful in rejuvenating the central area, which had a decidedly rundown look about it in the 1970s. The redevelopment of The Lanes in the mid-1980s, although sacrificing some of Carlisle's historic-but-dilapidated streets, has provided a shopping environment in keeping with the spirit of the old streets, and has certainly brought life back to the area. Figure 25 shows the arched entrance to the mall and the adjacent street frontage, all of which is incorporated into the Lanes shopping centre. But in bringing much-needed life to Carlisle, the rejuvenation of the central area has brought in more cars than either the city or its hinterland can accommodate without environmental loss. It is here that problems begin that are typical of most British cities.

Since bus deregulation in 1987 Carlisle has in effect had no say in the running of its public transport; and present Government guidelines on development control emphasize a presumption in favour of development. Therefore, Cumbria County Council, which is in

Fig. 25 The Lanes shopping centre, Carlisle

theory responsible for strategic planning, has little control over the growth of out-of-town shopping – in spite of the economic threat to the city centre and the environmental threat to the surrounding countryside from increased traffic. The result is that Carlisle already has two out-of-centre superstores and there are outstanding planning permissions for two more. By contrast, Freiburg has some control of its own destiny. It can control traffic congestion and environmental decline by improving public transport and by restricting the amount of parking space at the centre, and it can also resist the building of more out-of-town shopping if it can show that such shopping would threaten the prosperity of the city centre (*Trouble in Store*, TEST, referred to below).

Some shopping centres function well without creating traffic congestion and destroying the environment. Oxford Street in London leaves much to be desired but has the highest retail turnover in Europe and is served almost exclusively by public transport; and we have already seen that almost two-thirds of central Newcastle's shoppers travel by public transport. In the case of London's Kensington High Street, which remains well sited in relation to where people live, almost a third of shoppers walk there, almost a half travel by public transport and only eighteen per cent travel by car. A nearby superstore badly served by public transport is reached by thirty-seven per cent on foot, only three per cent by public transport, and sixty per cent by car – thus adding enormously to the problems of an already congested area.

The Nine Elms shopping centre in inner southwest London, which is not an area where people live and is poorly served by public transport, has taken twelve per cent of Chelsea's regular customers and ten and a half per cent of Brixton's. Shopping is in effect being taken away from where people live – surely a recipe for disaster in the long run, and a policy that no rational strategic-planning authority would allow. Without strategic-planning authorities, however, it is all too easy to understand the desire of borough councillors to do a deal with a retail developer: partly for fear of losing a planning appeal, but mainly to ensure that their borough is the one that benefits from any increased trade. Without a strategic-planning authority on which all boroughs are represented it is difficult to imagine rational decisions being made about the location of new shopping facilities.

Shops Where People Live

Small local facilities like pubs and shops will survive and be renewed in inner-city areas through the normal functioning of business enterprise, provided that planning authorities have ensured that population densities have not dropped to a level at which such facilities can no longer be supported, and provided that they have not allowed an excess of concentrated facilities like 'superstores' to be built just outside the locality.

In a group of local shops there can be no objection to a small, efficient supermarket; on the contrary, it can well have an invigorating effect on its surroundings. But the object of the new style of retailing is not so much customer convenience as dominance of the market or economy of scale. Whichever it is, it leads retailers to opt for a decreasing number of outlets, on sites increasingly remote from where people live. Even if it is within the built-up area of a town, a new superstore that is not part of an existing high street will seriously undermine the nearest high street to it. Not everyone will use the new store, but enough will do so to affect the viability of local shops and thus to threaten everyone's option to shop locally.

It is ironic that at a time when some local authorities are making strenuous efforts to decentralize certain of their town-hall activities to neighbourhood offices, it should seem almost impossible for them to prevent the general trend towards concentration of other activities, public and private. Whether such concentration and increasing remoteness is of shops or hospitals, it is a trend in the wrong direction. In resisting it, local authorities should receive guidance as well as support from Whitehall. At present the Government is ambivalent, supporting local-authority rejection of some projects that would threaten local shopping centres or generate too much traffic, allowing others to go through on appeal, but giving little guidance on the subject. As a result, the gradual erosion of local facilities continues, either because of an uncaring local authority or because of a Secretary of State who overrules a local authority that does care.

In 1986 the Anglo-German Foundation commissioned from TEST a report on retail location policies in Britain and Germany which was published in 1989 under the title *Trouble in Store*. The Report concludes that Britain was slow to adopt the fundamental changes in retailing but made up for lost time by sheer scale both in the size and number of developments: 'By the time it relaxed controls over out-of-centre retail development most European nations had been through that stage and substantially rejected it.'

The immediate advantages and the long-term disadvantages to the consumer of concentrating retailing into fewer outlets were described in Chapter 3 (iv), and they beg the question, 'How does one correct mistakes, however obvious it is that they were mistakes, when they have led to an apparently unstoppable trend?' The answer must lie in the fact that some cities in some countries have managed to do just that, with the aid of national legislation that encourages strategic planning and thus gives cities some control over their own hinterland. The major regulations affecting out-of-town retailing in western Germany date from planning laws of 1968 and subsequent amendments to them. TEST's report for the Anglo-German Foundation says: 'According to these amendments, shopping centres and superstores (in excess of 1,500 square metres) serving more than the market area of a local authority are only allowed to locate on core areas, or areas which have to be specially designated.' Needless to say, different regions interpret this law in different ways – and a city's ability to control its shopping patterns depends on its regional government. But at worst the regulations ensure that the impact of retail developments is considered, and at best, as in Freiburg and Stuttgart, they make it possible for the impact to be alleviated.

The trouble in Britain in 1990 is that 'looking ahead', 'research and development', 'strategic planning', whatever one calls it, is out of fashion. The result is that cities like Carlisle face a difficult dilemma. Although retailers are notorious for overestimating the proportion of people who shop by car, there can be little doubt that attempts to improve the environment by curbing the use of cars would lead to many shoppers deserting the city centre for out-of-town centres. If, on the other hand, nothing is done, then congestion increases, the environment deteriorates and customers are lost just the same. The large out-of-town superstores will suffer similarly in the long run, as customers tire of having to travel long distances in increasing congestion. By then, planning will almost certainly be back in fashion, but also by then shopping facilities in city centres and in local neighbourhoods could well be beyond redemption.

No one is going to benefit in the long run from the combined effect of shops being bigger, fewer and further away. It will always be true that large shops can provide a wider choice of products than small shops; but by definition they cannot be so well spread, and furthermore, the larger they become and the more they dominate the market, the more they reduce the consumers' choice of store. Much more significant in the long term, however, is the fact that out-of-centre retailing encourages low-density residential development which increases travel and dependence on the car which, in turn, will lead eventually to California-style suburban congestion, a deteriorating physical environment and a dangerous level of atmospheric pollution.

It must be better and cheaper for goods to be delivered in a small number of vehicles to a large number of retail outlets where people live than for a large number of vehicles to be used to collect each and every individual's shopping from a small number of remote outlets. Instead of being conned by retailers into collecting their shopping, the public should insist that the merchandise is distributed to their local shops or, in the case of large orders, to their homes. It is the more efficient and environment-friendly way of doing things, but it needs legislation on new retail outlets similar to that which already exists in Germany, and it requires sufficient restraint of non-essential traffic to give the operators of delivery vehicles the road space that was once taken for granted.

It is natural for retailers, like everyone else, to resist a change that requires reorganization. So far as they are concerned there is at present no incentive to change, because they are not having to pay for the environmental damage – both present and future – that is being caused by car-oriented shopping. Neither of course do they have to pay for their customers' petrol. It always has and always will fall to the Government to formulate the rules that are needed to ensure that traders operate with the general public interest in mind. In the same way that the Government protects historic buildings when they become threatened by the natural development of market forces, so the Government has to step in when the environment (and perhaps the survival of our planet) is similarly threatened. And in the same way that developers learned to make a profit out of converting historic buildings instead of demolishing them, so retailers will learn to make a profit out of shopping sited near where people live rather than on greenfield sites.

Traders have to be treated fairly, and new guidelines cannot take effect immediately; nor can all the necessary improvements to public transport be made overnight. All the more reason for the Government to reform – or, rather, reintroduce – strategic planning, so that British cities can begin to rationalize their policies on transport, retailing and the environment, along the lines of their European counterparts.

5 (v) METROPOLITAN GOVERNMENT

Strategic Planning, Land-Use Planning and Transport

With the abolition of the metropolitan counties, strategic planning and transport have become minor issues in political terms, unlikely to attract talented politicians for any length of time, and Britain's cities have become the only ones in Europe without directly elected governments responsible for strategic issues.

There is a great deal of sense in delegating as much local government as possible to a genuinely local level, and it can be argued that, for some of the services they provide, the district councils and London boroughs are too large. For this reason some local authorities have established mini-town halls to deal with their functions at neighbourhood level. But there seems to be a consensus that a population of 100,000 to 200,000 is about the right size for the smallest unit of local government in urban areas, and the 1974 Local Government Act saw to it that this is more or less the average size of our district and borough councils. However, where individual districts and boroughs are parts of an urban whole, it is necessary for cross-boundary issues such as land-use planning and transport to be dealt with on a city-wide basis. And, in order that the city authority that deals with such issues can command respect and attract the necessary political talent, it needs to be directly answerable to its constituents.

There are many people, not necessarily regionalists, who argue that, within national policy, transport should be a regional rather than a city responsibility. Some of the Members of Parliament who feel strongly about London's transport problems take this view. But

they are, *par excellence*, examples of those who see London through
the eyes of visitors rather than through the eyes of inhabitants. In
particular, they see London's roads as bottlenecks to be got through,
whereas Londoners – who account for ninety-five per cent of the
people making journeys in London – are more likely to see their
roads as places where they live. Those coming from outside want
the motorway to take them not just to the M25 but to Piccadilly
Circus or indeed to the House of Commons. But it must be left to
Londoners to decide whether this is either possible or desirable.
The same goes by analogy for all our cities.

A more plausible case has been made for regional transport
planning on the grounds that it would take into account the interests
of those who commute long distances. But in London's case these
account for only five per cent of the total number of journeys and, so
far as railways are concerned, it is not so difficult as it seems at first
sight to separate those services that operate mainly within the urban
area from those that are run mainly to provide access for people
living outside. Most of London's inner suburban services terminate
near the edge of the built-up area.

What is needed, therefore (regardless of the merits of some form
of regional government), is a strategic authority for each metropolitan area which can make decisions on the planning and transport
issues that transcend local-authority boundaries. Such an authority
need not be responsible for the day-to-day running of any services,
but it would provide the forum, make the decisions and have overall
control of policy on:

a) strategic planning, including the siting of major
   concentrations of activity, such as shopping centres;
b) major highway issues, including road-management policies
   which need to be city-wide;
c) public-transport services, including local services provided
   by British Rail.

These strategic-planning and transport authorities should be financed, like the old metropolitan counties, partly out of local taxes
and partly by central government grants, but with the difference
that it would be entirely up to the strategic authority to decide what
proportion of any grant it received for transport went on road

improvement and what proportion on improving public transport.

To give these new strategic authorities the necessary weight, to enable them to draw on the best available talent, and to make them answerable to the people of the cities they serve, their members must be directly elected. The present practice of leaving important decisions about the strategic planning of our cities to a Government minister, advised secretively by unknown Whitehall civil servants and little-known local appointees, should be brought to an end. Until it is, politicians are unlikely to take strategic planning as seriously as they do in Europe and, by comparison, Britain's cities will continue to decline.

We should aim to decrease our absolute dependence on transport and
the length and number of journeys; and to plan more consciously for
those who walk as well as those who use mechanized transport.

Government White Paper
on Transport Policy, 1977
(Cmnd 6836)

6 (i) MOBILITY AND ACCESSIBILITY

Unnecessary Travel

Mobility is often referred to as if it were a virtue not far removed
from godliness, and 'the mobile society' is thus seen as a blessed
state which we are fortunate to have almost within our grasp. The
fact is that urban mobility has been reduced in the last twenty or
thirty years. It is now more difficult for us to get around our cities, or
to get goods delivered, than it was in the 1950s.

But is it mobility, for its own sake, that we are seeking? In a
perfectly mobile society, everyone would be travelling for twenty-
four hours a day. Surely what we are really seeking is accessibility.
In other words, we would like our shops, pubs, bingo halls and
football clubs to be as close to our own front doors as possible and
preferably within walking distance. This may not be attainable, but
it should be striven for; and the Government White Paper of 1977
had the right idea.

Unfortunately the extract quoted above, like many similar expres-
sions of enlightenment before and since, has never been repudiated
but nor has it been reflected in Government policy. Instead,

mobility, at least for those with cars at their disposal, has been the aim. As an ironic result, we now spend more time travelling than ever. The saving in time which faster cars, lorries, trains and aeroplanes made possible has been more than offset – both by an increase in the average distance travelled by passengers and freight and by the resultant congestion. Far from trying to minimize the need for travel, governments have consistently done the opposite. Roads have been built which, although they have done nothing to ease congestion in urban areas, have certainly encouraged people to travel further; and tax concessions to those using company cars for private journeys have had the same effect.

The Government's decision in March 1990 to abandon the road-building proposals put forward in the London Assessment Studies (see Chapter 4 (iii)) seems to mark a recognition that road building within built-up urban areas is politically unacceptable. But it is by no means certain that this recognition applies outside London, and there could well be attempts to reverse the position in London: especially if the road builders could obtain private-sector funding. As recently as 1989 there was a spate of 'kite-flying' by contractors who, anxious to show that they could construct a system of tunnels across London, put up fictitious proposals to see how people responded. In the same year Peter Hall in his book *London 2001* (Unwin Hyman, 1989) suggested a rather more practical system of orbital toll roads in tunnels, for south London.

The cross-London tunnels were complete madness, and need to be mentioned only because they received favourable comment in some newspapers which may have influenced their more gullible readers. Tunnels could conceivably be used as very expensive bypasses: in London's case as a quicker route than the M25 from one side of the capital to the other. But because traffic travelling right across London is only three per cent of the total entering the metropolitan area (*Greater London Travel Survey, 1981*), such a scheme would be financially impractical. For tunnels to emerge anywhere near the centre would defeat the now universally accepted policy of discouraging extra traffic to that already overcongested area. Therefore the only possible use for them would be as part of a completely subterranean system of roads and car parks, unconnected to the existing surface network. But this too would be impossibly expensive. Underground railways could be built for a fraction of the cost.

Peter Hall's south London tunnels are designed apparently to redress the balance of advantage in favour of a transport-deprived area. But his own parallel suggestion of linking south London's existing underused inner-suburban railways to the Underground system is a much better and cheaper alternative. Hall seems to feel, however, that as there is a North Circular Road it is unfair on the south not to have a proper South Circular Road instead of the present series of signposts strung out along residential streets. But no fairminded person, having observed the wide belt of environmental disaster on each side of the North Circular, would wish to inflict a similar disaster on the south – except as a form of punishment. Some would argue that there is a need for more orbital travel in south London than can easily be provided by rail; but London, like all our towns, grew as a radial city with a strong centre, well served by public transport. To superimpose on this a strong pattern of orbital transport would be to court not just traffic chaos but environmental disaster as well. Indeed it could be argued that, although the North Circular is needed to provide access to its factories from the main radial roads leading into London, its use as a long-distance orbital route for all classes of traffic should be discouraged.

Rasmussen, the Danish town planner and author of *London: the Unique City*, felt very strongly that cities like London and Copenhagen, which grew round their radial transport corridors leading to the centre, should retain that pattern and emphasize it by extending their green belts towards the centre as 'fingers of green' running between the radial routes – separating them from each other rather than linking them via orbital routes. In this way each radial corridor (or linear city, as it was referred to in Chapter 2 (i)) would retain its own character and its own travel patterns. Rather than try to change the historic structure of our radial cities in the vain search for a complete orbital mobility that is unobtainable in a dense city, we should improve our radial transport and encourage people to travel in the manner that best suits the urban geography that we have inherited.

We know from Chapter 4 (iv), first, that our roads are being used less efficiently now than they were in the 1950s, and second, that by restraining car traffic and reverting to the 1950s level of public transport use we would be more mobile, goods could be delivered more efficiently, and we would enjoy a less polluted environment. We must recognize that road building without traffic restraint will simply suck in more cars without relieving congestion, and that with traffic restraint it is unnecessary. Instead we should be thinking in terms of improving public transport and providing people with incentives to use it. Above all, through better strategic planning we should be attempting to reduce the length of journeys that need to be made.

The Perceived Cost of Motoring

Many people persist in travelling by car to the central areas of our cities when it must be clear to them that everyone would get around more quickly if they did not. One of the reasons for this is that, quite apart from the environmental and macro-economic costs, they do not appreciate the cost to themselves.

It is obvious that those with a company car, who do not have to pay the full cost of their private journeys, will see the use of that car as a cheap way of travelling. But when considering the cost of making a particular journey, even those motorists who do not enjoy the use of a company car or parking space often think of the cost only in terms of the cost of the petrol. As a result, some of the congestion in our cities is caused by traffic which is there simply because the cost of making the journey by car rather than public transport has been underestimated. To overcome this exacerbation of the traffic problem it has frequently been suggested to governments that the Vehicle Excise Duty should be abolished and the revenue subsumed in an appropriate increase in petrol tax. Not only would this save the enormous cost of collection, it would also put an end to the frequent evasion of VED. If the car (purchase) tax could be treated in a similar way, and if car insurance could also be mileage-related, motorists would be encouraged to think twice about making a journey which was either unnecessary or could have been made by public transport.

It has been argued that such a policy might have an adverse effect on those living in rural areas where there is little public transport, so essential car mileage is greater. But the point of the policy would not be to increase the overall cost of motoring but simply to change the present annual payments to pay-as-you-drive payments. Calculation of the amount that would be added to the cost of a gallon of petrol could be based on the average private mileage of those living in rural areas. The fact that those who travelled less would have their motoring costs reduced would be compatible with a policy of encouraging a reduction in the need to travel.

The Need for Traffic Restraint

Even if a motorist's perceived cost of each journey were closer to reality there would still be a need to recognize the cost to the community of driving on congested urban roads. Congestion could be eliminated if enough people were persuaded to revert to public transport. Those commuting by car in central London make up the major part of rush-hour traffic but their number is small compared with the number travelling by train and Underground. A large proportion of motorists switching to public transport would therefore add only a small proportion to the total of public transport users, but would greatly reduce congestion on the roads.

It has been clear since the mid-1970s that this sort of solution was available to solve central-area problems in London, or any other city with a substantial railway system. What was not so clear was the impact that such a switch from private to public transport would have on the rest of the city concerned. In 1987 the London Centre for Transport Planning commissioned two studies of radial corridors leading to central London, to establish how traffic throughout London would be affected by a policy of traffic restraint confined to the central area (West End and City). The A1 Corridor Study, *A Case for Traffic Restraint in London*, by Stephen Plowden, was designed to show how many people would have to switch from car to public transport if it were decided that every car journey should be restrained where the costs inflicted on other road users in time and money exceeded the benefits to the person making the journey.

The figures arrived at were as follows:

77 per cent of car traffic   1¼ miles from the centre
50 per cent of car traffic   2¼ miles from the centre
34 per cent of car traffic   4½ miles from the centre
29 per cent of car traffic   6½ miles from the centre
20 per cent of car traffic 10½ miles from the centre

The A23 Corridor Study, *Croydon Corridor Two*, by Peter Bibby, was designed to show what proportion of car traffic would be removed from the roads of London generally if car commuters, whose journeys would take no longer by so doing, were to switch to public transport. The point chosen for the experiment was the Greater London Traffic Survey's inner cordon, six miles from the centre, and about halfway between central London and the edge of the built-up area. It was found that with a maximum increase in door-to-door journey time of four minutes, twenty-five per cent of car journeys could be switched to public transport – a figure remarkably close to the twenty-nine per cent of car journeys in the A1 Corridor (at a similar distance from central London) that in fairness to all travellers *ought* to be switched to public transport.

Of course, if public transport were to be improved the proportion of cars removed from the roads could be considerably increased. But the immediately possible reduction of twenty-five per cent is more than enough to allow for extensive bus-priority measures, which themselves would be more than enough to take the strain off the railways. The reduced road-traffic levels would also make possible the more efficient collection and delivery of goods, the elimination of 'rat-runs' through minor streets, and an improved environment for pedestrians and cyclists.

Area Bans or Road Pricing?

The vast majority of cars driven to the central areas of cities in the morning remain parked all day until they are driven home in the evening (over ninety per cent, according to the Croydon Corridor Study). They are clearly not being used for business purposes. Nevertheless, sixty-seven per cent of them in London are either company cars or have their journey to work subsidized by the driver's employer in some other way (see Gallup Poll (pages 189–90) and Chapter 4 (iii)). Writing in the *Independent* on 3 July 1990, Mathew Carter quoted the Reward Group's annual review of benefits, which showed that in spite of increased tax on the company-car perk, the additional salary needed to compensate for its withdrawal would be between £2,000 and £9,000 depending on the value of the car in question. One obvious way of reducing unnecessary traffic would therefore be to remove this perk (which sometimes also includes a free parking place, worth £5,000 per annum, and subsidized petrol) and instead institute an employer's contribution to the employee's public transport fare as in Paris (see Chapter 6 (iii)). In the meantime, to return our roads to maximum efficiency some form of traffic restraint is needed urgently. It will still be needed, even when the company-car perk has been eliminated, in order to improve conditions for pedestrians and to improve the environment generally – as has been demonstrated in Germany where the company car hardly exists.

There are many possible ways of discouraging or preventing people from driving cars into congested areas – from the enforcement of existing laws on parking to a complete ban on private cars from large areas of our cities. In view of the entirely disastrous effects of the motorcar on cities, the latter seems the more attractive. It was ultimately forced on Florence because no other way could be found of avoiding congestion, and after much foreboding the ban on cars is now seen as a blessing. Such a policy has always existed in Venice for geographical reasons, and the absence of cars has always been one of Venice's important attractions. If the ban were to cover large areas of cities such as London or Glasgow, which do not have a Venice-like system of canals, exceptions would have to be made for the proverbial doctors and plumbers who carry the tools of their trade with them. This could be achieved through changes in the licensing system which would allow the doctor's car to be treated as a quasi-ambulance and the plumber's as a commercial vehicle. In practice a system of permits would probably be necessary for the sake of the disabled, whose permits would be free, and for residents who lived within the area of the ban, who would be charged as they already are for street parking.

The obvious and much-discussed middle way is some form of road pricing. With tachographs already installed in lorries it is only a small step in electronic engineering to mass-produce for cars a sealed instrument which records, from sensors in the road surface, the distance travelled over the central area of a city. It has been argued that any form of road pricing is unfair to less well-off drivers. But in fact it is no different in essence from charging for a parking space or a bus ticket. Concessions could be made (and obviously would be made in the case of the disabled) in the same way as they are on public transport. Furthermore, charges could be set to make a profit, which could be used for capital investment in public transport or to reduce fares. The 1985–86 National Travel Survey found that the poorest section of the community (under £3,000 per annum at 1985 price levels) made only nineteen per cent of its journeys by car. This group also travelled more on foot and by bus than any other section of the community. It is this group that would benefit most from a policy of traffic restraint, plus improved facilities for pedestrians and the users of public transport.

Do We Need Cars in Cities?

Whatever the means used to achieve traffic restraint in our towns and cities there can be no doubt that a switch from private to public transport would bring us the same social, economic and environmental advantages now enjoyed by the German cities that made such a switch. Furthermore, it would not just be the city centres that benefited. The knock-on effect on the city's residential areas could be considerable. At present many quite short journeys that used to be made on foot are made by car, because the roads are seen as too unsafe or too unpleasant for pedestrians. If many of these car journeys were no longer necessary there would be a further reduction in traffic, and it should be possible, through traffic management, to return many of our urban streets to their original function of serving just their own properties, thus making them once again places where people, and particularly children, can meet in safety. School and shops would once again be safely accessible to all on foot or bicycle.

With less use of cars in cities, not only would there be a better local environment and a less polluted atmosphere but the main roads could be used more efficiently by delivery vehicles, buses and taxis. If this were achieved, fewer city dwellers would want to own cars. Those who made most of their journeys within the urban area, especially those without small children, would find it more economic to hire a car for the occasional out-of-town journey and to make all their local journeys by public transport – using taxis for awkward journeys or for journeys at awkward times or with awkward loads. Even as things are now, this argument makes sense for people living and working in inner London, if they do not have the use of a company car. Based on the Automobile Association's figures, the average annual cost of running a 1,000–1,400cc car that covers 10,000 miles a year is £3,132 at April 1990 prices, i.e. before the increase in petrol prices caused by the Middle East crisis (this includes the cost of the original car purchase spread out on an annual basis, but excludes the cost of garaging or parking). London Regional Transport's annual travelcard for Zones One and Two cost £364 in 1990 and allows unlimited travel on all forms of public transport in inner London (for example from Manor House to Putney, or Willesden to Lewisham, both distances of about ten miles). A couple without children, owning one car, would almost certainly spend between them at least this sum on public transport because they would not always be travelling by car to the same destination. Their total annual travel costs would therefore be at least £3,132 + £364 = £3,496. If they were to give up their car and buy two travelcards for Zones One and Two at a total cost of £728, they would make an annual saving of £3,496 − £728 = £2,768. They could spend this amount every year on journeys outside London by public transport, hired car or taxi, before it became more expensive than running their own car.

It is evident that for some time a statistically significant number of city dwellers have by choice not owned a car or, to put it another way, have chosen to live in cities although it imposes a restraint on car ownership. Figure 26 is taken from Mayer Hillman and Anne Whalley's *Walking* is *Transport* (Policy Studies Institute, 1979). It demonstrates, for example, that at the time of the 1975–76 National Travel Survey twenty-nine per cent of high-income households in high-density areas did not own a car, whereas only five per cent of high-income households in low-density areas were without a car. But to encourage more people to give up their cars by choice, not only does public transport have to be improved but the hiring of cars on the spur of the moment, and for short periods, has to be made easier, and places where one can hire a car need to be more plentiful. They could, perhaps, be obtainable at filling stations.

It must be noted, however, that people living near city centres are the ones least likely to travel to work by car. If road conditions are to be significantly improved, the traffic that needs to be restrained is that caused by people driving to the centre from the suburbs (and this is the traffic most easily transferred to public transport). A survey of such people was carried out in 1990 by the Metropolitan

Transport Research Unit, in association with Gallup, on behalf of three London boroughs and the London Planning Advisory Committee. The survey found that forty-five per cent of those driving to central London would prefer not to, and only did so because the alternatives were so bad. A further twenty-two per cent were prepared to switch to public transport if it were improved, and if environmental benefits came about as a result. These figures are surprisingly high when it is taken into account that a further question established that sixty-seven per cent of the respondents were receiving some form of company assistance for the purchase, running costs or parking of their cars.

Unfortunately the fact that a lot of people regard a particular course of action as a good idea does not necessarily mean that such action will be taken voluntarily – for a very sound reason. If one good citizen leaves the car at home it will make not an iota of difference to overall traffic congestion. The good citizen depends on a good government to provide legislation which ensures that everyone acts together, and that the action is therefore effective. It is such legislation that the Government can no longer avoid if it is to rescue our cities from strangulation by traffic congestion.

Households	Population Density Bands										All Bands
	Lowest									Highest	
	per cent										
High income no car	5	8	11	12	10	12	18	16	19	29	14
High income 2+ cars	43	31	29	36	32	22	25	30	15	7	28
High-medium income no car	15	21	23	20	27	31	31	36	39	56	29
High-medium income 2+ cars	17	12	8	7	8	7	6	3	4	2	8
Low-medium income no car	31	45	50	52	52	64	59	66	70	80	56
Low income no car	82	82	86	87	90	90	94	95	94	97	90

Fig. 26 Car ownership related to population density

6 (ii) WALKING AND CYCLING AS TRANSPORT

The High Proportion of Urban Journeys Made on Foot

Traffic restraint has been discussed above as a means of making more efficient use of our roads by relieving congestion. Improved mobility for everyone, through better bus services, would be one of the consequences of such restraint. Another would be the increased efficiency of industry through time saved on the collection and delivery of goods. But perhaps the most important consequence of all would be the improved environment for pedestrians and cyclists.

So far as walking is concerned, the 1985–86 National Travel Survey shows that thirty-five per cent of all the journeys made by people in Britain are made on foot and that they take twenty-eight per cent of the time spent in travelling (*Vital Travel Statistics, 1990*). In places of high population density, like the inner-city areas, the percentage of pedestrian journeys and the time spent on them are considerably higher. At the average overall 'town density' for Greater London (see Chapter 7 (i)), thirty-nine per cent of journeys are made on foot, and at the higher densities surveyed the figure rises to forty-five per cent. If we were to add to this the walking done at the beginning and end of journeys by car or public transport, and if we were then to take into account window-shoppers, tourists and people generally enjoying the town (or not enjoying it as the case may be), we would find that the majority of us see the town mainly from the pavement. If a town wishes to retain its residents and its workforce, and thus its prosperity, it clearly has to woo its pedestrians. Most towns in mainland Europe have taken steps to do so, but most towns in Britain have not.

The Healthy Journey to Work

It is, however, not just the social and economic health of the town that is at stake. Walking is also important to the physical health of the individual citizen. Before World War II and for some time after it, Dr Innes Pearce (who founded the Peckham Health Centre in 1935) campaigned for 'whole health' through physical and mental fitness. Her Peckham Experiment, as it was more usually known, was an experiment in prevention rather than cure – a health centre rather than a sickness centre (she referred to post-War planning as 'too often no more than a piecemeal correction of the mistakes of the past'). It is ironic that, more than forty years on, lack of everyday exercise should be a major cause of the most common serious illness – heart disease: a predominantly male affliction, since men tend to have the more sedentary occupations, sitting at desks and in cars. The British Heart Foundation in its 1991 publication *Exercise For Life* urges greatly improved conditions for walking and cycling which are, from the health point of view, the best possible forms of transport.

If for the sake of healthier citizens and a better environment our cities have to accommodate more pedestrians and cyclists, and if for the sake of urban mobility public transport is to be preferred to private cars, it follows that less road space will be needed for cars and that more space must be made available to pedestrians and cyclists.

Because of the switch from buses to private cars, the number of people travelling to central London by road in the peak period has been reduced from 424,000 in 1956 to 278,000 in 1988 (see Chapter 4 (iv)), in spite of increased road space and computerized traffic lights. If we exclude cyclists and motorcyclists from that figure it is reduced to 261,000, which is virtually identical to the number of people travelling in by bus in 1956 (see Figure 16). It follows that, without anyone having to transfer to rail or Underground, commuting by car to central London could be eliminated simply by restoring bus services to 1950s levels.

Two cars take up the space of one bus, but on average each car in London carries only 1.3 people, while each bus carries nineteen people (*Greater London Travel Survey, 1981*). In spite of this, cars take up only forty-five per cent of London's peak-hour road space when allowance is made for the space taken by commercial vehicles, but that represents a lot of spare road which could be used to improve conditions for pedestrians and cyclists; to speed up the remaining traffic; and to allow for the fact that not all cars, including those belonging to the proverbial doctors and plumbers, could be left at home.

In Hanover, when public transport was improved and park-and-ride facilities were introduced in 1985, a road to the central area with

three lanes in each direction was converted so that the lane adjacent
to the pavement became a belt of trees, the middle lane was given
over to buses and cyclists, and only the outer lane (in each direction)
was left for general traffic. There are probably not many cities in
Britain to which such drastic treatment could be applied but there is
certainly a lesson to be learned from the principle.

Cycling as a Mode of Transport

Cycling is becoming more popular as people become aware of its
potential convenience for short journeys in congested cities, and of
its beneficial effects not only on their own health but also on the
health of our planet. In 1969 (the earliest year recorded in London
Regional Transport's figures) only 4,000 people cycled to the central
area in the morning peak. The figure in 1989 was 10,000, having
reached a peak of 16,000 in 1982, then dropped to another trough of
7,000 in 1988. But even the 1989 figure represents only two per cent
of the total of those travelling to the central area and, in view of the
very much higher figure for cycling in European cities where
conditions are favourable, it almost certainly represents a suppres-
sion of the inclination to travel by bicycle, brought about by the
obvious dangers to cyclists inherent in current traffic policies. In
Copenhagen cycling declined when that city adopted car-oriented
transport policies similar to Britain's, and rose again when those
policies were finally abandoned (see Chapter 5 (iii)).

The London Cycling Campaign's immediate aim for the capital is
one thousand miles of strategic cycle routes uninterrupted by
dangerous stretches of road that cannot easily be avoided. It is
regrettable that such a campaign should be necessary, because
long-term policy should be to make all roads safe for cyclists – and
for everyone else. But it is difficult to imagine London or any other
British city quickly eliminating its roundabouts and other gyratory
traffic systems, let alone making bus and cycle lanes continuous.
Until this is done designated cycle routes are vital not just for safety
but also as an important part of any urgent policy to reduce traffic
congestion by encouraging more people to use bicycles.

It is a credit to the Government and to road users that Britain's
road-accident figures are comparatively good. But behind this good
and improving picture lies the appalling fact that in 1988 almost

forty per cent of fatalities were pedestrians (1,736) or pedal-cyclists (227), out of a total for all road users of 5,052 (*Transport Statistics Great Britain, 1978–88*). Although total fatalities are well below the European average, the figure for pedestrians is very much higher, and it seems that the only reason for the comparatively low fatalities for cyclists is that Britain's roads are now so obviously full of potholes, and generally unfriendly to cycling, that people are deterred from using it as a serious means of transport, in spite of the urgings of both the doctors and the environmentalists.

It looked as if the tide was turning when, in the early 1980s, the cyclists' cause was taken up in earnest by the Labour-controlled GLC, and endorsed by a Conservative Parliamentary Under-Secretary of State for the Environment, Sir George Young – who not only cycled to meetings himself but encouraged his senior civil servants to do likewise. But there is little to show for this sudden burst of enthusiasm. Although short stretches of safe route have been introduced along minor roads, there has been no attempt by the Government to promote cycling as one of the obvious ways of getting around our cities. With the possible exception of some university towns, the post-War new towns are the only places where cycling is positively encouraged.

Nevertheless the national Cyclists' Touring Club and its local affiliates have increasing political clout; and the European Cyclists' Federation is recognized by the European Parliament at Strasbourg as an important part of the transport lobby. Perhaps a straw in the wind is the recent decision by the Liberal-Democrat-controlled London Borough of Sutton to encourage its staff to use bicycles. They are offered loans on favourable terms for the purchase of their own machines and, where possible, they are encouraged to use them instead of cars for council business – the mileage allowance for using a bicycle being the same as it would be for using a car.

Time, however, is not on our side. If as an important part of the social and economic improvement of our cities we are to improve their image, our first and most urgent task is to make more space available to pedestrians and cyclists and to make their environment both safe and pleasant. By giving over a proportion of the carriage-way to this end, many European cities have reversed the decline of urban prosperity. Many North American cities are belatedly getting in on the act. It is time that British cities did likewise.

6 (iii) PUBLIC TRANSPORT

Land-Use Planning Comes First

Mobility is of no particular merit for its own sake, neither is it always necessary in order to achieve access to one's job, one's school or one's local shop. Accessibility is best achieved by making sure that the activity to be reached is within walking distance. It would be absurd, however, to deny that a great many journeys are necessary and that many of them, being too long for walking or cycling, need to be made with the aid of mechanized transport. But only a small proportion of people wanting to reach the central areas of our cities can be accommodated by car (see Chapter 4 (iv)) and then only at the cost of congestion, less efficient use of the roads, environmental destruction, and atmospheric pollution. Public transport has to be the answer to urban mobility, varying from buses-only in small towns to a combination of buses, Underground, light rail and conventional rail in the large cities.

Chambers Dictionary describes public transport as transport run in the public interest (not necessarily publicly owned), and in the context of cities the term must also imply an ability to carry large numbers of people with the minimum of pollution and the minimum use of space. It is the concentration of activities that makes cities what they are, and also makes the provision of high-capacity public transport so important. But if a city works best when it is served by public transport, so does public transport work best when it is serving a city.

Figures from the 1985–86 National Travel Survey make it clear (unsurprisingly) that people are better served by public transport in high-density urban areas than they are in low-density suburbs. In spite of the paucity of railway stations in some of our cities, at the 'inner-city' densities an average of forty per cent of households are within thirteen minutes' walk of a station, while at rural and outer suburban densities the figure falls to twelve per cent (*Vital Travel Statistics, 1990* by Potter and Hughes). Cities and public transport therefore go together – and access to the central area, and to large generators of activity outside the central area, should be designed around the city's public transport. For the last twenty years such a policy has been noticeable only by its absence, and one of the biggest causes of congestion outside city centres has been traffic-generating activity remote from good train and bus services.

The Canary Wharf development in London's Docklands is hardly typical as a development; but as an example of lack of foresight so far as transport is concerned it is all too typical. A development involving such a large increase in daily commuters should have been placed near the centre of gravity of the public transport system, so that it could be reached easily from all points of the compass. Instead it has been located three miles off-centre and connected only by a woefully inadequate light railway which is not even compatible with the rest of the Underground system, and therefore incapable of being used for 'through running'. The problem will be ameliorated, although not solved, by the extension of the Jubilee Line, but because of limited resources this will be at the expense of delays to the Chelsea–Hackney Underground Line and the north–south and east–west BR cross-routes, all of which were singled out by the Government's 1989 Central London Rail Study as the more promising options (see Chapter 4 (iv)).

The Government's enterprise zones provide developers with many incentives, such as 'rates holidays', but much more significant than the financial inducements is the complete waiving of planning control. The result is that, although developments in enterprise zones in London (Canary Wharf) and Newcastle (Gateshead Metro Centre) have been successful in rejuvenating specific derelict areas, they are prospective disasters for their cities, whose wider needs have not been taken into account. Nowhere is this more apparent than in transport. If we had to have enterprise zones they should have been designated in relation to the existing or proposed public-transport network, as was done in the case of La Défense in Paris. Instead the cart has been put before the horse, and land-use planning and transport policies have been tacked on as an afterthought.

Although the effects of large developments in enterprise zones like Canary Wharf and Gateshead are the most spectacular, and therefore the most discussed, they are really only the tip of the iceberg. Far more damaging to our national transport system and to our whole way of life are the run-of-the-mill planning decisions that place superstores, hospitals, county council offices, leisure centres and the like in situations remote from good public transport services. The 1985–86 National Travel Survey shows that in the sixteen-to-twenty age group only thirty-seven per cent of journeys are made by car, and that in the over-sixty-five age group the figure is forty per cent. Yet between them these people need to get to the sort of facilities described above. Placing such facilities in out-of-town situations where they are difficult to reach by public transport not only detracts from city life by reducing urban facilities, and from suburban life by increasing congestion, it also has the more tangible effect of denying access altogether for many of the old and young.

Our first step in providing a transport system worthy of our cities in the twenty-first century must be to ensure that the facilities we need to reach are sited in a position where they can be well served by public transport.

Subsidies and Comparisons with Europe

The need for efficient public transport in our cities is all too clear; but that need will never be met so long as our strategic land-use planning is unrelated to what public transport can do, and so long as we allow bus routes to be blocked by other traffic, much of which is unnecessary. Britain is not alone in allowing anarchy on its urban roads but at least in most other countries the consequential need to subsidize public transport in the form of railways or trams is recognized and acted upon.

The question of subsidies to public transport is one that generates much theorizing from little knowledge. In the same way that it is daft to be mobile just for the sake of it, so it makes no sense to encourage people, through subsidies, to make unnecessary journeys. For this reason free public transport for all was never a sound idea. On the other hand it is customary (or ought to be) for governments to give incentives to people to do sensible things (tax concessions to those making gifts to charity are a case in point). Because a city works much better socially, economically and environmentally when people are encouraged to make more use of public transport, city authorities in most of Europe encourage them to do so as a matter of policy. This is not seen as passive financing of services running at a deficit but as a positive incentive through either capital grants or revenue support to make public transport the generally accepted means of urban travel. In Britain, at the taxpayer's expense, we perversely pursue policies that cancel each other out. To relieve congestion we subsidize urban public transport (albeit at a very low level compared with our European neighbours), and we subsidize congestion by considerably more – through tax allowances to the users of company cars (see Chapter 4 (iii)). If it were pitched high enough, a tax on congestion along the various lines outlined in Chapter 6 (i) could render public transport subsidies in urban areas no longer necessary; but until such a scheme is put into effect, sufficient resources must be devoted to making public transport the popular way of getting round our cities.

The difference in what the farepayer contributes to the operating costs of public transport in London and Paris is demonstrated in Figure 27 (taken from Jane's Information Group's *Urban Transport Systems 1990*, which covers the year 1989). It will be seen that the Parisian passengers benefit more from the franchising of shops, advertising, etc. than do their London counterparts, but that they also enjoy more than double the subsidy. This needs some explaining because the national subsidy for transport in Paris is only twenty-five per cent – little more than London's national subsidy of twenty and a half per cent. The remainder is made up of local grants (twelve per cent) and the '*versement*'. The latter is a central Government tax which obliges employers to pay fifty per cent of the cost of their employees' season tickets: a remarkable contrast to the system in Britain which allows tax concessions on the use of company cars.

Sources of revenue in percentage terms

	Fares	Franchises	Subsidies	Total
London	74.1	5.4	20.5	100
Paris	32	15	53	100

Fig. 27 Financing public transport in Paris and London

London and Paris are examples of capital cities that are treated in very different ways so far as public transport is concerned, and London comes out very much the worse from the comparison: not just because of its obviously poorer services but also because of the effect that this has on the environment and efficiency of the whole city. It is surely a false economy to be cheeseparing on urban transport if the money saved is likely to be dwarfed by the money lost to the wider economy of the capital city through an inefficient transport system. The Governor of the Bank of England and other luminaries in the City of London are only too aware of the problem; but they and the rest of us are taking a long time to open the eyes of the Government.

Although it may be on the decline in relation to other capital cities in Europe, London is nevertheless still a powerful magnet in national terms and perhaps capable of surviving inept transport policies. It is therefore the effect of misguided transport policies on our provincial cities which should be concerning us more. Unfortunately because of bus deregulation outside London (see below) it is impossible to compare our provincial cities with their continental counterparts; but it is fair to say that most large European cities that do not have a suburban railway system, Underground, or Metro do have some form of light railway running like a tram through the city-centre streets and like a train on its own track outside the centre. In Britain, outside London, we have extensive suburban railway systems serving Glasgow, Liverpool, Manchester and Cardiff, and one for Birmingham which is being slowly reborn. But, apart from the excellent Tyne and Wear Metro (which is a light railway system that runs underground just at the very centre of the city) we have nothing to compare with the light railways of Europe apart from the trams at Blackpool, which still run along the sea-front, and the horse-trams at Douglas, Isle of Man, which do likewise!

Manchester's Metrolink now under contruction is fortunately the exception that proves the rule. It will consist of two-car trains running like trams on the streets in the central area and running on BR tracks outside the centre (see Figure 28); but similar and urgently needed proposals for Edinburgh, Sheffield, Birmingham, Bristol and Southampton are gathering dust while the cities they have been designed to serve are choking to death as their European rivals prosper.

Sheffield's Supertram proposals have in fact been approved by the Government, but the city has been told that no money is available. This is in marked contrast to the Government's 1989 White Paper 'Roads to Prosperity', which announced a ten-year programme of improvements to motorways and trunk roads worth £10 billion. The Treasury seems to be up to its ears in money – so long as it is for road building. If British cities are to reclaim their prosperity and their self-esteem they desperately need reinvigorated public transport systems and incentives to use them. Money already earmarked for transport should be diverted to the cities for this purpose.

The local mechanism for planning such a revival having been abolished, the Government has no alternative but to initiate the process itself (in conjunction with the surviving Passenger Transport Authorities), and at the same time to establish strategic-planning authorities for urban areas which can eventually take over.

Buses and Re-Regulation

The statistics given in Figure 27 include all public transport – buses, Underground and suburban railways. Since the deregulation in 1987 of all bus services outside London it has been impossible to obtain figures for Britain's bus services outside the capital; and since buses are such an important part of public transport in provincial cities, it is no longer possible to make international comparisons for any city other than London. For the sake of national prestige this is perhaps a

Fig. 28 Manchester's Metrolink

good thing, but it must be doubtful whether it was a major purpose of deregulation. Neither was it the Government's stated purpose that bus deregulation should lead to the continued decline in bus use, and yet the decline since 1987 has been sixteen per cent in the metropolitan counties and six per cent in the shires (*Have the Buses Caught Up?*, National Consumer Council and BusWatch, October 1990).

A different aspect of deregulation is the breaking up of transport systems, usually under the control of Passenger Transport Authorities, where bus and train services had been co-ordinated. Such services were not always successful, and stories were rife of bus drivers racing trains in order to get away from the station bus stop before the train passengers reached it. One of the systems that did work well, however, was Newcastle's combined bus and Metro service already mentioned in Chapter 4 (iv). Here, in order to alleviate central-area congestion, the bus services were deliberately stopped short of the centre at a well-laid-out interchange with the Metro, so that the latter carried the majority of passengers to the centre without requiring them to purchase another ticket. The doctrinaire abandonment of such a sensibly integrated system, and the ensuing traffic congestion, amounted to municipal vandalism; but even the less well-organized systems should have been improved rather than replaced by the anarchy of deregulation.

The general complaint about deregulation, however, which applies in rural areas as well as in towns and cities, is a lack of information about the availability of services. This is brought about largely by the fact that, with only forty-two days' notice required to withdraw a service, it is impossible for anyone to prepare a comprehensive timetable of local buses, let alone keep it up to date. With market forces gradually returning some areas to near-monopoly conditions, it may be that this will become less of a problem in future; but a degree of re-regulation is needed if public faith is to be restored in buses, not just as a local service but also as the means of reaching a specific destination at the end of a long journey by public transport. In particular, city dwellers without cars need to be able to plan the whole of their journey by public transport – not just the long-distance bit. Because of deregulation, inquiries about local services at the end of one's journey have gone from difficult to virtually impossible, and the concept of an integrated public transport service has been abandoned.

To condemn deregulation is not necessarily to condemn all forms of privatization. Exeter's buses were privatized in 1986, before general deregulation, and through switching most routes from half-hourly services provided by double-decker buses to services at five-minute intervals provided by minibuses, the new management secured almost a fifty per cent increase in passengers by employing forty per cent more drivers. When the same company set up a similar service in nearby Torbay it met with vociferous opposition from the local taxi drivers: surely a certain sign of success! Part of this success was due to the public's knowledge that frequent services were provided even in the evenings, and that there would be no question of being stranded in the city late at night (a common disincentive to bus use). This undoubtedly involved running some evening buses half empty. In effect the evening services that gave the public confidence that buses were always available were being subsidized by the rush-hour services: to the benefit of the image of the operation as a whole.

It is this sort of cross-subsidy between the rush-hour service and the evening service (and between the profitable route and the unprofitable route) which a city needs in order to provide a comprehensive network in which the public has confidence. Constant cutting of late services and services to outlying areas 'to tailor the service to customer demand' is a certain recipe for ending up with no customers at all. Deregulation as it stands allows local authorities to subsidize socially desirable services that are unprofitable; but, without the ability to offer an operator a profitable route as a quid pro quo, such subsidies become expensive.

Privatization can be in the public interest when it allows services to be contracted out via competitive tendering. But the authority, not the operator, should decide what sort of service is needed, and specify it clearly in the invitation to tender. Such a system needs to be run by a transport authority that is answerable to a strategic-planning authority, which is in turn answerable to the electorate on city-wide issues of land-use planning, public transport and highways. But however ingenious the transport authority and however efficient the operator, there is little they can do to run an effective service if the roads are congested and the planners have given permission for developments that are difficult to serve economically by public transport. Furthermore, unless the strategic authority is responsible for planning as well as transport, it is powerless to prevent our ever-increasing dependence on the car, let alone to provide those city dwellers without the use of a car the access to the countryside that they once had.

In December 1989 a conference held in Berlin by the embryonic European Academy of the Urban Environment stressed the need for normal access to city centres to be on foot, by bicycle or by public transport. The working-party report went on to say: 'The emphasis for urban public transport should not be on speed of travel, but on easy access to the network, which requires a high density and frequency of service. Buses operating on bus-lanes, and streetcars (trams), are therefore likely to be more appropriate than metros or suburban railways: except in very large cities. Artificially low fares are not necessarily desirable, since they can have adverse effects on the pattern of settlement: nevertheless subsidies to public transport should be maintained until other measures to restrain the use of cars have been implemented.'

These are not just the ravings of eccentrics from environmentally conscious cloud-cuckoo-land. We would do well to take note.

6 (iv) THE MOVEMENT OF GOODS

Avoidance of Unnecessary Freight Traffic

Although in some circumstances there may be good reasons for carrying freight very long distances by road, there is a strong case in some instances for production to be nearer the point of consumption, thus reducing the volume of goods traffic (see Chapter 4 (ii)). There can be no better example than the brewing industry whose product, however good, is ninety-five per cent water. It never made sense to carry so much water the length and breadth of the country in tankers, even during the nation's blessedly brief flirtation with the idea that all beer should taste the same. Now that variety is back in fashion it must be more economic in the long run to take the water element from the mains supply and do the brewing near the point of consumption, with short-distance deliveries from local breweries using small drays.

However, to achieve a significant reduction in road freight and to

restore the environment along secondary roads we have to do more
than increase the efficiency and reduce the transport needs of
individual industries, important though that is. First we have to
recognize that almost every town in Britain came into existence
because it was on a trading route and, although long-distance freight
is no longer the main traffic problem of our large cities, most small
towns on routes too minor to be duplicated by a motorway have
suffered at some time from a surfeit of heavy goods vehicles simply
passing through. The usual answer to this problem has been to
provide the town with a bypass (and there can be no doubt that all
towns and villages need a bypass for through-traffic), but this does
nothing for those living on the rest of the route who probably
enjoyed a reasonable environment before the switch of long-
distance freight from rail to road in the 1950s. Secondly we have to
remember that, after Belgium and Holland, England already has the
densest network of roads in Europe (2,100 kilometres of road to
every 1,000 square kilometres of land). There is thus a strict limit to
acceptable road building, even in rural areas.

Much could be gained, therefore, by getting long-distance freight
back on to the railways as in mainland Europe, and one of the main
justifications for the Channel Tunnel is that, by increasing the
average distance of freight journeys by rail, it will bring BR's freight
sector back into profitability and revitalize it. If, on the principle of
'the polluter pays', a charge were made for environmental damage
caused by road haulage it would be economic to transfer much
long-distance freight not only to the railways but also to coastal
shipping. (Freight bound for Europe from Ireland and Scotland
should have no need to be using the roads of Wales and England.)
Furthermore, much greater use could be made of the recently
widened Sheffield canal for sea-going barges from Yorkshire to the
Rhine. Similar ventures could be encouraged, which might bring
our use of inland waterways more into line with the very extensive
use made of them in the rest of Europe.

If the cost of avoiding transport-related damage to the environment were borne (as it should be) by the means of transport that
caused the damage, artificially cheap road transport would come to
an end, and with it the threat to local industry described in Chapter
4 (iv). The taxpayer would more than save on the cost of environmental protection what was lost on increased transport costs (see

Chapter 4 (ii)), and industry would be encouraged to use the more environmentally friendly transport modes (rail and shipping) for long-distance freight.

City-Friendly Lorries

Lorries in cities pose problems similar to those posed by cars. Although they are indispensable in a way in which cars are not, the disruption they cause can be just as great, if not greater. The damage that they do to roads is well known, and so is the effect that they have on dwellings near main roads. Nevertheless, it was once considered reasonable that most streets should be adapted so that they could accept whatever lorry was likely to be used for delivery. But, with the maximum-permitted gross laden weight for lorries now thirty-eight tonnes and due to be raised to forty tonnes by the end of the century, this proposition is no longer tenable. Instead, lorry fleets need to be adapted so that small, compatible vehicles can be used for collection and delivery in urban streets without blocking them. Either unsuitable lorries have to be banned from cities altogether (they are already banned completely from central Paris, and from most of central London except for the purpose of making deliveries), or there has to be some sort of discouragement by fiscal means. For example, vehicle taxation could be reformed so that instead of being charged annually it is charged on the basis of the miles covered and the sensitive nature of the roads used, in a similar way to that suggested for cars in Chapter 6 (i). The carrot to go with such a stick might be the right of small, city-friendly lorries, in off-peak periods, to use bus lanes from which cars are excluded all day.

What constitutes a city-friendly lorry, and what effect its substitution for 'unfriendly' lorries would have on the economic well-being of cities, has been a bone of contention ever since the demise during the 1960s of the 'mechanical horse and trailer'; but the only comprehensive study of the subject is the Wood Report (see Chapter 4 (ii)). The Report's conclusions on the long-term effects of a London-wide ban on lorries over seven and a half tonnes gross laden weight were as follows:

1. Lorry bans by themselves cannot remedy the complaint

that heavy traffic in London causes communities to be split in two.

2. The exclusion of heavy lorries from London will not cause a decline in London's economy generally.

3. Lorry bans may tip the balance in favour of moving out in the case of those industrialists who, for other reasons, are already contemplating this; but any land vacated, especially if located in London roads exempted from the ban (some main roads in outer London), will become attractive to firms whose main business is to serve the London market.

4. The main shopping centres will continue to thrive, the large department stores merely modifying their present transport systems to comply with the requirements of the ban.

Interestingly the Wood Report also found that, although a ban on all lorries in excess of seven and a half tonnes would lead to a five per cent increase in operating costs, if the ban were limited to lorries in excess of sixteen and a half tonnes there would actually be a small reduction in operating costs – since the benefits of using the smaller,

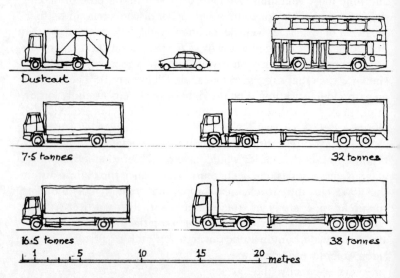

Fig. 29 Heavy lorries compared (typical lengths shown)

more economic vehicles would outweigh the extra capacity of the (then) maximum permitted thirty-two-tonne lorries, which were seldom fully laden.

Before the GLC was abolished in 1986 it successfully implemented the ban on heavy lorries at night and at weekends, but no further progress was made. It must be doubtful whether circumstances have changed much since the Wood Report in 1983, in which case there is no reason why the ban should not be made complete. In order to avoid the smack of unfair retrospective legislation, it would have to be introduced in stages allowing exemptions while lorry fleets are changed at their normal rate of replacement through wear and tear. Eventually the only exemptions would be for those who follow the well-established procedure for exceptional loads that require police clearance for specific journeys.

What is needed so far as London is concerned is a strategic-planning and transport authority that can take over, in this respect, where the GLC left off. As a temporary measure, if central Government is irrevocably opposed to such an authority, there could be a Minister for London with power to consult with the public and initiate the necessary legislation. There is certainly some point in dealing with London's problems first: partly because so much research has been done already in the capital, and partly because London is too big to be boycotted by recalcitrant hauliers. But the aim must be that all towns and cities should benefit from the more rational use of goods vehicles, and it is difficult to see how this can be arranged without strategic-planning authorities similar to the old metropolitan counties. When they have been re-established, one of their first tasks would surely be to set up their own equivalent of the Wood Committee, with a view to an ultimate ban on unsuitable lorries from their respective cities: perhaps along the lines of European cities, many of which have bans far more draconian than the Wood proposals.

In the meantime there is an urgent need for the reform of retail distribution, not just in large cities but in small towns throughout the country. It is more economic for the retail distributor to deliver locally than for individual customers to collect from a distant superstore (if you take into account total fuel costs as well as the cost of time spent by the consumer – see Chapter 5 (iv)). Small purchases are best distributed, therefore, by the supplier to local shops within walking distance of where the customer lives; and large purchases, whether of food or consumer durables, are best delivered to the customer's house. If we agree that any lorry under sixteen and a half tonnes is acceptable on urban roads, it follows that it should be able to make deliveries wherever they are needed. Even the residential streets should be able to accommodate such a vehicle occasionally for tasks like moving house, in the same way that they have to accommodate a fire engine or a dust-cart. However, it will almost certainly prove cheaper as well as more acceptable environmentally if the more typical delivery from local shops is made by electric vehicles similar to milk floats. Recent improvements in electric-vehicle technology have ensured that an increase in their use is not only desirable but likely.

Without lorries of one sort or another our cities would die, but that does not mean that cities have to continue to put up with vehicles that are badly designed for urban use.

6 (v) ACCOMMODATING TRAFFIC AND TAMING IT

Streets as Places, and the Dutch '*Woonerf*'

It has to be remembered that city streets do not exist just for the movement of people and freight. Indeed, unlike motorways, most of them do not have the carrying of vehicles as their primary function. They are first and foremost places where people live, work or do their shopping. Even in their role as a right of way, their function as carriers of services, drains and telecommunications is at least as important as their function as carriers of vehicles.

Ever since the introduction of the cul-de-sac in the 1920s, there has been some recognition that new roads on housing estates are primarily for the residents. But for a long time the cul-de-sac was an object of social scorn – something inferior to a proper road for proper people – and it was not until the Buchanan Report in 1963 that the principle of protecting residents from through-traffic was generally accepted (see Chapter 4 (i)). Buchanan's theory of environmental areas (like Alker Tripp's residential precincts, first mooted in 1942) anticipated the removal of through-traffic from minor roads and canalizing it on to the surrounding main roads. These would, where possible, be rebuilt without housing facing on to them directly. But with the complete rebuilding of our cities implicitly abandoned, virtually nothing happened in this direction until accidents to children, and the deterioration of the environment, brought public pressure to bear on local highway authorities. As a result, during the 1980s through-traffic has been removed from a few minor roads – usually those with the most vociferous residents – but virtually nothing has been done about conditions on the main roads, many of which are also largely residential. The way forward must lie in general 'traffic calming' as applied in varying degrees in West Germany and the Netherlands.

In a paper published by the South Bank Polytechnic in 1989, Tim Pharoah and John Russell define the main objectives of traffic calming as follows:

1. To reduce accidents and/or casualties;
2. To reclaim space (from the carriageway) for pedestrians and non-traffic activities, and to reduce the barrier effects of motor traffic on pedestrian movement;
3. To promote greater feelings of security: particularly among residents, pedestrians and cyclists and others engaged in non-traffic activities such as shopping or play;
4. To create environmental improvements and/or to promote local economic activity.

Describing traffic calming in the Netherlands, West Germany and Denmark, Pharoah and Russell say that it is 'promoted at the National and Federal level as part of an integrated transport policy, and specifically as a means of improving road safety and improving the urban environment. The policy aim of reducing the total volume of traffic is less clearly stated, especially in Germany, except as a desired consequence of investment programmes in public transport and cycle facilities. Some individual cities do, however, regard traffic calming as *part* of an explicit policy of traffic reduction.'

It is interesting to note that (in a conveniently forgotten appendix) the Buchanan Report suggested that twenty miles per hour or less should be the highest permissible speed for any roads that provide access to housing. It is ironic that this limit should now be accepted in principle by many European governments but not (yet) by the Government of the country that first suggested it in a Government-commissioned report nearly thirty years ago. It is one thing, however, to accept a principle and put up signs announcing a speed limit. Enforcement is another matter, and only in the Netherlands has it been tackled effectively on a large scale by designing roads in such a way that it is physically impossible to exceed the speed limit or, as in the case of the '*woonerf*', to exceed walking pace.

The *woonerf* (roughly translated as 'residential yard' or 'living street', depending on the translator) was originally designed only for roads that we would probably call 'access roads' in Britain. It was intended as an alternative to complete vehicle/pedestrian segregation, which had been possible, at least in theory, so long as comprehensive redevelopment was the order of the day, and traffic could be carried above or below pedestrian areas. The Rules of Conduct for *woonerven* are quoted by Pharoah and Russell (from the Dutch Ministry of Transport and Road Safety Directorate 1988) as follows:

1. You may walk anywhere on a road within a *woonerf* and children may play anywhere;
2. Cars must be driven at walking pace, as must mopeds and cycles;
3. Within a *woonerf*, traffic from the right always has priority and this applies to mopeds and cycles as well;
4. Anyone who drives a car or rides a moped or cycle within a *woonerf* must not impede pedestrians. But pedestrians and children at play should not obstruct or unnecessarily impede cars;
5. Parking is permitted only where indicated by the letter 'P'.

By 1985 the Dutch had established 4,000 *woonerven* covering 7,400 streets. Attention is now being turned to areas that are not necessarily residential, such as sections of road adjacent to schools or hospitals, or passing through the shopping centres of villages or small towns. In such areas the principle of making motorists aware that they are 'driving on the pavement' still stands, but through-traffic at walking pace is permitted, while some areas are given over

Before   *After*

Fig. 30 The people-friendly street in Germany

entirely to pedestrians. Figure 30 is a hypothetical example of the principle of the *woonerf* as applied in Germany. It is extracted from a traffic-calming manual published in Bonn in 1982 and illustrates well the possible transformation of ordinary urban streets.

Car-Free Areas and Traffic Priorities

The Dutch *woonerf* sounds almost too good to be true, but there are snags, mostly related to the accommodation of residents' cars. Although many cities in western Germany have used pedestriani-zation as a means of reducing the amount of traffic in the central area, general traffic-calming measures have seldom been seen as a means of reducing city-wide traffic levels. They have more often been implemented simply to make the roads safer and more pleasant. In Copenhagen both traffic and car ownership have been reduced through a combination of central-area pedestrianization, cheap public transport and high car taxes, but this has not happened to any extent outside the capital. In Holland, which has done more than any other country to improve residential areas, it seems that success is largely due to concentrating either on low-income areas where car ownership is less or on attractive historic areas where people are prepared to forgo the use of a car for the pleasure of living there. In areas of higher car ownership, garage courtyards are often built outside the *woonerf* and, although this does not generally lead to vandalism as it might in Britain, it does add to congestion on the surrounding roads.

The answer may lie in a proposal put forward by the working party on Environmentally Compatible Transport Structures to the 1989 Berlin conference (described in Chapter 6 (iii)). Paragraph 2.2 of the working-party's report suggests that 'every town should provide districts designed for people who want to live without cars. Such districts will normally be extensions of or adjacent to the pedestrianized town centre.' The great advantage of such a proposal is that it would overcome the objection that some people have to giving up their car if the road outside their house is still going to be polluted by other people's cars. Furthermore, if the idea became popular and such areas spread, not only would it be possible to walk on traffic-free roads to shops and pubs, but children would once again be able to cycle to school. The pedestrian routes would have to be designed on the principle of the *woonerf*, because it would still be necessary to provide access for milk floats and other delivery vehicles. However, provided car parking for visitors were provided on the periphery of the area there should be no need for car parking near the dwellings.

Combined with good public transport and a more readily available system of car hire, the car-free area could be an important beginning to the long-term recovery of our cities, and the precursor of good things to come. In the meantime we need policies that will benefit as many people as possible as speedily as possible.

In central areas the single most important role of the street must be to provide a civilized environment for the pedestrian, since almost half the journeys in the centres of our towns and cities are made on foot, and since most people judge a city centre not by the journey to it but by what it is like when they get there. The deterioration of the urban environment will not be halted, let alone reversed, until the needs of the pedestrian are given priority not only in residential areas but in urban streets generally. Only when the pavement has been designed to carry the foot-traffic generated by the centre's activities should the width of the carriageway and its capacity be decided. Clearly, narrow streets will be able to carry little more in vehicular traffic than is warranted by the delivery of goods to buildings in that particular street. In some cases it may be found that vehicular traffic can be accommodated only at night, or that it cannot be accommodated at all, and that deliveries must be made by mechanized hand trolley. On the other hand, wide streets can carry quite heavy volumes of vehicular traffic, as well as pedestrians, provided that the pavements are generous and, better still, are separated from the carriageway by trees.

Measures like those described above have been ruled out in the past because of the presumption that everyone should be encouraged to travel until they are physically stopped by congestion. But it was Chris Patten, Conservative Secretary of State for the Environment, who on 27 November 1989 echoed the spirit of the 1977 (Labour Government) White Paper quoted at the beginning of this chapter. Speaking at the Town and Country Planning Association, Mr Patten said, 'Transport isn't an end in itself. It is a means to an end.' With increasing concern about pollution and an increasing awareness (arising from London's Road Assessment Studies) that the old nostrums are politically unacceptable, the time is clearly ripe for a completely new approach to urban transport.

An assessment of what traffic is actually needed in a city, along the lines discussed in this chapter, would facilitate the setting of traffic priorities and total traffic levels: in such a way as to improve the environment for pedestrians and cyclists and to keep the remaining road space free for the buses and delivery vehicles that are the lifeblood of any city. If at the same time we could reduce our dependence on transport by bringing housing back to our inner-city areas, and if through imaginative land-use planning we could reintroduce a variety of activities to our central-area streets, we could make our cities safer and much more pleasant places in which to live, work and do our shopping.

Streets . . . give access to buildings, they provide an outlook from
buildings, they give light and air, they are the setting for architecture,
and they are the backbone of the everyday surroundings for many
people. It is impossible to maintain that these functions are subordin-
ate to the passage of vehicles.

Buchanan Report

7 (i) DENSITY AND COMMUNITY

What is Meant by Density?

The only reason that such an important issue as housing has been
left until the last chapter of this book is the apparent logic of arguing
from the general to the particular. The question of urban housing
does not arise in the first place unless we want our towns and cities
to retain their 'urban' densities. Before we can discuss urban-density
housing, however, we need to understand exactly what we mean by
density and how we measure it.

Most people would expect the population density of a town to be
expressed in terms of the number of people living in it divided by
the number of acres that the town occupies. Thus we would arrive at
a figure of x number of people per acre or, since metrication, per
hectare. (There are 2.47 acres in a hectare.) In the case of Ebenezer
Howard's garden cities (see Chapter 3 (i)) we can take the number
of people he intended to house in each city (30,000) and divide it by
the area allotted to it (400 hectares or 1,000 acres), and conclude that
the overall density of each city would be seventy-three people per
hectare (thirty per acre). But for the sake of the clarity of his thesis

and to prove that it was an economic proposition, the cities described in Howard's *Garden Cities of Tomorrow* were very precisely delineated: with exactly so much land allocated for industry, public buildings, schools, hospitals, open space, etc. Cities of the real world, as Howard was the first to acknowledge, are rather different.

Greater London, as defined by the old GLC boundary, covers 616 square miles, of which twenty-three per cent is green-belt land (Greater London Development Plan Report 1973). The 'built-up area' is therefore 474 square miles or 122,766 hectares. London's population is 6.7 million, and its 'town density' is thus fifty-five people per hectare (twenty-two per acre): a surprisingly low figure, but it has to be borne in mind that within the built-up area are many large parks and at least twenty-five square miles of derelict land (see Chapter 5 (i)). The area of the original new town at Milton Keynes is 4,434 hectares, which will ultimately house 200,000 people at a town density of only twenty-two and a half people per hectare (nine per acre); while the new Borough of Milton Keynes covers 18,100 hectares and will eventually house 237,740 people at a town density of thirteen people per hectare (5.25 per acre).

It is, however, not just the difficulty of measuring existing towns that makes town densities of little use as a planning tool. Even if we could calculate them rationally they still tell us little about people's circumstances. For example they give us no clue as to whether everyone is living in reasonably spacious accommodation or whether some people have more than enough room, at the expense of others who are overcrowded.

The 1943 County of London Plan seems to be the source of much post-War thinking about a method of calculating density that expresses the way that each family lives. The London County Council then covered an area of 30,200 hectares, and had a population of 4,094,500 (calculated in 1938). The overall town density was thus 135 people per hectare (fifty-five per acre). The LCC calculated that if about 600,000 people could be moved to new towns beyond London's green belt, the remaining population could be housed at a 'real' density of 240 people per hectare in the inner areas, 150 people in the outer areas and 187 people in the intermediate areas. Excluded from this calculation was all land that was not used for housing, but an allowance was made for the provision of community buildings and 1.6 hectares of public open space to every 1,000 people. The community buildings and the open space were then omitted, to arrive at a 'net density' of 247, 494 and 336 people per hectare (100, 200 and 136 per acre) for the outer, inner and intermediate areas respectively.

It is this 'net residential density' that is used by planning authorities in urban areas to control the number of people that can be housed on any particular site: usually assuming that the number accommodated in each dwelling will be equal to the number of 'bed spaces' provided, and that the area occupied by the dwelling, or dwellings, is simply the curtilage of the site plus six metres or half the width of any surrounding roads – whichever is the less.

The LCC thought that 336 people per hectare (136 per acre) was the optimum density for cities, taking into account the proximity of jobs, neighbourhood facilities, etc., and, with most housing authorities following the LCC lead, it became the generally accepted density to be aimed at for all inner-city areas. It was also assumed, however, that at this density two-thirds of families would have to live in flats rather than houses. This assumption was ill-founded, as we shall see later, but it contributed to the general acceptance of tower blocks during the 1950s and 1960s, and consequently to the reaction against them and against the '136 people per acre' that went with them.

During the 1980s, in the wake of the almost universal reaction against the housing of families in tall buildings, many inner-city planning authorities set their *maximum* permitted density at 247 people per hectare (100 per acre): a density that would eventually lead to a dramatic drop in the urban population and to the virtual suburbanizing of our cities, as local shops, etc. closed down through lack of sufficient customers to keep them viable.

Densities in London and Paris

The reason that so many people like the inner-city areas of Paris is not just that there is a good public transport system, but that there is always something going on; and the reason for all this activity is primarily the large number of people living there. Dr Martin Mogridge (Urban Studies 1985) has demonstrated that, in spite of a gradual fall in the population of both cities, Paris has consistently had a population density double that of London. For example, in

1970 London's population within a four-mile radius of the centre was less than one and a half million, while Paris's population within the same radius was three million. Closer to the centre, the contrast was even more marked, with the density of Paris almost three times that of London.

There is much to commend the Parisian way of living, close to where everything is going on. It entails most people being housed in flats because that is the way they like it; but at all levels of income such flats are usually well supervised, perhaps partly due to the uniquely Parisian custom of the poor living on the inferior floors above the apartments of the rich, but sharing the same entrance. This is almost unheard of in Britain and, as a result, it is only those with sufficient income to afford to live in a properly supervised building who are prepared to live in a flat; and then only if they are without children, and the flat is well placed in relation to work, shopping or entertainment. Nevertheless there are exceptions. In the less fashionable parts of west London people on only slightly higher than average incomes can afford the popular flats in enormous converted Victorian terrace houses which open on to mature communal gardens; and in Scotland, where urban housing has traditionally been more akin to Paris than London, there is not the same antipathy to apartments that there is in England. On the whole, however, the British, especially when they are living as a family, prefer to have their own front door and private open space. The irony is that with a little ingenuity this is achievable, even at densities approaching those of Paris.

7 (ii) THE ENGLISH HOUSE AND STREET

Renaissance of the Street

The twin tragedy of Britain's housing policies since World War II is that it was not necessary in the first place to abandon streetscale housing in order to achieve the LCC's 336 people per hectare (136 per acre); and neither is it necessary now, in the post-tower-block era, to suburbanize our cities in order to provide an alternative to high-rise living. The traditional urban street always had and still has the potential, even at this density, to provide a decent environment, with everybody's front door opening directly on to the street, and with gardens for family dwellings.

The reason street-style housing was abandoned after World War II seems to be fourfold. First, urban housing was generally overcrowded, in that living rooms were being used as bedrooms, and bedrooms meant for two people were being slept in by many more. Second, it was unhygienic: in the 1950s more than half of inner-city families still did not have their own lavatories and bathrooms. Third, and perhaps most important, the inhabitants had grown up in streets that were both overcrowded and unhygienic, and the very image of street living was, as a result, abhorrent to them. Finally, in the *ville radieuse* of Le Corbusier, there was a well-worked-out intellectual argument for trying something completely different.

Britain's unpretentious nineteenth-century streets, many of them slums from the outset, had a certain friendliness (something to do with the relationship between width of street and height of buildings), which was seldom recaptured in the housing that replaced them. Mothers could not shout to their children in the street from the top of a tower block as they could from the top floor of a three- or four-storey terrace house; and it is difficult to imagine one of those cheerful-looking VE-Day street parties taking place at the foot of a tall block of flats. However, although it might have been pleasant on a summer day to sit on the front doorstep of a nineteenth-century slum house and watch the traffic-free world go by, it must be remembered that the incentive to do so was often the chance of escaping the bugs indoors, which in the winter just had to be lived with. It is hardly surprising that the reformers and planners of the brave new post-War world followed their predecessors in the search for an urban ideal that broke away from the concept of the street. What *is* surprising is that, long after those who could afford to buy their own houses had rediscovered the potential of the street, those responsible for local-authority housing were still talking with pride of their longest or tallest blocks of flats.

If the first disaster of social housing in Britain after World War II was the mania for tall buildings, the second was that, just as the light was beginning to dawn and the megalomania of comprehensive redevelopment was giving way to piecemeal streetscale projects, the inner-city housing programme came to a virtual halt. During the

1980s, private-sector developments like those in London's Docklands, the limited number of housing-association projects, and the
more extensive programme of upgrading inter-War council estates
have not kept pace with the deterioration of ageing buildings.
Except in isolated cases (like Docklands), they have certainly not
changed the inner-city scene in the way that earlier housing
programmes had done.

The consolation for this state of affairs is that, with the fashion for
very low housing densities favoured by so many urban planning
authorities, our cities have been fortunate to escape the gradual
suburbanization that would have been their lot if the housing
programme had continued (see Chapter 3 (ii)). But the revitalization
of our urban housing cannot be delayed for much longer, and it is
important that, when resources are again available, they are used
wisely. Following the abolition of the metropolitan counties, and
the downgrading of strategic 'structure' plans in the shire counties,
local authorities in our cities have been required to draw up Unitary
Development Plans to replace the old two-tier system. We must
ensure that the new plans do not preclude the possibility of new
developments at proper urban densities.

Street Densities Illustrated

To illustrate the point about densities let us look at a Victorian street
pattern typical of inner London. We find that it is made up of houses
three storeys in height, with two-storey back additions and back
gardens, on plots about twenty-five metres (eighty feet) deep and
five metres (seventeen feet) wide. Goodness knows how many
people such buildings might have housed in the past, in overcrowded
and insanitary conditions but, rehabilitated, each building could
comfortably accommodate a four-person dwelling on the lower two
floors (using the basement entrance) and a two-person dwelling on
the top floor (using the original front door). The existing back
addition would provide a kitchen and bathroom for each dwelling,
and the road could be adapted on a 'pedestrian priority' basis to
provide one car-parking space for every two dwellings (see Figure
31). The accommodation provided would more than satisfy the
space standards set down in the Parker Morris Report (standards
that were recommended in 1961 as a minimum but which were, in

fact, treated as a maximum and which are now abandoned by the Government as too generous).

A total of six people is housed in the two dwellings provided by each building after conversion; and the site on which it stands is five metres wide and thirty-one metres deep (including half the width of the road for density-calculating purposes). The area of the site is therefore 5m × 31m or 0.00155 hectares, and the density is six divided by 0.00155, or 385 people per hectare (155 per acre). The five-storey Georgian houses illustrated in Figure 34 each accommodates nine people in two dwellings at a similar density because, although the buildings are taller, the spaces between them are greater.

It can of course be argued that the generally accepted way of

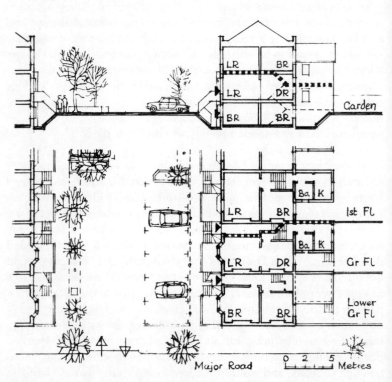

Fig. 31 Traditional high-density street: four- and two-person homes at 385 people per hectare (155 per acre)

calculating densities described above is difficult to apply to large
sites surrounded by roads or incorporating public open space, and
some of the examples illustrated below have been adjusted to reflect
this. But it has to be remembered that the number of people who
can be accommodated on a site has an important bearing on its
value, so the rules have to be clear. In any case it is not the purpose
of this chapter to defend or criticize the rules, but to show how they
arose and how they are applied, and to demonstrate the enormous
influence that a decision on maximum permitted densities can have
on the urban environment.

No planning authority is likely to refuse permission to convert
existing buildings in order to provide better accommodation, even if
the authority's recommended density is still exceeded. Nor is
permission likely to be refused for a single infill building similar in
height to those on each side of it. But it is not uncommon, when
redevelopment takes place over a wider area, for rules on maximum
permitted density to be enforced and for a suburban style of housing
to be the result. Houses like the Victorian and Georgian houses
illustrated in Figures 31 and 34 make up the majority of our urban
conservation areas. It is ironic that as new buildings they would not
now be permitted by most local authorities because they represent a
population density well in excess of 100 people per acre.

Figure 32 shows the cross section of a hypothetical four-storey
development designed to be in scale with a typical inner-city area. It
is based on a well-tried formula for converting nineteenth-century
houses (see Figure 34), and assumes two three-bedroom (five-
person) dwellings to each six-metre (twenty-three-foot) bay: one
dwelling with a garden, the other with a roof terrace, and each with
its own front door on to the street as in the Victorian houses
illustrated in Figure 31. It also works out at a similar density but,
because of the extra floor, can have wider frontages and a greater
space between buildings. This enables one car per dwelling to be
parked in the street (on the principle of the Dutch *woonerven*
described in Chapter 6 (v)). Nevertheless, like the Victorian
housing, it is fifty per cent above the maximum density of 247
people per hectare (100 per acre) permitted by many district and
borough councils, and would therefore be unlikely to be permitted
in present circumstances.

As a further illustration of the fact that it is not necessary to build

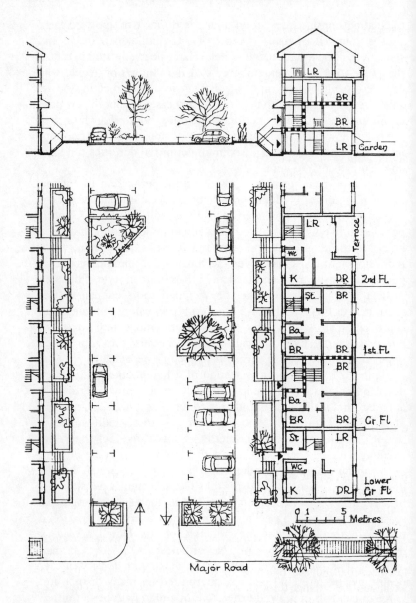

Fig. 32 New high-density street housing: five-person dwellings at 400 people per hectare (160 per acre)

tall in order to achieve high densities, Figure 33 shows the cross sections of three examples of housing built in the 1970s which demonstrate this thesis.

The Popham Street and Frederica Street estates were built for the London Borough of Islington to a density of 390 people per hectare (158 per acre) and 310 people per hectare (125 per acre) respectively. The latter was based on the idea of the mews, but neither estate represented a clear attempt to re-create the traditional urban street. Both, however, were limited to two- and three-storey buildings; both provided front doors on to public streets or alleys, and both provided private gardens for two-thirds of their dwellings. Popham Street gained, in some people's eyes, by having garages under one of the terraces and thus avoiding having parked cars on the estate, but some of its narrow pedestrian streets were too bleak. Frederica Street gained from the convenience of cars near homes (including some integral garages), but it suffered from the inevitable Sunday car maintenance, and from a long, bleak terrace facing one of the boundary roads. Both estates represented early attempts to build to 'tower-block densities' without building tower blocks (Popham Street was designed in 1967).

The density of the Queens Road estate in Richmond is not comparable, because of a considerable amount of open space within the site; but the design lends itself to the high-density urban street. It was built for the London and Quadrant Housing Trust and was the latest and most sophisticated of the three. It gives every dwelling a garden or roof terrace as well as its own front door on to the street, and it also provides a high proportion of integral garages.

All three estates provide for approximately one car-parking space per dwelling, and it would be difficult, even now, to imagine much new housing providing anything less in the way of car accommodation. Nevertheless, it seems that such a high provision in inner-city areas is not a good idea. Lower car use and improved public transport must eventually be the way to an improved urban environment and a better standard of living. Therefore, while noting that low-rise, high-density housing can provide one-for-one car parking, we should be aiming, through our transport policies, for a reduction in the use of cars in the long term, so that car-parking space within our cities can be cut down and allocated mainly for the use of hired cars (see Chapter 6 (i)) and visitors.

With or without cars, however, the examples mentioned above and illustrated in Figure 33 demonstrate that streetscale housing can be built to densities well in excess of one hundred people per acre. Therefore, provided that Unitary Development Plans with 'suburban' maximum densities do not rule it out, we can regain our close-knit communities, and with them the local facilities that depend on high concentrations of people.

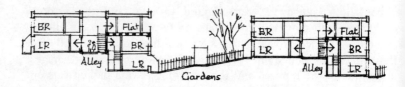

a. Popham Street, Islington

b. Frederica Street, Islington

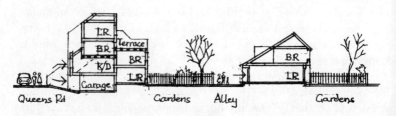

c. Queens Road, Richmond

Fig. 33 Examples of low-rise, high-density housing

There are of course those who do not wish to be part of a close-knit community but prefer Rayner Banham's 'community of peers' (see Chapter 5 (i)). They see 'community' as parochial, with everyone knowing too much about everyone else's business. But parochial can also mean a preparedness to help those in the community who are in trouble. It is probably the juxtaposition of these two aspects of parochialism that has kept people interested for so long in the goings-on of that famous village of Ambridge near Borchester. Whether such a village still exists must be open to doubt, because even villages depend on a certain concentration of people to keep them alive. There are, in fact, probably more 'village' communities remaining in our inner-city areas than there are in the countryside. What keeps us interested in Ambridge (or, for that matter, Coronation Street), is that we see it as a community, small enough for us to feel that we know everyone, yet large enough for it to support the pub and corner shop so vital to its creators for setting up chance meetings of unlikely people. Most urban streets used to have their 'Rover's Return' with singing on Friday and Saturday evenings and few customers who did not live in the immediate neighbourhood. With the present concern about drinking and driving, there is a strong case for the return of the genuine 'local'. The local, however, needs a locality. We must see to it that, when urban regeneration gets under way, our urban villages, new and old, are sufficiently compact and identifiable for people to know one another, and to support the 'local' as well as all the other local facilities that people expect to find in a city.

7 (iii) NEW HOMES FROM OLD HOUSES

Nineteenth-Century Houses

Most of the irredeemable slums that we inherited from the nineteenth century were demolished between 1930 and 1970. It is true that, as a very sad part of the brave new world of post-War housing, we built ourselves some brand-new slums, but many of our surviving urban streets are worth saving. They may need thermal insulation, but the fact that they are deteriorating is less to do with their construction than with bad management and lack of resources for maintenance.

Much of our old urban housing has been repaired and converted to suit twentieth-century needs and standards. Some of it has been done very well, especially in the case of buildings that have been treated with special care because they are of architectural and historic interest. But some of the run-of-the-mill Victorian and Edwardian houses, which could have made just as good homes as the 'historic' buildings, have been converted so unimaginatively (with narrow, artificially lit internal corridors and awkwardly shaped rooms) that they remain slums. The resources spent on structural repairs have therefore been wasted.

Figure 34 illustrates a good example of the conversion of five-storey Georgian houses, listed as being of architectural and historic interest. Situated on the slopes of Pentonville, little more than a mile's carriage drive from the City of London, they were part of a large estate built for the increasingly prosperous middle classes in about 1820. Each house was designed for one large family, with servants working in the basement and sleeping in the attic. They probably survived as family houses until the second railway boom of the 1860s enabled well-off families to move to more remote suburbs. From then until the 1970s, like similar houses in the area, they were split up into small tenements with shared washing facilities. Unlike some of their larger Victorian counterparts, these Georgian houses are too small in area to provide reasonable flats on each floor, and much too large overall for a single modern family. Hence each house has been divided in two, with the dwelling on the lower two floors having the garden, and the upper dwelling having a roof terrace in place of the rear attic room. The upper dwelling uses the original front door and lobby which are isolated and insulated from the lower dwelling's ground-floor rooms, and the lower dwelling has its front door in the basement area. On this estate, with its generous basement ceilings, the living rooms of the lower dwelling are in the basement and the bedrooms on the ground floor. The more usual arrangement is the other way round, as in Figure 31.

Figure 35 illustrates the rehabilitation of Kirkdale's late-Victorian streets named after flowers, and usually referred to collectively as 'the Flower Streets'. They formed one of Liverpool's General Improvement Areas and the work was carried out during the 1970s

for the Trustees of the James and William Evans Estates. The
rejuvenation of these tightly packed terraces demonstrates that in
some circumstances even two-storey housing can, with ingenuity,
provide reasonable accommodation at a density well in excess of the
old 'tower-block density' of 136 people per acre. It also represents a
rare example of private-sector housing upgraded for renting.

When the Flower Streets were rehabilitated, many of the houses
adjacent to Commercial Road were demolished in order to provide a

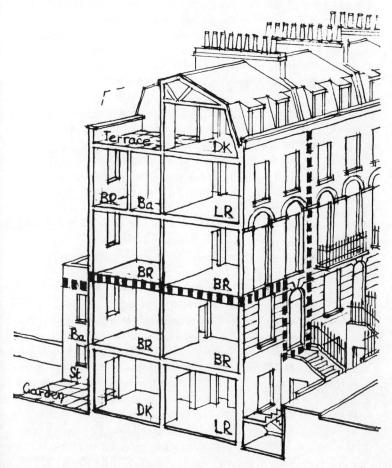

Fig. 34 Conversion of Georgian houses in Islington

landscaped barrier, which not only protected the streets from intrusive heavy traffic but also prevented their use as 'rat runs' by motorists on their way to work. The roads that serve the houses are thirteen metres (forty-three feet) wide, but there are no front gardens; and although the houses provide generous rooms, with little space wasted on corridors, there is not much space at the rear between houses: the main back walls are thirteen and a half metres (forty-four feet) apart, and the back additions are only eight metres (twenty-seven feet) apart. Furthermore, the back alleys, which in the south of England would be eliminated for fear of vandalism, leave little space for the rear yard or garden. Nevertheless, the houses and their back additions are cleverly staggered to avoid

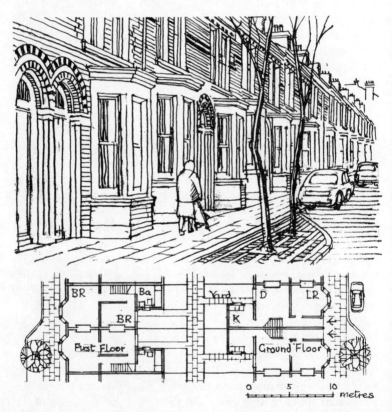

Fig. 35 Liverpool's Flower Streets

overlooking, and they provide four- and five-person family dwellings in excess of Parker Morris standards, at a net residential density of 400 people per hectare (160 per acre).

Inter-War Council Estates

The one widespread success in urban housing during the barren 1980s was the upgrading of many of the inter-War council estates; and one of the formulae that worked out most successfully was that developed in the 1970s to cope with the ubiquitous four-storey blocks in the London Borough of Islington. Figure 36 illustrates the oldest of these blocks, built in the early 1920s. The conversion is not especially interesting architecturally, largely because the original buildings were rather nice and there was therefore no call for the spectacular addition of 'charm', which has been so successful on the more stark estates. Indeed it could be argued that the rather clumsy refuse chambers are not as sympathetic to the original buildings as they might have been. It is interesting nonetheless not only for the imaginative redistribution of accommodation described below but also because it provides one of the first examples in Britain of traffic calming along the lines of the Dutch *woonerf*: not actually applied to an existing street but to one of the little-used tarmac drying-yards-cum-playgrounds which ran for 200 metres between the main blocks. It became the new approach to the blocks, the backs of which were used to provide private and communal gardens.

The principle of the Halton Mansions conversion was that the ground and first floors, which originally consisted of ordinary single-level flats, were combined to form self-contained, two-storey dwellings with their own front doors, their own private gardens at the rear and, of course, their own internal staircases. Thus on the lower two floors each spacious two-storey dwelling took the place of two very cramped flats. Flats were retained on the two upper floors and continued to be served by the original staircase, now protected by a system of entry phones, but some internal partitions were removed to provide fewer and larger rooms for smaller families. The tarmac areas between the blocks that were not used for access were sufficiently wide to provide, as well as the individual private gardens mentioned above, a large garden for the use of the occupants of the upper flats, which was accessible directly from the main staircases.

The disadvantage of this type of conversion is that the small dwellings on the upper floors, although they avoid the need for access balconies, still have shared entrances and staircases; but all the small dwellings are together, and all the family dwellings have their own private gardens and entrances. The combination seems to work well, and it became the precursor for the upgrading of many three- and four-storey council estates.

Halton Mansions had originally been built to a very high density but as a result of the conversion it was reduced from 550 people per hectare (240 per acre) to 365 people per hectare (148 per acre) – again demonstrating the absurdity of the suggestion that any density above 250 people per hectare (100 per acre) is too high.

It is probably no great surprise that five-storey Georgian houses,

Fig. 36 Upgrading of Islington's inter-War estates

much sought-after in certain parts of our cities, can be converted to provide more modest family dwellings suitable to our age. But it is all too easy in trying to meet a particular housing need, such as that for single people or retired couples, to attempt a conversion for which the particular building involved is not suitable. Perhaps because they do not command the respect of Georgian houses, a great many Victorian houses similar to the one illustrated in Figure 31 have, as mentioned earlier, suffered from ill-considered conversions which have done nothing to further the cause of living in cities. We have seen, however, that some local authorities have not only made a success of converting one of the most unpromising of all our inheritances from the past – the inter-War housing estates – but have included in these conversions the much-needed small dwellings, which are often difficult to provide satisfactorily in nineteenth-century buildings.

The comprehensive developments before and after World War II have left us with large council housing estates on which many people feel divided from the rest of the community but which usually have one great advantage: although they may be unpleasantly close to busy roads, they seldom have heavy traffic running through the estate itself. On the other hand, many nineteenth-century streets, apparently more promising as the providers of modern homes, are incapable of providing a civilized environment in the more general sense because of the traffic that uses them as alternatives to the main roads. For this reason, if for no other, it is important that housing and transport are looked at together and that traffic is 'tamed'.

It also has to be borne in mind that when existing streets or housing estates are rehabilitated it is seldom possible to find additional off-street car parking, and that (as with new housing described earlier) residents' parking requirements are met only with difficulty and at the expense of a good environment. If the arguments for transport reform put forward in Chapter 6 were to prevail, car ownership in urban areas would probably fall, as in Copenhagen; but if it were to increase, extra parking would have to be provided, either in specially built garage courts (on land that would otherwise be designated for housing or open space) or under new buildings. The latter is the more usual option adopted in European cities, where it is well managed and does not suffer from the stigma attached to it in Britain. But improved public transport, easier car hire, falling car use in urban areas and an improved environment for pedestrian and cyclist must be the best way forward for our cities: not just in transport terms but also for the sake of better housing, in streets where children can play and everyone can enjoy more pleasant surroundings.

7 (iv) NEW URBAN HOUSING

Low-Rise, High-Density Housing

Although many of our older buildings are worth retaining and improving, many of those built recently already need to be replaced. Furthermore, although continuity and familiarity are part of the essence of cities, another part of that essence is change. There will therefore always be a need for new urban housing.

We have seen that public dissatisfaction brought to an end the high-rise industrialized building of the 1960s and led eventually to the suburban housing densities in the local-authority development plans of the 1980s. It did not lead immediately to the abandoning of comprehensive redevelopment, in spite of the disruption which that had caused. The new schemes were less tall but sometimes even more complicated; and the attempts of their designers to create an interesting environment often led to a system of pedestrian streets which, although potentially charming, finished up as 'mugging alleys'. Eventually, in the late 1970s, housing managers began to see the merits of simple, high-density, inner-city housing schemes built piecemeal on small sites, as an integral part of the existing street pattern. But, coincidental with the new enlightenment, political considerations brought much local-authority housing, and therefore most new urban housing, to an end.

The need to house large numbers of people quickly and in an interesting environment was not the only reason for the survival of comprehensive redevelopment after tower blocks were abandoned. Another important justification for big and complicated schemes was the assumed necessity of separating vehicular and pedestrian traffic in any new housing. Such separation had been pioneered in a 1930s low-density housing project in Radburn, New Jersey, and pursued in many of Britain's post-War new towns. It was based on the principle that the main approach to a dwelling was by footpath from a linear park that ran through the housing estate, and that the 'garage court' was hidden away at the back. The idea worked well so long as most people arrived on foot: but it lost much of its point when nearly everyone came by car.

Nevertheless the 'Radburn' principle of separating pedestrians from vehicular traffic took a firm hold on the minds of those responsible for largescale housing projects who, when they came to apply the principle in high-density areas, did so by providing pedestrian access on a 'deck' above street level. This could be done only where comprehensive redevelopment was possible over a large area, and even then it made sense only if it was assumed that the whole town would eventually be redeveloped in the same way. This was certainly the assumption made in the Barbican area of the City of London, and the attempt to extend pedestrian decks outside the Barbican was finally abandoned only in 1986, by which time it had become accepted that in residential areas it was better to make vehicular and pedestrian traffic more compatible than to separate them altogether.

One of the last high-density, low-rise housing projects to be built in London before the cutback in urban housing in the 1980s, and one of the few not to suffer from pedestrian decks and other forms of over-complication, was that at Wood Lane for the Borough of Hammersmith (see Figure 37). This project is interesting primarily

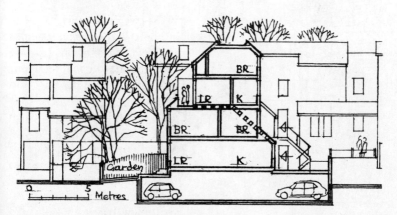

Fig. 37 High-density housing in Hammersmith

because, in spite of its density of 360 people per hectare (140 per acre), it was built to two, three and four storeys, with every dwelling having its own front door on to a public street, and each family dwelling having a private garden. It also attempted to solve the difficult problem of car parking, without cluttering up the streets, by putting residents' cars under some of the dwellings: a system that worked perfectly well when applied by the same architects to similar housing in Germany (see page 240), but which, as is all too common in this country, was marred by vandalism due either to insufficient supervision or to the inherent ill-discipline of British society.

Another project of the same period as the Wood Lane housing was that built by the GLC on the site of the old Odhams Press in the middle of Covent Garden (completed in 1981). The architectural style is severe and, because of hooliganism, some of the first-floor alleyways designed to give 'street' access to every dwelling have had

Fig. 38 Odhams Walk, Covent Garden

Fig. 39 Princes Reach housing, Preston

to be closed to the public. But the Odhams Walk development, with its shops at ground-floor level, is well integrated into the old four-storey street pattern, and it shows that modern design can add character to historic streets and can be much more satisfactory than pastiche: especially in areas like Covent Garden which are renowned for their variety. It accommodates public car parking (which is not abused) and public recreation facilities at basement level. Furthermore, most dwellings have private open space in the form of a terrace, yet the density achieved is 470 people per hectare (190 per acre).

One form of high-density housing that did survive the 1980s was the project related to the reclaiming of derelict industrial land. There were many such projects built by the private sector in London's Docklands enterprise zone and another at Chelsea Reach; but although they were interesting projects, which certainly contributed to London's river scene, they did not set out to solve the generally perceived problems of inner-city areas. A project that seems to combine the reclamation of derelict land and contribute to inner-city housing in a more general way is the Princes Reach scheme in Preston's old docks, built for Lovell Urban Renewal Ltd (see Figure 39).

Princes Reach does not attempt to provide everyone with a front door on to a street because, although it is not a high-rise scheme, neither does it pretend to be part of the existing street pattern.

Instead it takes maximum advantage of its unique riverside position and provides all dwellings with balconies overlooking the water. It is not easy to imagine people at Princes Reach doing without cars, and there is more than one parking space per dwelling ingeniously fitted into a series of well-landscaped courtyards. But in spite of the space taken up by car parking (which in similar circumstances in Europe would have probably been put below ground) the scheme achieves a density of 290 people per hectare (120 per acre), with buildings that vary between three and five storeys.

New 'Street Housing'

If, as mentioned above, improved public transport and falling car use can once again make our existing urban streets pleasant places to live in, it follows that new residential developments can be small in scale and part of the existing street pattern. Thus they can be more easily integrated into the existing community.

In fact, one of the other modest successes of the 1980s was the development of small 'street infill' housing schemes which worked especially well when they were built on comparatively quiet roads. The housing at Clerkenwell Green, close to the City of London, built by the London Borough of Islington, provides pleasant housing in a conservation area largely given over to offices, light industry and a few shops and pubs. It makes good use of an awkwardly-shaped site (which had lain derelict for many years) by developing both the Clerkenwell Green frontage (illustrated in Figure 40) and the frontage on to Clerkenwell Close at the rear, with a paved courtyard joining the two frontage developments. Being a central-area project, it is not designed for families with children and there are no private gardens, but the central courtyard provides a secluded environment in the middle of a busy business district. Seventy-five people are accommodated at a density of approximately 370 people per hectare (150 per acre).

The buildings shown head-on in the illustration are all part of the housing scheme, and demonstrate the way that it has been broken down into small elements (with shops at ground-floor level) to reflect the higgledy-piggledy nature of Clerkenwell Green.

Another example of new high-density housing, built as part of an existing street, is that in St Mark's Road, North Kensington, built by the Kensington Housing Trust (see Figure 41). The three- and four-storey buildings are not as high as their Edwardian neighbours, but they make intensive use of the space available and attain a density of 395 people per hectare (160 per acre). The essence of the scheme is the repeated pattern of two tall narrow-fronted family dwellings behind each gable, with one two-person flat at lower-ground-floor level. The family dwellings have private gardens at the rear, and the flats have small gardens on each side of the front steps. Because the site is on a corner, access for car parking behind the back gardens is available from a side road.

Describing the St Mark's Road housing in an *Architectural Review* article in 1980, Bob Allies wrote: 'If on the mainland of Europe they have rediscovered the piazza, in England we may rediscover the street.' It is ironic that in the same article he also mentions the view of Jeremy Dixon (the scheme's architect) that there is really no true tradition of urbanism in Britain, but 'a sophisticated and rich

Fig. 40 Infill housing, Clerkenwell

Fig. 41 Infill housing, North Kensington

tradition of suburbanism'. This is true to the extent that few people live in the very centre of our cities as they do in Europe. It is also true that St Mark's Road and Wood Lane, unlike Covent Garden and Clerkenwell, are by no means part of the central area. They are, however, 'urban' in the sense used in this book: they are built to a sufficiently high density to support basic facilities like pubs and shops within walking distance, and they are within the area where good public transport services should render the motorcar a luxury rather than a necessity.

New Housing in Central Areas

There were brave attempts in the 1960s to develop a truly urban form of housing that could accommodate families with children in the centres of our cities. The Park Hill Estate on a steep hill near the centre of Sheffield was one of the more glorious failures. Its access ways, wide enough to carry milk floats, started at ground level but, because of the sloping land, quickly became streets in the air, which added a new dimension to urbanism but failed to become streets in the community sense. Similarly, the Byker development in Newcastle had its 'Wall': a tall, irregular block of flats sheltering close-knit communities of low-rise housing (which are really the essence of the project) from a motorway which was, in the event, never built (see Figure 42). Although Byker seems to be deservedly popular with its residents, most of these very large housing projects from the 1960s and 1970s have become the sort of places that people leave if they have the resources to do so.

The one very large inner-city housing project from that era which can be regarded as a success is the Barbican estate in the City of London, but it is hardly typical. Its success is due partly to its being within walking distance of one of the most sought-after commercial centres in Europe and partly to the large sums of money lavished on its construction and management (which put its rents out of the reach of most people). Projects like it could therefore no more solve the housing problems of London as a whole than could Henry Roberts's 'Model Homes for the Working Classes'. Moreover, it is difficult to believe that the Barbican provides the sense of community that can be generated in an ordinary London street. It does, however, demonstrate that lifts and underground garages are not a problem where there are sufficient resources to manage them properly, and it shows that there is still a role in housing for tall buildings, provided that they are in the right place and for the right people: not for families with small children.

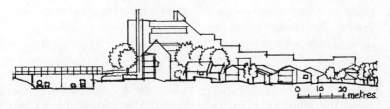

Fig. 42 Newcastle's Byker Housing

The three central-area housing projects at Park Hill, Byker and the Barbican all date from the 1960s. To find any central-area housing on a similar scale that has been built more recently one either has to look at projects on derelict industrial land, like the dockland schemes described on pages 235–6, or one has to look abroad. It is ironic that the response to a request for such material from Germany produced the Bohnenviertel housing in Stuttgart: designed by the British architects for the Wood Lane project described earlier.

At Bohnenviertel the surrounding streets are urban, busy and noisy; but they are not quasi-motorways carrying heavy, fast-moving traffic. The housing project could, indeed had to be integrated into the existing urban fabric. This was done successfully by following the pattern of existing streets and allowing the peripheral blocks to provide shops which were designed to blend with the existing streetscape while, at the same time, protecting the central common garden (on to which most dwellings faced) from the inevitable street noise (see Figure 43). The project can fairly be described as 'social' housing, having been trade-union subsidized and designed for the families of people working in central Stuttgart for comparatively low wages. This did not prevent the provision of properly managed underground car parking, as it probably would have done in Britain, in spite of the fact that car ownership is less necessary than it is in British cities because of Stuttgart's superior public transport.

The housing at Bohnenviertel enhances the vitality and diversity of the city. Its residents can choose between being part of this vitality or retiring to the private side of their dwellings where they can enjoy quiet. The family dwellings overlook their own private gardens, and the smaller dwellings overlook their roof terraces and the communal garden beyond. Whether Bohnenviertel will prove successful in the long run or whether, simply because it is subsidized housing, it will ultimately become a ghetto for those who cannot afford to live anywhere else, only time will tell. But it does demonstrate that it is physically possible to provide in the centre of a city a decent family environment at a high density of population.

If our cities in Britain are to regain their vitality, housing for all income groups has to be brought back to the inner areas. Where this cannot be achieved through market forces, subsidies of some sort will have to be used, as has been found necessary all over the world.

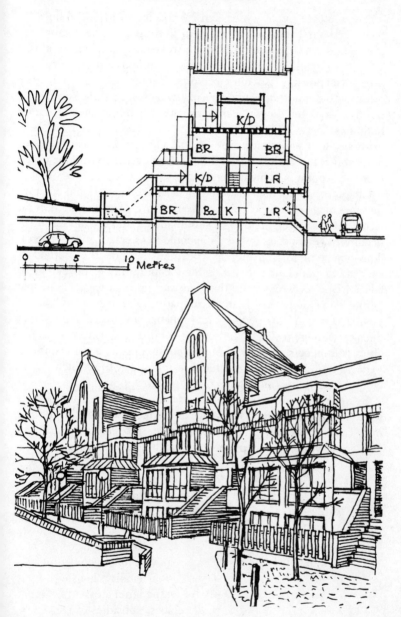

Fig. 43 Central-area housing, Stuttgart

There is a case for very high-density housing in high buildings for those without children who want to live right in the commercial centre and who thus can contribute to keeping the centre 'alive'. This is the justification for the Barbican, although it provides very little social housing. But our most important task must be to find the means of providing attractive housing *throughout* our inner-city areas, through new buildings or through the rehabilitation of existing buildings. New building need not be tall but must nevertheless maintain, and sometimes increase, the population density so as to re-establish the high concentration of local facilities without which there is no point in living in a city.

Chapters 5 and 6 demonstrated the social, economic and environmental advantages of keeping our cities as compact communities, rather than allowing them to be suburbanized through the setting of maximum densities as low as 247 people per hectare (100 per acre). The object of this chapter has been to describe the method of calculating population densities for the purposes of development control, and to demonstrate that densities up to at least 320 people per hectare (130 per acre) can be compatible with the sort of housing people want. Many people are probably already living at that density without realizing it. Forcing suburban densities on to our cities is unnecessary from a housing point of view, and to continue to do so would be an unmitigated disaster for city life, which thrives on diverse activities and plenty of people to support them.

By enhancing our urban tradition of close-knit street communities we can maintain the form of city we have inherited and still have our own front doors and private open space. We can also keep our friends, as well as our shops and pubs, within walking distance.

SUMMARY AND CONCLUSIONS

The ease of long-distance information increases the need for face-to-face contacts. The cities provide this through their density and their role as transport hubs . . . Strategies which emphasise mixed use and denser development are more likely to result in people living close to workplaces and the services they require for everyday life. The car then becomes an option rather than a necessity.

Commission of the European Communities
Green Paper on The Urban Environment,
Brussels, June 1990
(Cmnd 90/218)

In feudal times the cities of Europe provided the first oases of freedom and were at the forefront of all civilized endeavour, from learning to trade. Nevertheless the urban population was only five per cent of the total. The Industrial Revolution heightened the magnetism of cities, which continued to attract people to them until the latter half of the twentieth century; but it also led to the abject poverty and overcrowding that marked the beginnings of urban decline.

It is commonly assumed that the trouble with Britain's cities in the 1990s is that they are still overcrowded. This is not so. Because they were able to dispense with fortified walls long before their European counterparts, they have never been so crowded as most other cities, and this is certainly the case now. Although there may still be overcrowding in individual buildings, our cities suffer not from a surfeit of people but from a steady decline of the urban population: a decline that threatens the viability of the close-at-hand amenities that should make city life worth living.

It is also assumed that congestion on the roads and railways of our cities is caused either by too great a concentration of people working in the central area or by insufficient capacity on the roads serving it. Neither is true. In London, as in most other cities, there are now fewer people travelling and less freight being moved than twenty years ago but, because of the decline in public transport and excessive reliance on the private car, congestion has increased. Urban road building, designed to relieve congestion, has almost invariably made things worse, and damaged the environment in the process. It is no solution to the problems of transport in cities and should not be pursued.

Britain's urban public transport used to be the best in Europe. Now it is amongst the worst, thanks to a Government which, in contradistinction to its European counterparts, gives more in subsidy to the users of company cars than it does to the users of public transport. This has proved to be a false economy, with dire effects on our environment and on our prosperity. It has even led to urban roads carrying fewer people than they used to, as buses have been replaced by cars.

If the present policies on planning, housing and transport allow chaos and uncertainty to continue for much longer, almost the only people left in the cities will be those trapped there because they cannot afford to move out. This can be avoided and cities made congenial places in which to live and work if, instead of just reacting to situations as they develop, we make use of our ability as rational beings to plan ahead. Without necessarily reverting to the imperfect state of affairs prior to the abolition of the GLC and the other metropolitan counties, some form of elected authority is needed to oversee and co-ordinate the strategic planning and transport of our major cities.

If cities are to be reinvigorated they must retain their concentration of people and diversity of activities, without which the whole point of urban living is lost.

Major commercial areas must be at the centre of gravity of the public transport system. All shopping centres, major leisure activities and public institutions must be close to a frequent train or bus service.

A proportion of space in the central area must be allocated to service industries, low-cost housing, shopping and leisure activities which may not be able to pay market rents but which are nonetheless necessary to the prosperity of the centre. This requires an extension of policies that already protect open space, historic buildings and certain shopping frontages.

Local shops must be retained and encouraged to improve. The tendency for retail outlets to become larger, fewer and further away must be resisted. Large out-of-centre stores, which cater mainly for those shopping by car, threaten existing shopping centres and generate traffic congestion. They should not be permitted.

We need another retail revolution which reinstates a proper delivery service to local shops and a home-delivery service for large orders. Not only would this provide a better service for the customer, it would also be better environmentally, and in terms of fuel consumption, than the present trend of requiring every customer to collect by car from a distant warehouse or superstore.

Cars are a blessing to many people. Even in cities they are useful for carrying awkward loads to awkward places; but their advantages are far outweighed by their disadvantages. They have polluted the atmosphere, destroyed the urban environment, inhibited the freedom of children to play near their homes and, ironically, they have made those who live and work in cities less mobile.

Many residents living in central city locations already forgo the use of a car by choice. Their number would increase if public transport were improved and car hiring for exceptional journeys were made easier. Large car-free areas, which include shops, schools, etc., should be established so that those who give up their cars can enjoy the benefits of so doing.

We therefore need to improve public transport and land-use planning so that all activities can be reached without the need for cars. Car traffic can then be eliminated gradually through traffic restraint. Even now it is only a small proportion of commuters who travel to city centres by car, but they are a major cause of urban congestion. This abuse of the roads should be ended quickly and roads given over to buses, delivery vehicles, pedestrians and cyclists.

The medical profession sees our too-sedentary way of living as a major cause of ill health. It sees walking and cycling as the healthiest forms of transport. They are also the least polluting, and should therefore be encouraged – especially in towns where they are potentially at their most effective.

Lorries and vans are the lifeblood of a city, but they must be designed to fit the street in which they are collecting or delivering. They should be small, city-friendly vehicles which can be given priority on the roads – perhaps by allowing them to use, in off-peak periods, bus lanes from which cars are excluded all day. The development of electric delivery vehicles based on the principle of the milk float should be encouraged, and lorries over sixteen and a half tonnes gross laden weight should be banned from cities (except under existing police powers for dealing with exceptional loads).

Five per cent of Britain's urban land is derelict. If this 890 square miles (almost one and a half times the area of Greater London) were put to good use, pressure for development on green-belt land and on the countryside generally would be relieved and our cities would regain their concentrated form, and thus their vitality.

Dereliction in central areas should be reduced by ensuring that permission to demolish is part of the planning process, so that existing buildings on a development site survive until the development is ready to proceed. The current practice of using such land as temporary car parking not only blights the area concerned but also attracts more traffic and therefore contributes to urban road congestion.

A safe and pleasant urban environment should reduce the need for public open spaces as palliatives for deprived cities. However, each district or borough needs a park large enough to allow unprotected areas of grass and some wilderness. Housing at urban (as opposed to suburban) densities will help to ensure that there is land available for such a park. Although small, supervised local parks also have an important role, urban greenery should in the main be provided by extensive tree-planting in streets, squares, other small paved areas and private gardens.

Housing densities in the inner areas of towns and cities must be at a level equivalent to the typical three- and four-storey urban street: a level at which it is still possible to provide each dwelling with its own front door on to a public street, and to provide gardens for all family dwellings. Densities in the central area for those without families can be higher. There is plenty of suburban housing around our cities for those who prefer it, and there is no reason to dilute the inner-city areas by suburbanizing them as well.

Retaining 'urban' housing densities should ensure the survival of local facilities like shops, pubs, primary schools, doctors' surgeries and bus stops within walking distance of everyone's front door. Large shops and other public facilities should be concentrated in existing centres where there are good public transport services.

Most important of all, our city streets must be treated first and foremost as places. In primarily residential areas it should be safe for children to play outside their front doors and to cycle to school. In shopping and commercial centres, even when they are on a main road, first consideration must be given to the pedestrian. The person who lives in or has business in an area should always have priority over the person passing through.

It is not everyone who wants to live in a city and it is not everyone who has to. Many people enjoy the lifestyle of scattered, car-oriented communities, especially if, as at Milton Keynes, the car has been properly accommodated from the start. But if everyone deserted the cities in favour of dispersed communities, traffic congestion, fuel consumption and atmospheric pollution would increase and our densely populated island would no longer work socially, environmentally or economically. We simply cannot, especially in the south of England, accommodate everyone at new-town or suburban densities and still have sufficient land left for civilized agriculture and recreation. Instead of suburbanizing our inner-city areas and dispersing their inhabitants we should be attracting people back to the cities by reviving our traditions of streetscale housing and revitalizing our public transport.

In scattered communities every activity outside the home involves a journey that has to be planned. There is great potential vitality in close-knit urban communities where social activity can be spontaneous and where the necessities and pleasures of life are close at hand.

BIBLIOGRAPHY

History

BAIROCH, PAUL *Cities and Economic Development*, Mansell
    Publishing, 1988
BURKE, GERALD *The Making of Dutch Towns*, Cleaver-Hume,
    1956
CLAPHAM *An Economic History of Modern Britain*, Cambridge
    University Press, 1926
DYAS AND WOLF *The Victorian City – Images and Reality*,
    Routledge and Kegan Paul, 1973
FISHER, H.A.L. *A History of Europe*, Eyre and Spottiswoode, 1935
LIPSON, E. *The Economic History of England*, A. and C. Black, 1931
MANTOUX, P. *The Industrial Revolution in the Eighteenth Century*,
    Jonathan Cape, 1928
MORTON, A.L. *A People's History of England*, Victor Gollancz,
    1948
MUMFORD, LEWIS *The Culture of Cities*, Secker and Warburg,
    1938
TREVELYAN, G.M. *English Social History*, Longmans, Green and
    Co., 1944
TREVELYAN, G.M. *History of England*, Longmans, Green and
    Co., 1945

Planning

CHERRY, GORDON *Urban Change and Planning (from 1750)*, G.T.
    Foulis and Co., 1972
CIVIC TRUST *Urban Wasteland Now*, 1988
COOPER MARCUS, CLARE and SARKISSEN, WENDY *Housing
    as if People Mattered*, University of California Press, 1986

GEDDES, PATRICK *Cities in Evolution*, Williams and Norgate, 1949

HALL, PETER *Urban and Regional Planning*, 2nd edition, Allen and Unwin, 1985

HALL, PETER *London 2001*, Unwin Hyman, 1989

HOWARD, EBENEZER *Garden Cities of Tomorrow*, new edition, Attic Books, 1985

JACOBS, JANE *The Death and Life of Great American Cities*, new edition, Pelican Books, 1984

LONDON COUNTY COUNCIL *County of London Plan*, 1943

MOGRIDGE, MARTIN *Transport Land Use and Energy*, Urban Studies, 1985

RASMUSSEN, STEEN EILER *London: the Unique City*, Jonathan Cape, 1948

SUTCLIFFE, ANTHONY *Towards the Planned City*, Basil Blackwell, 1981

TRANSPORT AND ENVIRONMENT STUDIES (TEST) *Quality Streets*, 1988

TRANSPORT AND ENVIRONMENT STUDIES (TEST) *Trouble in Store*, 1989

Transport

AUTOMOBILE ASSOCIATION *Motoring Costs*, April 1990

BIBBY, PETER *Croydon Corridor Two*, London Centre for Transport Planning, 1987

THE BRITISH HEART FOUNDATION *Exercise for Life*, 1991

THE BUCHANAN COMMITTEE *Traffic in Towns*, HMSO, 1963

DEPARTMENT OF TRANSPORT *Transport Statistics Great Britain, 1964–74, 1975–85, 1978–88*, HMSO, *National Travel Survey Report*, HMSO, 1988

HAMER, MICK *Wheels Within Wheels*, Routledge and Kegan Paul, 1987

HILLMAN, MAYER and WHALLEY, ANNE *Walking is Transport*, Policy Studies Institute, 1979

JANE'S *Urban Transport Systems 1990*, Jane's Information Group, 1990

LONDON REGIONAL TRANSPORT *Central Area Peak Count Data*, 1989

NEWMAN and KENWORTHY *Cities and Automobile Dependence*,
  Gower Publishing, 1989
PHAROAH, TIM and RUSSELL, JOHN *Traffic Calming*, South
  Bank Polytechnic, 1989
PLOWDEN, STEPHEN *Taming Traffic*, André Deutsch, 1980
PLOWDEN, STEPHEN *Transport Reform, Changing the Rules*,
  Policy Studies Institute, 1985
PLOWDEN, STEPHEN *A Case for Traffic Restraint in London*,
  London Centre for Transport Planning, 1988
POTTER, STEPHEN and HUGHES, PETER *Vital Travel
  Statistics, 1990*, Transport 2000, 1990
THOMSON, MICHAEL *Great Cities and Their Traffic*, Victor
  Gollancz, 1977
TYME, JOHN *Motorways Versus Democracy*, Macmillan Press, 1978

INDEX

Abercrombie's Greater London Plan, 94–5, 103, 109, 115
Accessibility, 181–90, 195
Accidents, 193–4
Agriculture, 26–8, 53–6, 58, 61, 68
Amsterdam, 45

Bairoch, Paul
  Cities and Economic Development, 25–8, 40, 59, 65, 75
Baltimore, 46
Banham, Rayner, 151, 225
Barbican, London, 159, 233, 239, 242
Barlow Commission, 90–1
Bath, 45, 58, 70
Beeching Report, 121
Bibby, Peter
  Croydon Corridor Two, 186
Birmingham, 58, 72, 76, 80, 134, 170, 199
Birth rate, 61, 104
Black Death, 54, 69
Blandford Forum, 70
Booth, Charles, 83
Booth, William, 84
Boston, 46
Bournville, 78
Bradford, 72, 75
Brewing industry, 203
Brighton, 71
Bristol, 51, 52, 70, 199
Britain
  in Roman times, 29–30
  medieval, 30–6
  and town planning, 165
Buchanan Committee, 116–19, 125, 126, 137, 142–3, 165, 208, 209
Building regulations, 80
Burke, Gerald
  The Making of Dutch Towns, 43
Buses, 113, 118, 138, 139, 192, 200–3
Buxton, 70
Bypasses, 204

Cambridge, 110
Canals, 63, 204
Canary Wharf, London, 154, 196
Canterbury, 52
Capital cities, 38, 43
Carlisle, 172–4, 176
Cars, 16, 91, 92–3, 111, 112–43, 165, 221, 223, 245
  choosing not to own, 189, 212
  company, 127–9, 184, 186–7, 198
  cost of, 184–5, 189
  hire of, 189, 212
  parks and parking, 155, 231, 234
  restraints on, 167, 168, 185–8
  tax on, 184, 198
Channel Tunnel, 204
Cheltenham, 71
Cherry, Gordon
  Urban Change and Planning, 69, 70, 72, 75, 77, 78, 90–1, 94, 148, 149
Chichester, 52
Children, 16–17, 141–2, 156, 212
Churches, 47, 69, 136
Cities
  definition of, 25–6
  density of, 40
  as living place, 43–6
  size of, 27, 35
  as works of art, 40–3
City Commuters' Group, 140
Clapham
  An Economic History of Modern Britain, 64
Coal, 59, 63
Commercial developments, 108–11, 152–4
Communities, 97–103, 151–2, 225
  see also Street communities
Company cars, 127–9, 184, 186–7, 198
Congestion, 42, 244
  see also Lorries, Roads, Traffic, Transport
Conurbations, 87
Co-operative housing, 102

Copenhagen, 168–70, 211, 231
Cost-benefit analysis, 130
Cottage estates, 88
Cottage industry, 43, 49–50
Cotton, 60, 72
Council estates, 229–32
Countryside, 150
    see also Green belt
Covent Garden, 163, 234–5
Coventry, 114–15, 170
Craig, James, 71
Crawley, 91
Crossman, Richard, 97
Croydon, 108
Cul-de-sacs, 208
Cycling, 142–3, 158, 191–4, 245

Danelaw, 31–2
Danger from thugs, 161
Decentralization, 84, 101
Decision-making on transport, 132–6
    see also Planning
Demolition, 100
Density
    of population, 40, 85, 101, 102, 152,
        214–17, 219–25, 246
    of roads, 204
    see also Overcrowding
Department of Transport, 132, 140
Derelict land, 154–5, 160, 235, 246
Dispersal, 107–11, 150, 156
Dublin, 44

Edinburgh, 44, 110, 134, 171, 199
    New Town, 71
Electric vehicles, 208
Enclosures, 55
Enterprise zones, 196
Environment, urban, 164–6
    see also Planning, Street communities
Exeter, 52, 202

Factories, 50, 73, 107
    housing around, 72–3, 98
Fairs, 50–1
Festival of Britain, 1951, 13
Films about housing, 88–9
Fisher, H.A.L.
    A History of Europe, 33, 36, 39, 52–3
Florence, 39–40, 137
Frankfurt, 161
Freiburg, 167–8, 172, 174, 176
Freight movement, 119–25, 134–5, 203–8
Fuel efficiency, 157–9
Future possibilities, 18–19

Garden cities, 84–7, 108, 214–15
Geddes, Patrick, 87
Geneva, 46
Genoa, 33
Gentrification, 100
George, Henry, 84
Germany, 52–3
    see also Freiburg, Hanover, Munich,
        Stuttgart
Good life, the, 13
Government intervention, 67–8, 77,
        103–6, 177, 190
    lack of, 125, 129, 131
Greater London Council, 105–6, 124, 137,
        194, 207, 244
Greater London Development Plan, 1970,
        117–19, 125, 126
Great Fire of London, 41, 69
Green belt, 87, 103, 113–14
Growth of industrial towns, 72–3, 74
Guilds of craftsmen, 32–3, 49–50
Gunpowder, 38–9

Hall, Peter, 148, 151
    London 2001, 182–3
    Urban and Regional Planning, 87, 103, 130
Hammersmith
    Wood Lane, 233–4
Hampstead Garden Suburb, 85, 86
Hanover, 192–3
Hanseatic League, 53
Harlow, 91, 92
Holland, 43–4
Holy Roman Empire, 34, 39, 53
Home/work relationship, 36, 47, 49–50
Horse-drawn traffic, 119–20
Houses
    in Holland, 43–4
    in London, 44
Housing
    Action Trusts, 102
    by-laws, 79–80
    in city centres, 164
    in commercial areas, 161
    estates, 44, 72
    Trusts, 80, 223
    urban, 214–42
Howard, Ebenezer, 84–7, 91, 108, 148–9,
        214–15
    Garden Cities of Tomorrow, 147, 215
Hughes, Peter
    Vital Travel Statistics, 127, 141, 158,
        191, 195
Hygiene see Sanitation

Industrial Revolution, 57–68
Iron smelting, 59–60
Islington, 74, 101
  Clerkenwell Green, 236
  Halton Mansions, 229–30
  Frederica Street estate, 223
  Packington estate, 100
  Popham Street estate, 223
Italy, 34, 37, 39, 53
  see also Florence, Genoa, Rome, Venice

Jacobs, Jane, 26, 161
  The Death and Life of Great American
    Cities, 155

Kensington High Street, London, 174

Laissez-faire planning, 67–8, 77, 83, 91,
    150, 165
Land ownership, 85, 100
Land use, 159–64
  control of, 103–4, 160
Lansbury Estate, Poplar, 13
Layfield Report, 117, 140
Le Corbusier, 14, 95, 218
Leeds, 118, 150, 170
  Quarry Hill Estate, 89
Leitch Committee, 135
Letchworth, 85
Lincoln, 52
Lipson
  The Economic History of England, 49, 51
Liverpool, 102
  Flower Streets, 226–9
Local government, 178–80
Location-of-offices Bureau, 109–10
London, 18, 30, 33–4, 41–2, 46
  commercial activity, 152–4
  conditions in 19th century, 76–7
  development in 18th century, 70
  Greater London Council, 105–6, 124,
    137, 194, 207, 244
  Greater London Development Plan,
    94–5, 117–19, 125, 126
  Great Fire, 41, 69
  Planning Advisory Committee, 106–7
  Priority Route Network, 131, 133
  prosperous centre of, 110
  and railways, 66–7
  revival of, 148–51
  size and growth of, 65, 73–4, 92, 149,
    215
  see also individual areas and streets
London County Council, 215–16

cottage estates, 88
Greater London Plan, 94–5
Lorries, 121–5, 205–8, 246
Los Angeles, 151

Magna Carta, 34, 51
Manchester, 72, 150
  Metrolink, 138, 199
Manufacturing, 48–52, 60
Market forces, 159, 163–4
Markets, 50–1
Mass housing, 84
Mearns, Andrew, 84
Medieval England, 28–36
Metropolitan counties, abolition of, 105–7,
    132
Metropolitan government, 178–80
Milton Keynes, 91, 92–3, 157, 215, 247
Mobility, 181–90, 195
Mogridge, Dr Martin, 216
Morris, William, 84
Morton, A.L.
  A People's History of England, 60, 62
Motorways, 115, 117, 121
  inquiries, 130–1
Mumford, Lewis
  The Culture of Cities, 37, 46, 68
Munich, 46

Nancy, 44
New Brutalism, 14
Newcastle, 52, 134, 170, 172, 174, 196,
    201
  Byker development, 239
New Lanark, 78
New towns, 90–3, 149–50, 151
New Urban Housing, 232–42
New York, 46, 154, 158
Nine Elms, London, 174
Noise, 122–3
North Circular Road, London, 183
North Kensington
  St Mark's Road, 236–7
Norwich, 52
Nottingham, 52

Office accommodation, 152–4, 159–60
Old buildings
  modern use of, 225–32
  value of, 162–4
Orbital roads, 117, 183
Osborn, F.J.
  New Towns After The War, 91, 94, 97,
    103

Osen, Donald
   The Victorian City, 72
Out-of-town shopping centres, 136, 166,
   167, 174, 175–8, 245
Overcrowding, 40, 78, 95, 137, 243
Owen, Robert, 78
Oxford, 52, 110
Oxford Street, London, 174

Paddington, 74
Paris, 39, 40, 75, 129, 137, 161, 187,
   198, 205, 216–17
Parker, Barry, 85
Parking offences, 133
   see also under Cars
Parks *see* Public open space
Parliamentary reform, 76–7
Party walls, 69
Patten, Chris, 213
Paving, 36
Peabody Trust, 80
Peckham Experiment, 191–2
Pedestrianization, 166–72, 211
Pedestrian precincts, 114–15
Pedestrians, 141–3
Pentonville, 226
Perth, Australia, 158
Peterborough, 65, 170
Pharoah, Tim, 209–10
Phoenicia, 28, 48
Planning, 103–7, 163, 166–72, 244
   blight, 99–100, 155
   responsibility for, 132–6
   trend, 129–30
Playgrounds, 156
Plowden, Stephen
   A Case for Traffic Restraint in London, 185
   Taming Traffic, 125–6
   Transport Reform, Changing the Rules, 128
Plymouth, 170
Pollution, 159, 166, 177
Porritt, Jonathon, 17
Port Sunlight, 78
Potter, Stephen
   Vital Travel Statistics, 127, 141, 158,
      191, 195
Poverty
   rural, 61–2
   urban, 80, 83
Preston
   Princes Reach scheme, 235–6
Privacy, 46–8
Privatization, 202
Public Health Acts, 77–8
Public inquiries, 130–1

Public open space, 46–8, 155–7, 246
Public transport, 137–40, 167, 185–6,
   189, 195, 198, 244 *see also* Buses,
   Railways, Underground
Pubs, 225

Quality of life, 76
Quality Streets (TEST), 166–72

Radburn, New Jersey, 232–3
Radial cities, 66–7, 183
Railways, 63–7, 73, 74–5, 119, 120–1,
   150, 159, 179
   suburban, 199
Rasmussen, Steen Eiler, 183
   London: the Unique City, 14, 19
Recreation, 162
Redcliffe Maude Commission, 105, 148
Redditch, 91
Redevelopment, 98–103
Refuse disposal, 36, 39
Reith, Lord, 94, 148
Renaissance, the, 36–48
   in England, 57–8
Retailing, 172–8
   see also Shops
Retail Price Maintenance, 110, 111
Ribbon development, 73, 88, 113
Richmond
   Queens Road estate, 223
Road Assessment Studies, 131–2, 140, 182
Road haulage, 120–5, 134–5, 203–8
Road pricing, 187–8, 205
Roads, 63, 99, 110, 113–17, 134
Roberts, Henry, 79, 239
Roehampton, 95–6
Rome, Ancient, 27–8
Ronan Point, 97, 152
Roundabouts, 142, 193
Rowntree, Seebohm, 83–4
Runcorn, 91
Russell, John, 209–10

Salt, Titus, 78
Sanitation, 36, 47, 73, 77–8
Satellite towns, 85, 94
Saxons, 29–31, 54
Sharp, Thomas
   Town Planning, 91
Sheffield, 138, 150, 170, 199
   Park Hill Estate, 239
Shopping precincts, 114–15, 116
Shops, 16, 20, 110–11, 172–8
   local, 207–8, 245
   out-of-town, 136, 166, 167, 174, 175–8, 24

Sitte, Camillo
  The Art of Building Cities, 84
Skeffington Committee, 130
Skylines, 153–4
Sloane Square, London, 156
Small-scale housing, 95
Southampton, 199
South Bank, London, 162
Spa towns, 45, 70–1
Speed limits, 209–11
Stamford, 51, 64–5
Steam-engine, 62–3
Stevenage, 91
Stockholm, 154
Street communities, 14, 15, 88, 112,
  156–7, 161, 188, 208, 217–25, 247
Street infill, 236–8
Stuttgart, 166–7, 176, 240–1
Subsidies, 197–200
Suburbs, 19, 66, 67, 73–4, 87–8, 90, 108
Suburbanization, 102–3, 152, 219
Subways, 141
Superstores, 110–11, 175–8
Superstition, 38

Telford, 91
Textiles, 60–1
Thomas, Ray, 147
Thomson, Michael, 117
  Modern Transport Economics, 130
Tower blocks, 14, 15, 97, 152, 218
  expense of, 15
  see also Ville radieuse
Towns
  in medieval times, 32–5
Townscape, 153–4
Townshend, 'Turnip', 58, 61
Trading, 26, 27, 28, 30–1, 35, 38, 48–53
Trade unions, 121
Traffic, 42, 98, 116
  calming, 209–13, 231
  efforts to ban, 42
  see also Buses, Cars, Lorries, Transport
Trains *see* Railways
Trams, 74, 75, 167
Transport, 15–16, 27, 63–7, 74–5,
  105–43, 181–213
  of freight, 119–25, 134–5, 203–8
  planning, 179
  public, 137–40, 167, 185–6, 189, 195,
    198, 244
  see also Buses, Cars, Railways,
    Underground railways
Transport Act, 1968, 121
Transport and Environment Studies

(TEST), 166–7, 175–6
Trees, 156
Trevelyan, G.M.
  English Social History, 54–5
  History of England, 30
Tripp, Alker
  Road Traffic and Its Control, 114, 165
  Town Planning and Road Traffic, 114, 116
Tunnels, 182–3
Tyme, John
  Motorways Versus Democracy, 130
Tyneside Metro, 137–8

Underground railways, 74–5, 118, 137,
  139
Unitary Development Plans, 219, 224
Unité d'Habitation, L', 95
Universities, 35, 37
Unwin, Raymond, 85, 87, 103
Urban environment, 164–6
  see also Planning, Street communities
Urbanization, 64
Urban poverty, 80, 83
Urban reform, 69–75
  in 19th century, 75–80, 84

Venice, 33, 35, 39, 137, 187
Vienna, 137, 170
Villages, 225
  in medieval times, 31–2
Ville radieuse, 95–7, 218

Walking, 42, 141–3, 158, 188, 191–2, 245
  see also Pedestrianization
Walter, Hubert, 34
Wars, 53, 61–2
Washington, DC, 67
Washington (England), 91
Wealth, 67–8
Welwyn Garden City, 85
Westminster, 32, 52
Westway, London, 125–6
Whitehaven estate, 70
Widdicombe, David, 130–1
Winchester, 52
Wolverhampton, 170
Wood Report, 124, 205–7
Wool
  industry, 60
  trade, 51–2
Woonerf (Holland), 210–12
Wren, Sir Christopher, 42, 69
Wythenshawe, 86, 88

York, 52, 83